W9-BVQ-417

BODILY DISCURSIONS

SUNY Series, Postmodern Culture

Joseph Natoli, Editor

BODILY DISCURSIONS

GENDERS, REPRESENTATIONS, TECHNOLOGIES

EDITED BY
DEBORAH S. WILSON
AND
CHRISTINE MONEERA LAENNEC

STATE UNIVERSITY OF NEW YORK PRESS

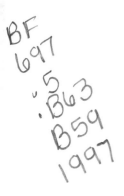

Published by
State University of New York Press, Albany

© 1997 State University of New York

Printed in the United States of America

For information, address State University of New York Press,
State University Plaza, Albany, N.Y. 12246

Production by M. R. Mulholland
Marketing by Bernadette LaManna

Library of Congress Cataloging-in-Publication Data

Bodily discursions: genders, representations, technologies / edited
by Deborah S. Wilson and Christine Moneera Laennec.
p. cm. -- (SUNY series in postmodern culture)
Includes bibliographical references and index.
ISBN 0-7914-3187-8 (alk. paper). -- ISBN 0-7914-3188-6 (pbk. :
alk. paper)
1. Body image. 2. Mind and body. 3. Body, Human (Philosophy)
4. Body, Human--Social aspects. 5. Women--Psychology. I. Wilson,
Deborah S., 1955-   . II. Laennec, Christine Moneera, 1960-   .
III. Series.
BF697.5.B63B59 1997   96-33798
306.4--dc20   CIP

10 9 8 7 6 5 4 3 2 1

For Carolyn L. Kemery and Mary Beth Meyers
and
For Michael Syrotinski

CONTENTS

IV. The Body-Mind Connection

V. Disease in the Body Politic

ILLUSTRATIONS

ACKNOWLEDGMENTS

No intellectual enterprise takes place in a vacuum; *Bodily Discursions: Genders, Representations, Technologies*, is no different. First, we thank Carola F. Sautter, a more gracious and patient editor would be hard to find. We also thank Ronald J. Fortune, Chair of the Department of English at Illinois State University, and Charles B. Harris, former Chair of the Department of English at Illinois State University, for the generous support that allowed us to produce this manuscript so expeditiously. Finally, we thank Jean C. Lee, formerly Director of the Publication Unit at Illinois State University, and now an M.F.A. candidate in Louisiana State University's creative writing program. Her technical assistance during earlier stages of *Bodily Discursions*'s production proved invaluable.

We would also like to thank the following people for granting us permission to reprint the illustrations used in this book: Carol Christianson, Permissions Manager for the Doubleday division of Doubleday Bantam Dell Publishing Group, Inc., New York, New York for use of Edward Steichen's 1927 photograph of Marion Morehouse, used by permission of Doubleday, a division of Bantam Doubleday Dell Publishing Group, Inc.; Diane Edkins, Conde Nast New York; Georgina Knight, *Vogue* London, for permission to reprint Edward Steichen's 1932 *Vogue* cover photograph, Andre Durst's 1936 photograph of surrealist fashions, and Toni Frissell's 1939 photograph of a woman in front of Henry Dreyfuss's locomotive; Lorraine Mead, Permissions Editor of Conde Nast/American *Vogue* for use of Edward Steichen's 1925 photograph of abstract fashions, George Houyningen-Huene's photographs of the girl with the hoop, 1932, and beach fashions, 1930, respectively; and Edward Steichen's photograph of the woman in the stairwell courtesy *Vogue*, copyright 1935 (renewed 1936) by Conde Nast Publications, Inc.

We also thank Andrea Salwen and Barbara Snow, Vice President for Communications, Planned Parenthood Federation of America to reprint their advertisement, "Will the Supreme Court's next decision be written in stone?", and Williams and Wilkins, A Waverly Company, Baltimore, for use of before and after photographs from Darrill Hodgkinson, M.D. and Glen Hait, M.D., "Plastic Vaginal Labioplasty," in *Plastic and Reconstructive Surgery* (September 1984).

INTRODUCTION

Deborah S. Wilson and Christine Moneera Laennec

One thing is made clear in the essays you are about to read (and it should be equally clear even if you only look at the pictures): the body is, indeed, and has been for some time, a screen onto which various ideologies are projected, a battlefield for competing discourses. Even the definition of "the body" is becoming uncertain: it is difficult, given the often incredible reports from the front lines of medicine and technology at the close of the twentieth century, for us to say exactly where our "natural" bodies end and some technologically enhanced body begins. The increasingly common use of transplants, prosthetic and/or mechanical body parts, and various reproductive technologies (not to mention developments such as virtual reality) bring into question what our bodies are, and thus what our relationship to them might be.

There are no certain answers, but rather, another set of complex questions at the crux of such inquiries. Where does the natural body end and the prosthetic body begin? Can we use such terms as "prosthetic" and "natural" unselfconsciously? Can we use these terms together and yet avoid reiterating them as the very binaries we wish to put into question? Recorded inquiries into and meditations upon the nature of the body, on how it mediates experience, sensory or social, and how, in turn, consciousness relates to it, date back at least to Aristotle in the Western tradition; they have also long been an integral part of many non-Western traditions. Indeed, inquiries from a variety of cultures, disciplines, and historical periods focus again and again on the body. They bring to bear upon it all manner of *technics*, both to better understand its functions and to mould it into conformity with prescribed social or cultural roles. It is very important to place any discussion of technology and the body in a historical context, and for this reason we have chosen to open the collection with a piece that focuses on the English Renaissance, "Female Bodies Misbehaving" by Torri L. Thompson. This essay, quite rightly, implicitly questions the smug assumption that we need go back only as far as the nineteenth century to understand the social and cultural impact of technology.

Technology: It's All Greek to Us

Perhaps not coincidentally, the English Renaissance saw the Western rediscovery of ancient Greek. Indeed, our English word, *technology*, derives from the ancient Greek, *technikos* (skillful), as, of course, also do our words *technique, technician,* and *technic.* While a technic is a tool, it is a highly specialized one, for it demands the trained hand of the artist, the artisan, or the technician. It is designed not so much to accomplish a specific task, but instead to perform that task in direct service of realizing some larger project. If we use the words *technic* and *technology* more broadly, we can then apply them not only to some mechanical thing or mechanized process, as well as to a variety of discursive practices and projects as well. Fashion magazines, literature, and extra-textual discursive practices, conjoin with the tools—literal or figurative—that we design to reshape the body or modify the behavior that emanates from the body in question. In short, under these conditions, discursive agenda, implemented through the technics appropriate to specific technologies, become themselves a sort of template that the "technicians" using them superimpose over both the body and that body's behavior: to identify points of defect, deviance, even subversion, with the object of correcting or even eliminating them.

Let us illustrate our point through an extreme example: the *Malleus Maleficarum*, written by German monks in 1484 as a handbook for clerical inquisitors in service of the Roman Catholic Church, specifies the stages and procedures designed to wring confessions from both accused witches and warlocks. The authors quite straightforwardly offer the *Malleus Maleficarum* as both technic and template. All women, they argue, are potential witches; superimpose their guidelines upon any woman, and you will find if not her manifest, then certainly her latent witchery.[1] However, the authors also made clear that men are just as susceptible to the devil's wiles. Strictly speaking, Satan's recruitment of women is merely an intermediary gesture: through women-turned-witches he could most easily reach men and make them warlocks, thus recuperating the whole human race. Consequently, if the *Malleus Maleficarum*'s authors, Fathers Jacobus Sprenger and Henry Kramer, seem to espouse the clerical misogyny so pervasive in the European Middle Ages, we must bear in mind that their overriding concern is for *human* salvation. Yet their focus remained on the "weak link," as it were, in the Great Chain of Being: woman.

In an irony that was perhaps not lost on either Sprenger and Kramer or their contemporaries, one could only save a soul through the living body that housed it. Mortification of the flesh had been a Catholic tradition long before the Inquisition; after the Reformation it became more broadly a Christian one. Penance could not necessarily be affected only through prayer; the tongue alone could not bear the whole of the body's disciplinary burden. For invaluable though a single soul may be, it was the Church's responsibility to recruit as many as possible to advance the cause of heaven. Therefore, it was paramount that the devil's minions be identified and eliminated, lest they corrupt Christian society. In an excess of zeal, great injustices were perpetrated primarily against women during the European witch-hunts and these witch-hunts became the cornerstone of the Inquisition. Expanded to include Jews and heretics, no one, male or female, necessarily escaped suspicion.

We think it very much worth noting that conduct books and advice manuals of later eras make arguments remarkably similar to the *Malleus Maleficarum* about a variety of perceived social problems. Often identified as diseases, deviations, or even subversions—in either or both sexes—certain designated problematic "disorders," real or imaginary, are thought to harm not merely individual health, but the very body politic: for example, in seventeenth century Massachusetts Bay Colony, witches' covens;[2] in nineteenth century Britain, masturbation;[3] in the twentieth century United States, homosexuality and lesbianism,[4] Communism,[5] and more recently, co-dependency,[6] and cultural literacy.[7] All these have given rise to social issue books, guides, manuals, and advice books, whether written for professionals (such as physicians, psychiatrists, social workers, law enforcement officers, and teachers) or a more general public. We certainly *do not* claim that such publications advocate using the Inquisition's fiendish physical and psychological tortures as a means of getting to the "truth." Yet they generally concur with Sprenger and Kramer on two essential points. First, they frequently claim that the perceived threat is far greater than we might at first think. Indeed, it may, in some instances, even be part of a massive conspiracy.[8] Second, the text sounding (or echoing) the alarm claims to offer an appropriate diagnostic template for identifying both the cause(s) and culprits. For example, during the early 1980s, when the hysteria over the McMartin Preschool Case reached its zenith, wildly improbable charges of ritual, even satanic, abuse, involving a vast national network of pedophiles and pornographers, who were said to be victimizing the children attending the school, gained wide credibility. In response, a number of purported experts and victims, affirming that the threats posed by devil-worshipping pedophiles had long been with us, became ubiquitous guests on the talk show circuit. Print media —and not just the tabloids—quickly entered the fray, offering books and articles that claimed to help concerned parents properly read the "warning signs" of possible ritual abuse, which could be any-thing from moodiness to bad dreams to bed-wetting to sex play.[9]

A Handbook for the Age of (Gender) Anxiety

The notion of gender identity is likewise increasingly com-plicated in our time: "androgyny" and "gender-bending" are currently valorized terms, at least in the fashion and entertain-ment industries. The success of such films as *Paris Is Burning, The Crying Game*, and *Orlando* provide evidence of a late twentieth-century questioning of gender and sexual identity. This ques-tioning and refashioning of the body coincides with a number of fierce political battles that are currently being fought over issues of personal freedom and control of the body. (These include struggles over abortion rights, HIV/AIDS policies, sexual harassment, gays in the military, and arguments surrounding the ethics of new reproductive technologies.) It seems very clear indeed that the body is a contested cultural site.

Rather than trying to assemble an anthology that would present a single theoretical approach, we, as feminist editors who want to actively resist theoretical hegemony, have deliberately encouraged a diversity of voices and perspectives. *Bodily Dis-cursions*, being organized along thematic lines, analyzes the dis-cursive practices surrounding these issues from a variety of critical and theoretical perspectives. This anthology demonstrates that, historically, cultural conflicts seem to coalesce most insistently around the female body. Consequently, the contributors to this volume analyze a wide range of discursive practices as they inscribe themselves primarily—but by no means exclusively—on issues involving the bodies of women. Fashion and the concomitant refashioning of women's bodies to suit a prevailing standard of beauty, social placements and displacements of women's accounts of pregnancy and childbirth (and their function as metonyms of society's fear and mistrust of the female or maternal body), plastic surgery, and other medical interventions in the human body's etiolations each serve in their turn here as a locus for feminist inquiry.

We do not, however, claim a unifying thread or overarching theoretical purview between the essays presented here, even if they are all feminist in their outlook. Literary criticism, social theory, psychoanalysis, cultural studies, art history, and the history of rhetoric all attest to the diversity of the approaches taken by the eleven essayists. The individual contributions tacitly demonstrate that each contributor takes the term "feminism" to mean different things: to some, it may mean a hyphenated ideology, whereas to others, it is a methodology—a technic. Yet in their different ways, the essayists anthologized here all make rigorous inquiry into the emergence of truly entrenched and deeply conflicted cultural discourse(s) surrounding the body, traditions of oppression that are themselves framed through institutional practice. As a result of this conflict, the body has been technically and rhetorically manipulated throughout history in response to cultural and social anxieties that are specific to a given historical moment. Moving from the English Renaissance to the European Enlightenment and up through our own *fin-de-siècle* twentieth-century, the scholars whose work appears here all analyze how these anxieties have been played out, literally as well as figuratively, upon the proving ground of (primarily) women's bodies. This phenomenon can be seen in the physical punishment enacted upon the female body, from the Renaissance "scold's bridle" to the plastic surgeon's scalpel. Indeed, the body—whether female or male—can be seen to disappear, as in late twentieth-century technologies such as virtual reality. The maternal body in particular begins to become transparent, invisible, and even expendable. This phenomenon can be seen in accounts of reproduction and birth dating back at least to the nineteenth century, as well as in current medical and ethical approaches to pregnancy, which focus almost exclusively on the foetus, literally or figuratively looking straight through the body of the pregnant woman.

The contributors to *Bodily Discursions* focus on the politics of gender and sexual difference as those rubrics apply to women primarily, and to men secondarily. For it is the cultural constraints and social codes that depend, systematically and institutionally, upon differentiating hierarchically between the sexes, that in turn give rise to other hierarchies, whether as a social order or as a tradition of oppression. We are not saying that these last two terms are interchangeable, any more than we are saying that all men oppress all women. The issues this volume, taken as a whole, discursively addresses are far too complex for us to reduce to simplistic, sexually coded notions of oppression, victimization, and collaboration. By focussing on the female body, the essays here implicitly open up debate on the male body. Angela Wall's contribution offers several perspectives on the male homosexual body in particular. Indeed, Naomi Wolf's comment to male readers of *The Beauty Myth* is wholly pertinent to this collection. Men are warned to pay attention to what is happening to women because "Their turn is next" (288).[10]

No Pain, No Gain

Just as *Bodily Discursions* does not have relevance for women only, we do not wish to discuss gendered difference in narrow terms of sexually distinguished cultural and social surveillance. Such a strategy would not merely be naive, for it would evade questions of systematic control and institutional practice, but it is ultimately counterproductive. It assumes that Plato was right: reality and representation remain separate and discrete, one from the other, and what is more, the former is necessarily superior to the latter. In *Nostalgia and Sexual Difference*, Janice Doane and Devon Hodges forcefully reject imposing binaries of any sort; their point has vital implications for feminist analyses of power, authority, and enfranchisement, whether collective or individual.

Opposition is a power game. The opposition *male/female* . . . is also typically hierarchical. The disparaged term, "female," helps preserve the value and integrity of the privileged term, "male." Those . . . who want to maintain the reality of a distinct male identity need to keep the terms "male" and "female" separate and opposed. It is not always obvious that the "female" sphere is being disparaged, but once we see how *female* is placed in a system of opposition that aligns it with the degraded term of other oppositions, such as *image* (which is opposed to *reality*), *fiction* (which is opposed to *truth*), or *the present* (which is opposed to *the past*), we can see how male identity and formulations of the real are secured and their importance maintained by woman's traditional place and speech (9).

We concur with Doane and Hodges that "we have yet to see how the promotion of fixed sexual differences—whether they are described as natural or culturally constructed—does anything but maintain an all-too-familiar system of oppositions and stereotypes" (11–12). To put it another way, simple role reversal, making the "bottoms" exchange places with the "tops," as it were, accomplishes nothing, for it activates and transmits power and authority through repressive hierarchical structures. Admittedly, avoiding oppositional discourse can prove very difficult indeed, but the contributors to *Bodily Discursions* have attempted to avoid such oversimplifications.[11]

In addition, as editors we remain deeply suspicious of essentialist arguments; yet at any given cultural or historical moment, and in respect to any of the issues referred to above, we keep returning to the same question: Does the material body truly exist or can it only really exist as a social construction? Since we all must live in our bodies, this question becomes imperative. The body, whether a natural phenomenon or a socially constructed entity, is mutable and, we would therefore venture to speculate that, perhaps, it has always been so. On the other hand, is it *absolutely* mutable? Have Dolly Parton and Michael Jackson—going beyond cosmetics, camera angles and lighting, diet, and exercise—remade themselves entirely by turning to plastic surgery as well? By the same token, can we argue that Madonna, who apparently draws the line at plastic surgery, reinvents her public self and her body any less successfully? Is it enough to say that our bodies, modified by heredity, fashion, health, environment, self-regard, and evolution, remain first and last not so much instruments as technics? Perhaps then the question is not whether the body is "natural" or "socially constructed," but, instead, if we regard our bodies as technics, who, then, are the technicians who would make use of them? Should we count ourselves as technicians, assert that we all manipulate other bodies—from friends giving each other diet and exercise advice to medical researchers experimenting with gene therapy? As feminists, we remain suspicious of totalizing arguments, yet undeniably we have to recognize that we too are part of cultural, economic, and social, not to mention environmental, ecosystems. In an attempt to avoid facile relativism on the one hand, and too absolute a reading of over-determination on the other, we return first to questions of gendered bodies and look for fresh points of departure.

In all the essays in this book, the contributors question how the body relates to issues of societal control and ideological domination. It is clear that "technologies of misogyny" (to use Deborah Wilson's phrase) are consistently operative from the Renaissance through the present day: the tradition of oppression, particularly as it is enacted upon the female body, has been remarkably continuous. Both Cynthia Huff's essay on childbirth in the early to mid twentieth-century, and Julie Shaffer's essay on female virginity and the married woman's chastity as commodities in the eighteenth century, point to the same conclusion. Whether virgin, pregnant, or otherwise sexually claimed through marriage, a woman's body serves as a primary locus for patriarchal control. In our own time, as Susanmarie Harrington demonstrates, the example of Kimberly Bergalis shows the body as a machine for the production of ideology. It is equally revealing that both Torri Thompson discussing the Renaissance, and Cathy Peppers analyzing postmodern cyberculture's interventions on the gendered (and in Adams's and Peppers's cases, to a much lesser extent, the racial) body, focus on its malleability for both cultural and political reinscription(s). Both these studies make clear that, in divergent ways, the body is literally moulded; unquestionably, it becomes, to paraphrase Teresa de Lauretis, our only technic and possession ("Desire" 132).

The inscription of the public agenda on the body has been and continues to be a very visible and tangible one. As Angela Wall's inquiry into competing AIDS discourse(s) shows, it is so highly politicized that it configures and reconfigures the full spectrum of polemical discourse, from the Reagan administration's public health policies to ACT-UP's extended critiques of those policies. In this collection, we hope to ask some new questions that will go beyond reducing the body, and the discursive practices that apply to it, to a simplistic binary argument.

Several of our authors, in speaking of very different historical periods, ask whether women can in fact subvert society's efforts to patrol their bodies. To cite one example, Cathy Peppers's analysis of Gina's situation in *Synners* problematizes the issue of control and invasion by asking whether we should identify the use of Gina's synning capabilities as an act of rape. It is important not to oversimplify issues of control, for they are anything but simple. Recognizing the complexity of these issues, many of the essays here implicitly ask such questions as what constitutes consent? Or violation of personal space? And most importantly, what constitutes personal space? If "personal space" is now no longer "sacred," was it ever? We can see clearly—in cyberpunk fiction, plastic surgery, and virtual reality, as well as in the current political debate over reproductive freedom—that the notion of an inviolate "personal space" has become at best a debatable concept.

This line of inquiry is not unrelated to the issue of how one considers technology. Can we use technology to our own ends?—clearly, women and men have benefitted from technologies in many ways—or will it ultimately destroy us? In the conclusion of her essay, Cathy Peppers points out that it is not enough for us to divorce ourselves intellectually from technology, since, as Gina observes, "All appropriate technology hurt somebody . . . *Fire* for Christ's sake [hurt somebody]" (183). And of course she is right: we cannot disavow "technology" as some Frankensteinish Other not of our making, unrelated to the many devices in modern life that allow us to travel more easily, to communicate more efficiently, and, perhaps, to lead richer lives.

It seems then that we should consider the possibility that technology could be used to contest totalizing cultural imperatives. Judy Wajcman, in *Feminism Confronts Technology*, observes that

> a recognition of the profoundly gendered character of technology need not lead to political pessimism or total rejection of existing technologies. The argument that women's relationship to technology is a contradictory one, combined with the realization that technology itself is a social construct, opens up fresh possibilities for feminist scholarship and action. (x)

If we juxtapose Wajcman's observation with Mary Shelley's ironic gloss on science and technology's progressive march forward ("The labours of men of genius, however erroneously directed, scarcely ever fail in ultimately turning to the solid advantage of mankind"), we might achieve an appropriately and usefully ambivalent attitude toward current technological advances in medicine, communication, travel, and education.[12] On the one hand, as feminists we resist a totalizing, monolithic construction of scientific and/or technological progress. On the other hand, we would be fools to argue that such progress can so rigidly over-determine our cultural situation(s) that the only use we can make of technology is to articulate more fully the terms of our own oppression.

The question posed by Gina about rape foregrounds another consideration implicit in many of the essays in this collection: How do desire and technology "interface"? Cathy Peppers examines the ambiguities inherent in cyberpunk's envisioning of the desiring body's radical separation from desire itself; Christine Laennec's essay addresses the profound ambivalence in the image of the (man-made) Assembly-Line Love Goddess; Alice Adams's and Deborah Wilson's work analyzes the male desire to achieve maternity through mechanical means. There are several kinds of desire analyzed in these essays. In critical readings of William Gibson's cyberpunk novels (Peppers), Brian De Palma's *Body Double* (Schreyer), and James Burt's "love doctoring" (Adams), we see male sexual desire as misogynist domination. In *Body Double* and in advertising practices alike we also find the idea of female sexual desire predicated upon a male gaze. Men's desire for control and manipulation of women is manifest, for example, in the use of the Renaissance scold's bridle, in Locke's manipulation of the figure of Rhetorica, in eighteenth-century conduct manuals for women, in childbirth practices, in fashion photography, in plastic surgery, and in AIDS discourse. At the same time, we can see that some women have considered what we might term patriarchal control of their bodies in a positive light. Examples of this per-spective can be found in the practice of "churching" (discussed by Torri Thompson), in Gina's "synning" (in Cathy Peppers's essay), as well as in Roberta Schreyer's analysis of the character of Holly Body, who, like some of her real-life counterparts, does not con-sider her work in porn films or her status as a porn movie star degrading, but rather, empowering.[13]

Not Merely Academic

These issues of control may at first seem like idle professorial chit-chat, but they are in fact questions that women deal with in everyday life. Are we being exploited in a job, or are we gaining valuable professional experience? If we have prenatal testing, are we taking the first step down the garden path of eugenics, or preventing future loss and heartache? Is it a sign of complete hypocrisy for feminists to wear makeup? Conversely, can they be politically effective if they have moustaches? (Apparently so, to judge from the emergence of Frida Kahlo as the new middlebrow pop feminist icon for the 1990s.) How serious should we be, and how many jokes at our expense should we laugh at—or make? Perhaps, as with racism and homophobia, the question should not be whether we have internalized the terms of our own oppression, but rather, to what degree. Once we accept that we cannot transcend our own overdetermined cultural moment, we still have to decide whether and/or where to draw a line.

For this reason, it is important for us to try to understand what is happening at this point in our history. To do so, we must analyze the past, and also realize that we will always be hindered by a cultural blind spot with regard to our own time. What conclusions are we to draw, for example, from the coincidence of Twilight Sleep maternity homes (which Cynthia Huff discusses) becoming popular at the same time as S. Weir Mitchell's famous "rest cure," a practice that similarly infantilized women and induced them to forfeit control not just of their bodies but also of their minds, to male doctors?[14] The fact that upper- and middle-class women were treated in this way confirms that the long-enduring social need to control and repress women was focused on their "unruly" bodies. However, while we build our own understanding of how the body has been manipulated in earlier periods of history, we must not distance ourselves from the past experience of others. We may not be able to identify personally with choices made by people in the past, but we should stop to reflect that we, too, (men and women) are operating within cultural pressures of which we cannot fully be aware.

In questioning, as Torri Thompson does in the opening pages of this volume, what history is and how it gets written, we are confronted with the issue of representation, which is central to this anthology. Throughout the collection, questions relating to perception and the viewer's gaze are raised, in such diverse media as advertising and fashion photography, AIDS discourse, and film. Challenging the predominance of representation, the essays also consider the body not only as the object of a gaze, but as the source of voice, as a speaking subject (albeit often, paradoxically, deprived of the power of speech).[15] These challenges merge forcefully in Thompson's essay on the forcible and sadistic silencing of women, in Huff's essay on the "anesthetizing" of the maternal voice (both in birthing practices and in the practices of literary historians), and Harrington's and Wall's essays on AIDS discourse and the body. Wall's analysis of the male homosexual body, as the 1990s equivalent of Freud's hysterical female body, presents another instance of a voice (in this instance that of AIDS activists), which has been denied, erased, and explained away as the result of physical deviation from the norm. On the other side of the same coin, Harrington shows how Kimberly Bergalis's "innocently infected" body, carried on a stretcher to Congressional hearings, simultaneously speaks for and embodies, figuratively as well as literally, the right-wing stance on AIDS.

The work in *Bodily Discursions* opens up many avenues of inquiry. In doing so, it focuses primarily on women; it also reflects on class, and to a lesser extent, race. As editors, we are aware of the collection's limitations, but we feel that the questions raised here resonate equally through issues of class and race, and hope that they might open up new avenues of study in these directions. For, as has often been pointed out, gender, class, and race are not discrete issues, but remain in many striking instances inextricably linked. Yet, as the historian Joann McNamara has quite correctly remarked, scholars tend to "see women as gendered and men as people."[16] Just as it is important to keep in mind that gender does not refer solely to women, it is equally important to remember that sexism, racism, homophobia, and classism are all manifestations of the same hatred and fear.

The fate of the body in the late twentieth century has much to teach us. Is it possible that the idea of the masculine as a norm from which women deviate is being replaced by a new ideal, a perfect or perfected (once machinomorphic, now technomorphic) body from which everyone else deviates? Perhaps our era, in which many upper-class girls get nose jobs for their sixteenth birthdays, is exposing a formula that has been operating in Western society for a long time. We seem to be a long way from being able to "recognize each other as different *and therefore exciting,* imperfect *and as such enough*" (Chapkis 175). But it does seem that, if we want to better understand our culture and our history, they are to be found written on the body, not only for us to read but to learn from, and not only to learn from, but, subsequently, for us to act upon.

Notes

1. See Evelyn Fox Keller's analysis of the cultural impact of the witch hunts in Europe, especially as they evolve through the political economy of academia generally, and the scientific disciplines particularly.

Evelyn Fox Keller, *Reflections on Gender and Science* (New Haven: Yale U P, 1985), 59–61.

2. See Marion Starkey's *The Devil in Massachusetts: A Modern Inquiry into the Salem Witch Trials* (Magnolia, MA: Peter Smith Publishers, Inc., 1969), still a standard work on the Salem Witch Trials, mass hysteria, and the motivations of the accusers.

3. For their classic analyses of Victorian anxieties over "self-abuse" (the Victorian euphemism for masturbation) as debilitating to both the individual and therefore to her/his society at large, see Steven Marcus, *The Other Victorians: A Study of Sexuality and Pornography in Mid-Nineteenth Century England* (New York: Basic Books, 1966), 19–22; and Ronald Pearsall, *The Worm in the Bud: The World of Victorian Sexuality* (New York: Macmillan, 1969), 417–21.

4. See John Gerassi for his analysis of hysteria over a "homosexual ring" operating in Boise, Idaho, in 1955: *The Boys of Boise: Furor, Vice, and Folly in An American City* (New York: Collier Books, 1968), especially 28–86. Although his psychology is very dated, Gerassi's inquiry is thorough and sympathetic, and he makes a forceful and—in the context of his time—progressive argument for decriminalizing homosexuality between consenting adults.

See also Jonathan Katz's interview with an anonymous man who was unjustly accused of sexually exploiting young boys during this period of scandal in Boise. Jonathan Katz, *Gay American History: Lesbians and Gay Men in the U.S.—A Documentary* (New York: Thomas Y. Crowell, 1976), 109–19.

Both Katz and Gerassi present overwhelming evidence that the Boise "scandal" was blown up entirely out of proportion, and that the subsequent miscarriages of justice were many and far-reaching. Katz's interviewee asserts that the furor originated in a cynical and cowardly effort to discredit a local politician, whose brother was notoriously gay, and that no "ring" of adult male homosexuals conspiring to corrupt adolescent boys existed (109).

In a military context, see Randy Shilts, *Conduct Unbecoming: Gays and Lesbians in the U.S. Military—Vietnam to the Persian Gulf.* (New York: St. Martin's P, 1993). Shilts argues that in the view of the N(aval) I(ntelligence) S(ervice), all female marines and naval personnel are potential lesbians. His argument is most compelling as he compares NIS investigative guidelines for ferreting out lesbians with the *Malleus Maleficarum*'s guidelines for ferreting out witches, 625–38.

Shilts also presents overwhelming documentation of anti-gay and anti-lesbian purges in the U.S. Armed Services, and the concomitant search for "rings" and "conspiracies," whose object was to "subvert," through seduction, "unsuspecting innocents," especially 383–93, 411–22, 499–509.

Gerassi, Katz, and Shilts all fully document the complete disregard for the civil rights of suspected lesbians and gay men, the appallingly coercive tactics—even psychological torture—in civil and military contexts respectively: sleep deprivation, isolation, imprisonment without access to legal counsel, and other violations of individual rights to due process.

5. There are of course any number of excellent sources on the anti-Communist hysteria of the McCarthy era, HUAC, and their political and cultural legacies. Victor S. Navasky's *Naming Names*, (New York: The Viking P, 1980) is particularly strong in its analysis of the rhetoric and representations of "communist subversion" in public discourse and popular culture during the McCarthy era; see also Nicholas von Hoffman, *Citizen Cohn* (New York: Doubleday, 1988), more specifically, for his close analysis of Cohn's political relationship with Senator Joe McCarthy, and, specifically, his role in the Army-McCarthy Hearings, 234–45.

6. The literature and media cultures of co-dependency, self-actualization, and recovery focus primarily—and too often deleteriously—on women. Wendy Kaminer notes that "According to one publisher, the co-dependency market is 85 percent female" (15). She also asserts, in her bracing critique of the "recovery movement," that

There are differing feminist perspectives on this mostly female phenomenon. Stressing that women should not be submissive and self-effacing, the recovery movement includes some popular feminist ideals. But calling femininity a disease obscures the fact that many women are trapped in abuse by circumstance, not weakness. They enter abusive marriages unwittingly, out of bad judgment or bad luck, not masochism; they remain because they can't afford to leave, perhaps because they've had less than equal educational opportunities or because they have young children and no day care. Problems like these are political as well as personal; they require collective as well as individual action, and objectivity, as well as introspection (15).

In other words, angry, dissatisfied women may not be dismissed (or persecuted) as witches any more, but instead run considerable risk of being judged as "dysfunctional," rather than being encouraged to identify the circumstances of their own oppression and direct their anger outwards.

Wendy Kaminer, *I'm Dysfunctional, You're Dysfunctional: The Recovery Movement and Other Self-Help Fashions* (Reading, MA: Addison-Wesley Publishing Company, 1992).

7. See E. D. Hirsch *Cultural Literacy: What Literate Americans Know* (Boston: Houghlin Mifflin Company, 1987).

8. As in the following specific instances: Salem, MA, in the 1690s; Boise, ID, in 1955; the Army-McCarthy Senate Hearings in 1954; the lesbian and gay purges in various branches of the armed forces since World War II, but especially in the 1950s and mid-to late 1970s.

9. Hirsch's book offers a checklist, composed of an arbitrarily selected collection of facts, allusions, dates, and personages, that the reader can use to discover whether or not s/he is "culturally literate," 146–215.

Similarly, many self-help guides and confessional books also offer checklists and questionnaires that purport to offer the reader quick, straightforwardly diagnostic templates to determine whether or not the reader, the reader's family, adult partner, friends, or even work environment are "dysfunctional" or "co-dependent." Thus, they urge the reader to score her/his reading on scales that determine levels and types of dysfunction.

The problem, as Kaminer points out, is that often the terms are made too elastic, and that they become so inclusive as to be meaningless. According to Kaminer, one such term would be "child abuse." "If child abuse is every form of inadequate nurturance, then being raped by your father is in the same general class as being ignored or not helped with your homework. When everything is child abuse, nothing is." (Kaminer 26–27).

10. While men have not infrequently turned to plastic surgery for cosmetic reasons, their numbers seem to be growing, and plastic surgery for male beauty seems to be gaining more acceptance. See, for example, Richard Alleman, "Waist Not," *Vogue* (June 1993), 126–27.

On the other hand, for the last twenty years, major cosmetics companies in the U.S. have developed full lines of cosmetics for men, but have not yet determined how to market them. The exceptions would be "personal care" products such as shaving lotions, shampoos, colognes, and more recently, lines of skin care products, such as Clinique's lines of facial scrubs, creams, and toners for men.

Of course, whether the average male will come to accept mascara and lipstick as part of his daily grooming ritual remains to be seen.

11. Nonetheless, the rhetoric of opposition remains firmly entrenched, even in the most provocative, sophisticated, and challenging texts engaged in critiques of the body. For example, in his introduction to *Body Politics*, Michael Ryan insists on localizing (em)body(ied) oppression in "The heterosexual white males who largely shape and run our world," whom, he claims,

don't like bodies. They prefer the abstractions of moral mythography, which transform people and things like welfare mothers, communism, Saddam Hussein, gays and lesbians, homelessness, economic inequality, and the like into allegorical figures like "Evil," "Individual Responsibility," and "Political Correctness." Those people and things are thereby denied the complex modes of representation they deserve, modes that elude moral allegorization. Moral allegorization is especially difficult when one is connected bodily to the people and things one represents (xi).

While Ryan's point about "the abstractions of moral mythography" remains valuable, and, therefore, should be given serious attention, we must interject that, by categorically dismissing heterosexual white males as chief villains and world oppressors, he is engaging in the very sort of discursive practice he wishes to repudiate. Michael Ryan, "Introduction," in *Body Politics: Disease, Desire, and the Family* (Boulder: Westview P, 1994, xi–xiii).

See also Arthur and Marilouise Kroker, "Scenes from the Last Sex: Feminism and Outlaw Bodies," in Arthur and Marilouise Kroker, eds., *The Last Sex: Feminism and Outlaw Bodies*. (New York: St. Martin's P, 1993), 1–19, for a similarly entrenched oppositional discourse.

That important work on the cutting edge of cultural criticism resorts to a simplistic rhetoric of opposition underscores just how difficult it is to redefine critical perspectives and terms.

12. Professor Waldman to Victor Frankenstein, just prior to Victor's creation of the creature. Mary Shelley, *Frankenstein*, ed. by Johanna M. Smith (Boston: Bedford Books of St. Martin's P, 1993), 49.

13. Andrew Ross, *No Respect: Intellectuals and Popular Culture* (New York: Routledge, 1989), 188.

14. See Ellen L. Bassuk, "The Rest Cure: Repetition or Resolution of Victorian Women's Conflicts?" in *The Female Body in Western Culture: Contemporary Perspectives*, ed. Susan Rubin Suleiman (Cambridge: Harvard U P, 1986), 139–51.

15. Feminist criticism—particularly the work of French critics such as Luce Irigaray and Helene Cixous—has argued that women's voices are in no way disconnected from their (female) bodies. Along similar lines, Belenky, *et al.*, in *Women's Ways of Knowing*, using Carol Gilligan's work as a departure point, study how women from various backgrounds are able or unable to speak for themselves, and to articulate—or not to articulate—an autonomous subjectivity.

16. Comment made during a question and answer session at a conference on Women and Gender in The Middle Ages and The Renaissance, the Newberry Library, Chicago, Illinois, May 3, 1991.

I

THE DISCIPLINED BODY

1

FEMALE BODIES MISBEHAVING: MORTIFICATION IN EARLY MODERN ENGLISH DOMESTIC TEXTS

Torri L. Thompson

An Introduction

More than sixty years ago, Virginia Woolf noted in *A Room of One's Own* the seeming contradictions between the strength and agency of Shakespeare's female characters compared to her perception of actual women living in early modern England. Woolf looked to historians to provide her with an explanation for the differences, but she discovered only disappointment. Unfortunately, we still are unable to definitely respond to Woolf's dilemma, although perhaps the question has changed somewhat. We no longer expect history to provide certain answers because the post-modern world has redefined history as an ideologically determined social construct; thus literary and historical texts are historically situated cultural artifacts. Both of these concepts make it impossible to reconstruct a definitive understanding of the female body in early modern England. Fortunately, however, literary critics and social historians have at their disposal an alternative discursive tradition of sixteenth- and seventeenth-century prescriptive domestic texts that consistently re-present the early modern female subject, or as Ruth Kelso once called her, "the Lady of the Renaissance." Constance Jordan, Linda Woodbridge, Barbara McManus, Katherine Henderson, Lynda Boose, and Valerie Wayne, among others, recognize the importance of textual sources that traditionally have been considered nonobjective, biased, inferior, nonliterary, and, basically, inadmissible evidence. As Wayne argues, "becoming alert to alternative discourses that are present at a particular historical moment and the variety of textual forms associated with them may enlarge our notion of what is available to us as we reconstruct history and politics in our own present" (174). This essay presents three texts that help to negotiate a context for the mortification or public disciplining of the female body in early modern England: William Heale's *Apologie for Women* (1609), Thomas Bentley's *The Monument for Matrones* (1582), and the anonymous *Certaine Questions by Way of Conference Betwixt a Chauncelor and a Kinswoman of His Concerning Churching of Women* (1601).[1]

Unfortunately, the feminist project of providing basic cultural information about English women from 1540 to 1640 still remains incomplete because, as Mary Astell noted long ago, histories are "writ by [men] . . . and they recount each other's great exploits, and have always done so" (Kelly 84). Not only has history been male focused, but also traditional historical methodology has privileged sources that, by definition, record a male past. These sources include church and military histories, and legal, consti-tutional, and political histories. The traditional historical sources seldom include domestic life and female experience.

Domesticity

Domestic prescriptive texts have traditionally stood outside the margins of accepted scholarly discourse, whether historical or literary. Domestic texts are those that attempt to define social desire within the domestic realm. Rather than providing us with an accurate portrayal of early modern English domestic life, it is more likely that these texts, most of which are male authored, present their readers with a picture of what a patriarchal society wanted or needed domestic life and relations to be like. However, at the same time, because these texts are written for a popular audience, it is essential for the persuasive purposes of behavior modification that the audience be convinced that the texts repre-sent life as it is rather than life as culturally imagined. Thus, the twentieth century reader should be aware that these works are just as complex and require just as careful an analysis as do more traditionally literary works. The texts include a number of dis-cursive formats, such as prayer and devotional texts, practical home guides and marriage manuals, and legal and historical documents of an unofficial nature.

In addition, early modern English domestic texts provide twentieth-century readers with alternative modes of critical discussion that allow us to move beyond traditionally agon or strife-centered scholarly discourse, the either/or proposition that has forced the entire critical debate over women's history into a binary opposition. I critically find it more productive to think in terms of alternative sources, multiple perspectives or "vantage points," and reader as ally, based on the work of Joan Kelly. I want to suggest, in this essay, that mortification of the early modern female body made public the perceived or constructed private lapses in women's behavior. Punishments such as the scold's bridle and the ducking stool, both of which included a procession through town, signify private bodily sin that is interpreted as having public consequences.[2] Lynda Boose discusses several physical means of controlling women's bodies and the attendant social justification in her article, "Scolding Brides and Bridling Scolds: Taming the Woman's Unruly Member." In this essay, she insists on the necessity of critically acknowledging the *physical* nature of male discipline or mortification of female bodies when one is attempting to analyze dramatic or literary genres. As Boose's historical contextualization of *The Taming of the Shrew*[3] suggests, men seem not to have been relieved of their anxiety concerning domestic authority over their wives, in spite of the marital contract. The wife's position of absolute marital subjection is clearly expressed in early modern English domestic texts:

> as for their husbands, them must they obey and cease from commanding and perform subjection. For this surely doth nourish concord very much when the wife is ready at hand at her husband's commandment, when she will apply herself to his will, when she endeavoreth herself to seek his contentation and to do him pleasure, when she will eschew all things that might offend him. (Klein 17)

Although the above quote from *An Homily of the State of Matrimony* makes the wife's role very explicit, the number of prescriptive texts focusing on female subordinance suggests that early modern England needed the repetition of ritualized discipline to insure that no one forgot the female body's subordinate status. However, the binarism suggested by this perspective is perhaps eroded by Linda Fitz in "What Says the Married Women," which suggests that perhaps women were not conforming in the required ways (11). And the large output of domestic prescriptive texts is thus explained by need resulting from women who are transgressing social codes. The three texts to be discussed in my essay provide discursive examples of early modern England's attempts to contain the female body, but at the same time, suggests how those attempts possibly were mediated.

An Apologie for Women. or An Proposition to Mr. Dr. G. his
assertion. Who held in the Act at Oxforde. Anno 1608. That it was
lawfull for husbands to beate their wives, 1609

In this polemical pamphlet, William Heale argues against the physical abuse of wives; however, his title may reflect multiple social apprehensions of the female's innate nature: in addition to "for" women, Heale could be appropriating the female speaking subject in his role as white, male protector; he could also be apologizing to men because women "all are defectives" (Smith 68), and he does describe at length the "appropriate" use of authority and discipline. While making his apology, he does encourage husbands to use Christian compassion in reforming their inherently fallible wives; yet, he neither defends nor proposes the equal status of the two sexes. Finally, *Apologie* is surely also a reference to the rhetorical category of *apologia*, which is defined as a formal defense of an idea, religion, and so on. Yet, any critical analysis of Heale's text should take into account the perception of English male culture that he was overly protective of women, and thus, weak. As one text describes him, he was "a zealous maintainer of the honour of the Female Sex . . . He was always esteemed an ingenious Man, but weak, as being too much devoted to the feminine Sex" (Wood 314).

The introduction to *An Apologie* addresses issues of class and education. Heale says that he is writing in response to a Mr. Dr. G. who publicly supported at Oxford, husbands' legal right and duty to beat their wives: "But nowe this bad cause hath gotten better patrones: especially when in the Universitie, in the open Act, in publike disputation their names are called in question, their capacitie thought unfit for learning, themselves adjudged worthie of blowes" (3). The public nature of Mr. Dr. G.'s comments is mirrored by much of the mortification of the early modern English female body. The family, state, and church participated in events designed to function as pedagogical spectacles; these events included victims and audiences: everyone participated, either in a classical cathartic sense, or, often, literally in the administration or reception of punishment. Heale, arguing against wife abuse, recognizes very self-consciously the connection between "private" or women's domestic behavior and the correspondent performative nature of public discipline: "And as the private event of this action must needs be inconvenient unto ourselves, so the publike example thereof is dangerous unto the common-wealth. For whatsoever in this kinde is committed within our own family, is acted (as it were) on an open theater, where wee have store of spectators: our children, our servants, our neighbors" (16).

Another public form of wife abuse that Heale addresses is the discursive tradition of misogyny prevalent in the Middle Ages as well as in Renaissance England. Heale suggests that one source of motivation for wife abuse is the large number of texts written to attack women's reputations:

> it is a custome growne so common to under-valew their [women] worth, as everie rymer hath a libell to impeach their modestie; everie phantastike a poeme to plaine their unfaith-fulness . . . . None . . . upon anie iust cause, have yet filled the world with pamphlets, things most idle in themselves, and most disgracefull unto women (1, 2).

Interestingly, Heale does not distinguish between popular and "high" art. He also accuses the Renaissance theater of reproducing misogyny for an audience which was at least partially "illiterate," through playwrights who "likewise . . . make ostentation of their wit unto the stage" (2). He attempts to establish intertextual links between private and public, as well as diverse rhetorical situations: poems, pamphlets, plays, public argumentation, and the literal beating of women by their husbands.[4] Heale's discussion of the multiple sources that contribute to wife abuse within his society reinforces our understanding of the public nature of much of the wife abuse, justified as discipline, in early modern England. In this sense, corporeal punishment is a public arena in which the gender politics of the period are played out, and a tight link is forged between civic and domestic discipline.

Although Heale's defense of women is often based on their supposed natural debilities, his text is much more palatable than William Whately's *A Bride-Bush, A Wedding Sermon*, 1623, which suggests: "Is this to erre in her love, to smite her on the face, or to fetch bloud or blewnesse of her flesh? But yet if a wife will put upon her selfe even servile conditions; if she will abase her selfe to foolish, childish, slavish behavior; I see not why the rod, or staffe,

or wand, should not be for the fooles backe in this case also"
(107).[5] Conversely, Heale attempts to mediate the physical abuse
of women within a culture that consistently defends its right and
duty to reform and control the female body through corporeal discipline. This culture is allowed to define women as either redeemed
or sinful, to the extent of life and death: "a husband taking his wife
in adultery might lawfully kill her" (Heale 51).[6] Because of the
female's innately sinful condition, the husband is duty bound to
redeem his wife through mortification: "so hee must not looke to
find a wife without a fault, but thinke that she is committed to him
to reclaime her from her faults" (Smith 68).

The Monument of Matrones: conteining seven severall Lamps of Virginitie, or distinct treatises, 1582

Thomas Bentley's *The Monument of Matrones* is a multi-
volume devotional text that was composed for the seemingly
straightforward reason of aiding women in their private daily religious exercises or contemplations. However, in the section of the
text discussed in this essay, it is clear that any rhetorical analysis
of Bentley will be most effective when performed on multiple
rhetorical levels. Although this is a devotional text, it is rhetorically
framed in order to perform particular cultural work: in this case,
the reinforcement of male sexual control over the female body, but
through self-management; in other words, the disciplinary goal is
for women to internalize the cultural message concerning adultery.
The text is rhetorically directed to a gendered audience by presenting itself as a devotional manual written explicitly for women,[7]
and the reproduction and almost infinite replication of sinful
females in this text suggests that women are constantly in need of
reformation. If the female is gender-defined by its need for re-form,
then the early modern male is gender-defined by his duty to reform in a god-like fashion—truly man (i.e., male) is made and
makes in the image of the Judeo-Christian creative god. The
female is ultimately malleable in her capacity to be re-formed, but
also in her susceptibility to de-forming influences.

The complete title to the fifth and sixth lamps[8] of Bentley's
text directs the audience to the object of reformation: "The Fift
Lampe of Virginitie: Conteining sundrie forms of christian praiers
and meditations, to bee used onlie of and for all sorts and degrees
of women, in their severall ages and callings; as namelie, of
Virgins, Wives, Women with child, Midwives, Mothers, Daughters,

Mistresses, Maids, Widowes, and old women." Although the vast bulk of this large book is directed towards women, the sixth lamp does contain a brief discussion of husbands' duties toward their wives, but it is significant that men are not mentioned in the title page of the fifth and sixth books in spite of the frontispiece's mention that the book is necessary for both sexes. The frontispiece's visual rhetoric is likewise instructive: Elizabeth I's initials are showcased in the visual center of the page, right and left. Obviously this attempt to flatter the monarch might also suggest that in spite of her royal prerogative and her constant assertions of princehood and body politic, that ultimately even Elizabeth is a daughter of Eve, as are all women, and would benefit from such a collection of religious devotions.

Standing in contestatory relation to this reading is the long, flattering dedicatory epistle to Elizabeth which denies her need of reform because she is already a good woman and has written and/or translated her own devotional texts. In connection, Bentley repeatedly addresses what he fears is the audience's potential perception of a superfluity of devotionals or "domestical libraries" (sig. B.i.); not only do many other devotionals already exist; moreover, many are written by women. This concern suggests that the binary opposition between men and women, especially regarding authorship, is at least problematic enough that Bentley feels the need to textually authorize his position as male author. However, in addition, he is preempting the issue of Queen Elizabeth having written devotional texts herself. Apparently, though, his worries did not ultimately prevent him from producing one more handy, male-authored collection of moral exempla designed to tell women how to read their own lives.

The *Monument of Matrones* offers a variety of discursive traditions to its female audience: a section on the duties of women; a dictionary of women in the Bible; and a series of prayers for women in their various domestic and social roles, based on male definition of the female body: for example, the daughter in law, or "anie woman, when she is woed of anie man to be his wife" (46); "the wife for hir husband being a Captaine or Souldiour, and gone a war-fare," and the like (79). Just as male subject positions determine those of the women in the culture, in this text, male values are normative, or, in other words, the position from which female values are determined. Although Bentley suggests the sins committed against normative standards may occasion physical punishment, the text is most interesting in its attempts to logocentrically mortify the female body. While not openly advocating physical beating, the text just as effectively batters women into subordination through male-authored confession. Bentley's prayers concerning women's failings, especially those of the body, are psychodramas in which women are not voicing their own experience, but are forced to incriminate themselves through male-authored, predetermined confessions.[9] By putting the prayers in first person, Bentley manipulates the text so that it appears that the women themselves are authoring these confessions of sin and shortcoming. As Foucault reminds his readers in *Discipline and Punish* (although he specifically refers to torture and capital punishment by the state, and his choice of pronouns is always masculine), the public exhibition and confession by "the body of the condemned man . . . [is] the herald of his own condemnation" (*Discipline and Punish* 43).

It also has been suggested that the women represented by Bentley's text have perhaps no voice at all, due to what may be multiple submerged references to the scold's bridle and the ducking stool.[10] In the beginning of the prayer entitled "A lamentation of anie woman, virgin, wife, or widowe, for hir virginitie or chastitie, lost by fornication or adulterie: not unapt also to be used of anie Christian sinner, or sinfull soule adulterated and fallen awaie by sinne from hir spirituall spouse Christ Jesus," the female persona describes the thwarting of her linguistic desire: "And how can I speake, when as the tong is tied, and the lips dare not once moove or wag? The tong doth not his office; the throte is dammed up; all the senses and instruments are polluted with iniquitie" (*fift lampe* 13). On a narrative level, the woman wants to beg God for forgiveness, but she is unable. This disability is supposedly due to her throat being blocked by the sin that has polluted her body; thus, she is forced to ask the saints to verbally intercede for her. However, Bentley's description of her physical sensations mirrors a Quaker woman's testimony that describes wearing a scold's bridle: "'three barrs of Iron to come over my face, and a peece of it was put in my mouth, which was so unreasonable big a thing for that place as cannot be well related, which was locked to my head, and so I stood their time with my hands bound behind me with the stone weight of Iron upon my head and the bitt in my mouth to keep me from speaking'" (Boose 206). Bentley's text is a tremendously conflicted document: a man "writing" a female character who *says* metaphorically that she is unable to speak, but then goes on to "speak" for fourteen pages, according to what is literally a predetermined script.

In the lamentation that forms the bulk of the prayer, the woman rhetorically asks, "what shall I saie?" "what have I felt?" "how am I fallen?" "how am I thus come to naught" and then proceeds to answer, almost like a catechism, each of her (character) / his (author) / their (readers) questions in ways that damn her beyond any doubt. Hence, the female "narrator" fulfills the desire of the author/culture by becoming a self-condemning mouthpiece. The voice reveals that it has polluted itself and hopes that "the sowe may be washed from hir filthines; the dog eate of the crumbs that fall from hir maisters table, and a sinner worse than Marie Magdalen . . . be saved" (15, 26). Just as the Quaker woman's description of the "iron bitt" suggests oral or fellatial rape, so Bentley's preauthored devotions *cum* confessions are forced into the linguistic cavities of his female personas, giving new and very sinister life to the expression "putting words in someone else's mouth." In a phallocratic culture, the woman's "unruly member" is depressed/replaced/rescripted in this prayer, through confession. The sinner's questions (1) are rhetorical in the sense that the character/author/readers know the answers; (2) are nonrhetorical because they provide a linguistic space to question what often seems to be a crushingly over-determined subject position; (3) are more than "rhetorical" in that they represent the inability of the nonspeaking, speaking subject to identify her subject position. Perhaps in allowing the questions, the author has left open the author-ity of his text, unintentionally refuting the seamless whole it appears on the surface to be.

This same prayer is complicated from yet another perspective: the woman's sexual sin is narratologically obfuscated because of vague pronoun referents and a convoluted plot line:

> Wherefor after much alluring . . . they promised me . . . craftie conveiances to avoid the subtiltie of Satan; but afterward, the Divell in the same night transformed into an Angell of light, reasoned with me, saying, When thou art alone, get thee up and go unto them . . . condiscend, and harken unto them, do it, and cease not, neither stagger thou at the matter, till they be satisfied . . . . I, oh unhappy creature, skipping out of my bed at the dawning of the day, could not finish my wonted devotion . . . but following too much mine own fleshlie affections, folded and wrapped myself in the snares of the Divell. I got me unto the bed of the wicked, and required of them to perform the covenants

in the night, which we had made the day before. (fifth lamp
17; my modernization)

A mysterious "they" urges her to fornicate, and the devil appears as
an "Angell of light" to convince her. For reasons not made clear, the
woman assumes agency and "skips" out of bed the next morning,
demanding that "they" fulfill the agreement made the night before,
even though earlier in the narrative, Satan seems to be trying to
convince the female character to satisfy "them," rather than
demand that they satisfy her.

The narratological confusion of *The Monument* may also be
due to the fact that Bentley's "dramas" are necessarily hypertextual
because they are designed to fit a number of sinful occasions and
types of sinners rather than one specific woman's sexual
transgression, thus, the polymorphous nature that results from the
author's attempts to shepherd his sixteenth-century readers down
the most appropriate narratological paths. The sinning woman's
choice would be determined by her *own* sinful state or experience,
but the general reader of devotions not using these prayers as
forms of confession and repentance could choose and construct a
scenario. The performative nature of the text, thus evident, encourages readers to participate in the formation of narrative structure
and also leaves it open to reader intervention—in this case, the
female reader. The submerged erotic effect of this prayer is obvious
as it encourages the reader, by leaving the narrative vague and
confused, to quite literally fantasize the sexually explicit details. The
rhetorical source of this capability to mentally re-create mirrors the
medieval tradition of *memento mori*, imagining Christ's death and
by extension one's own death in order to create the appropriate
desire for repentance. The possibility of the reader's imagination
leading to sexual titillation and stimulation in the Bentley text is
clear. In 1703, Ned Ward, commenting on the public beating of
nude women by men, criticized the punishment "as if it were
designed rather to feast the eyes of the spectators than to correct
vice, or reform manners" (Burford 79).

In conclusion, much early modern English discipline had
humiliation and the public display of the female body as its goals.
Thus, Bentley's female persona acknowledges that she probably
will be publicly displayed, perhaps by being forced to wear a white
veil and walk through the village so that everyone can witness her
guilt: "bewaile me that am taken awaie and made a publike
example of reproch to all women" (24). However, the humiliation in

this text is not finite because (1) it takes on a perpetual presence for the audience, whether female or male, each time they read the printed lamentation; (2) they relive it each time another early modern Englishwoman is literally punished; or (3) the women have internalized it themselves, whether they "sin" or not; since the text includes all classifications of women, the females in the multiple social roles designated by the title all confess to sexual sin. The textual voice resonates refrains of guilt and sorrow, and is multi-generational in its cry of "Wo is me, O mother." Although the actual narrative describing the sin is intriguingly specific, the echoing choir of voices seems to endlessly replicate the sinful nature of all women, all daughters of Eve.

Certaine Questions by way of Conference betwixt a Chauncelor and a Kinswoman of his concerning Churching of Women, 1601

This Puritan text concerning "Popish custome and ceremony" is an argument against the Anglican practice of *churching*, inherited from ancient Judeo/Christian purification rituals.[11] The process was the manner in which the Church of England read-mitted women to the church after they had given birth (*Certaine Questions* 21.)[12] In *Certaine Questions*, the woman and the chancellor are arguing over who has the right to define and prescribe the post-parturient body: the individual believer, or the church and the male interests it protects? When traditional Protestant conscience-based arguments for personal religious and even political autonomy are taken to the ultimate logical extension, they necessarily entail an argument for women's authority concerning their own bodies and souls; however, I do not want to argue that Protestantism in itself recognized the autonomous female subject or made any allowance for such a position. In fact, the tract's very title argues against such extension: the *kinswoman* is defined by her relationship to the *chauncelor* who has a freestanding title of social and religious authority.

The female speaker in this text argues against churching from a traditional Puritan understanding of the role of conscience; this capacity is provided by God to guide the believer through the complexities of a fallen world. By applying her conscience, the speaker identifies the gendered nature of churching and its role in defining the female body because it does not apply to men. She uses this point to argue against the chancellor's definition of churching as thanksgiving: "I holde my husbande a farre more

woorthy member of the Church then my selfe, and therefore I see
no reason why yee should not cause him to bee Churched as well
as me, and so all others in our parishe that have escaped either
drowning or danger of death" (58). However, in spite of the gender
hierarchy reflected in this statement, embedded within its logic is
an argument for equity: the female speaker demands the theoretical rights of all individual Christians to determine her or his own
salvation and relationship to God and the community of the
redeemed: "I doe well assure my selfe it were a sinne and wickednes
in mee, because it is against the light of mine owne conscience"
(45–46). This Protestant notion of autonomous "reading" of the
word/world allows for the perception of the female body as text,
leading the reader to ask, "Who has the authority to interpret it?" It
also creates a space into which arguments for gender equity will
develop in subsequent generations. Additionally, the proto-feminist
submerged argument is a solid challenge to early modern English-
men's privileges of religious and social authority expressed through
the Anglican Church's doctrine and customs; thus, such arguments are sites of potential liberation, even though the feminist
argument was subordinate and unconscious at the time the statement was composed.

The female speaker's claim to autonomy in decisions regarding her body stands in contrast to the early modern English definition of women's bodies within legal, ecclesiastical, and marital
discourses. Historically and discursively, we can trace a line along
which women's bodies have been defined as the material possessions or chattel of their husbands. One author argues, in 1542,
that "the beasts won't be subservient to their husbands, but rather
take upon them to rule, as though not only their goodes, but also
themselves were not their husbands and at his commandment"
(*Golden Boke* Biiii). The further combination of capitalism and
Protestantism strengthens this philosophy by redefining marriage
as contract, wife as commodity, and discipline or mortification as
the reshaping of a defective product, all in the service of the
Protestant capitalist state. Marriage becomes a religious duty rather
than an optional and less perfect state as it was understood by
Catholicism. And the products of that union (children), all potential
new Christians, further position women as commodities.

As such, women's ability to exercise religious authority was
in general totally denied by the English church. Although in early
Puritan separatist groups, women often had a more active role in
the daily administration of the church, their leadership often dis-

sipated when (1) entire sects were marginalized to extinction; (2) for survival, the dissenting church attempted to align itself a little more closely to the Anglican Church in regards to the regulation of women's voices; or (3) the fledgling movements gained enough strength and solidity to no longer need women's active participation. In some groups, such as the Quakers, women maintained linguistic identity as speaking subjects in spite of tremendous pressure and punishment from civic and ecclesiastical authority. Boose notes such an example in a collection of Quaker texts entitled *The Lambs Defence against Lyes* in which a woman is "bridled," imprisoned, and beaten, even though "they had not any thing to lay to my Charge" (206). Bridling, punishment specific to scolds, obviously attempts to control women's ability to religiously define themselves and achieve agency through language. It is no surprise that this woman was a Quaker, one of the few religious groups that allowed women at least limited ecclesiastic and linguistic equality. However, in the majority of Puritan sects, women's religious roles gradually were deleted and condemned, a decision justified by early modern culture's definition of women as inherently sinful, signified through the blood of menses and childbirth.

These bloody signifiers provided proof of women's incompetence for social and religious leadership.[13] Women had domestic authority, but only that delegated by or a correlate of male authority. The chancellor reminds the female speaker, "what a devil should you medle with any of these matters? It were much fitter for such as you are, to medle with your spindle and your wheele, and soberlie to attend your trades and vocations, then thus in the pride of your heartes to controlle your betters, and to deale in Church causes which belong not unto you" (67). However, the chancellor's attempts to verbally reduce the female speaker to subjection are futile because in this text, she is positioned as rhetorically dominant (not because she is a woman, but because she is a Protestant mouthpiece). She provides reason-based arguments, while the chancellor finally resorts to bribery and, then, threats.

The female speaker argues that the church defines women as unclean because of its insistence on churching, regardless of women's determination of their bodily and spiritual status. She argues that the church uses childbirth to disqualify women from the fellowship of believers: childbirth and the attendant blood taboo differentiates them and defines them as unclean in spite of the chancellor's insistence that the ritual only represents, in the

Reformed Church, a thanksgiving for the safe delivery of the child
and preservation of the mother. The female speaker retorts, "for
what may Purifying I pray you presuppose, but some former
uncleannesse? Likewise, that a woman is helde for the time as an
excommunicate person, and therefore most solemnly be receyved
agayn into the church. For what may Churching presuppose but
some former excluding, shutting out and cutting off?" (23). Her
use of the passive grammatical construction of "a woman is helde"
emphasizes her inability to make choices regarding her body on
the basis of religious conscience because the church is making
those choices through doctrine and social custom.

Her argument that childbirth is neither polluting nor requires
ecclesiastical thanksgiving is supported by the *felix culpa* that led
to Mary's birth of Jesus. Ironically, however, childbirth signifies,
for the Anglican church, women's need for recurrent public mortification. Such impurity, however, carries great political and cultural significance beyond the churching ritual: many midwives
were burned at the stake as so-called witches because they and
the women they cared for represented and exercised very literally
the power of life and death over the male capitalist possessions of
wife and child. Thus, the parturient female body signifies in early
modern England a marginalizing, yet empowering experience, a
marker of inequality, but a sign interpreted by male authority as
innately subversive. In order for the Anglican Church to reappro-
priate reproduction, women are constructed as sinful and in need
of redemption from the most obvious signification of their
differentiated status. Churching is a stripping away, a divesting of
the power that childbirth confers; churching is the "some such
marke to be known by, which is a manifest signe . . . " that the
Church requires as visible, tangible tag so that it can interpret and
define the female body (*Churching* 21). Without it, women are not
recognized as readable texts by sixteenth- and seventeenth-
century English male culture.

In conclusion, the early modern Anglican Church, socially,
legally, and cosmically, defines the female body as sinful and never
allows it to escape its post-lapsarian status. The church's continuing insistence on the necessity of churching for all post-
parturient women persists with energy and strength because the
ritual is economically and culturally advantageous. Churching,
whether manifested in domestic texts through the author, in
ecclesiastical texts such as in the *Book of Common Prayer* or the
homilies, or in social participation through church membership,

represents a power differential. Ian Maclean, in *The Renaissance Notion of Woman*, notes that women's "natural infirmity" in regards to menstruation and childbirth was seen to categorically disenfranchise them; thus the impurity of the female body is established, opening a way to socially construct a naturalized position of disempowerment (17–18). Ecclesiastical and cultural mortification of the female body, in all of its diverse forms, enabled sixteenth- and seventeenth-century English society to reinscribe women as sinful, justifying their exclusion from positions and institutions of power. Churching publicly dramatized a definition of the female that was otherwise discursively bestowed. In *Certaine Questions*, the female speaker's argument against churching is an insistence on self-knowledge rather than the obedient acceptance of canonized definition.

A Conclusion

The need for mortification or physical discipline of the female body resulted from Aristotelian physiological definitions of the female as incomplete at best, and evil at worst.[14] Thus, the early modern female was seen as constantly in need of reforming and reshaping, which ensured indefinite social control of women's bodies; mortification thus becomes a form of definition, of identification for culture at large, and unfortunately, perhaps also self-identification for the female cartesian subject, whether in a group or as an individual: "I am punished, therefore I am." However, as these texts have demonstrated, although direct forms of contestation are not always possible, the texts themselves reveal gaps into which female resistance can be figured. And if New Historicism is correct in its assumptions, these discursive gaps are indicative of stresses and fissures within the larger society.

William Heale's *An Apologie for Women* creates for its readers a perspective on early modern English culture that is terrifying in its implications: this is a society in which the beating of women occurs with great regularity, if we base this assumption on (1) the role of corporeal punishment in the culture; and (2) the great number of discussions of wife abuse that appear in multiple discursive forms: Heale's text, the overt purpose of which is to directly attack the practice of wife abuse; *An Homily on the State of Matrimony* which, in its larger discussion of Christian marriage, exhorts men not to beat their wives; and William Whately's *Bride-Bush: A Wedding Sermon*, which encourages its male readers to try all other methods of character reformation before resorting to beating, but suggests that some women will be reformed no other way. However, what this expansive discourse of corporeal punishment for women suggests is that the subject is being debated across the culture. And we need to remember that early modern England condoned and practiced corporeal punishment in all its forms, from whipping posts in every village center, to public executions. So to even debate the justice of beating women suggests that the culture is beginning to shift in regards to the female body and its treatment.

Bentley's *The Monument for Matrones* presents a much more difficult critical task if one's goal is to avoid binarism. In the prayer entitled, "A lamentation of anie woman, virgin, wife, or widowe, for hir virginitie or chastitie, lost by fornication or adulterie . . . " (13), the text so explicitly positions the female body within transgressive sexual space, that it is almost impossible to make an argument for anything but the binary opposition of dominance and oppression regarding women's bodies. However, this prayer is only one of many in the complete text and placing it within the larger context of the whole book might mediate its affect. In addition, Bentley does mention in his introduction that many women, including Queen Elizabeth, have written devotionals. This would place women in an active authorial role and challenge the dominance that Bentley as author represents.

However, it is within the anonymous *Certaine Questions* that we find the strongest challenge to the binary opposition of male = good, female = bad. It is not simply a matter of subversion or containment, or that some women had power to make choices and others did not. Rather we need to ask how much and in what forms women did exert agency. In *Certaine Questions*, we can look at the female speaker's arguments against the churching ritual, and through a feminist analysis of this primarily Puritan text, discover a nascent feminist subtext. Foucault's discussion of power relations between the dominant and the subordinate is particularly relevant to this project:

> power is exercised rather than possessed; it is not the "privilege," acquired or preserved, of the dominant class, but the overall effect of its strategic positions—[there are] innumerable points of confrontation, focuses of instability, each of which has its own risks of conflict, of struggles, and of an at least temporary inversion of the power relations" (26–27).

Early modern Englishwomen's lives were clearly mediated, restricted, obstructed, qualified, and relativized by patriarchal politics. However, as Foucault suggests, the disempowered usually are not totally without will. This essay has attempted to work out ways in which domestic texts provide a unique locus for investigating not only negative discursive constructions of the female body, but also ways in which those very discourses betray their own instability.

Notes

1. These texts can be accessed through the microfilm series corresponding to *Pollard and Redgrave's Short Title Catalogue*. The STC number must be looked up in the cross-referenced reel catalogs.

2. As Lawrence Stone notes in *Family, Sex, and Marriage in England, 1500–1800*, during the early modern period, private life was only beginning to be recognized and valorized. In contrast, we find maintained in many domestic texts an intertextual union of family, church, and state. For example, William Gouge, in *Of Domesticall Duties*, 1622, notes that "a familie is a little Church, and a little common-wealth, at least a lively representation thereof, whereby triall may be made of such as are fit for any place of authoritie, or of subiection in Church or common-wealth" (18).

3. See Lawrence Stone, Susan Amussen, Alan Macfarlane, David Underdown, and Florence King, among others, for gaining information about early modern English social and domestic history.

4. Ester Sowernam, in response to Joseph Swetnam's violent attack on women, notes the same intertextual connection between literary discourse and the mistreatment of the female in early modern culture: "it hath even been a common custom amongst Idle and humorous Poets, Pamphleteers, and Rhymers, out of passionate discontents or having little otherwise to employ themselves about, to write some bitter Satire-Pamphlet or Rhyme against women" (234–35).

5. Whately's *Bride-Bush* is a perfect example of the care needed in using domestic literature: the 1617 edition, not authorized by Whately, is 48 pages in length. The authorized version, published by the author, is 223 pages, and is much more violent and abusive in tone towards women who are perceived as opposing male authority in any way.

6. This puts critical readings of *Othello* in a whole new light. Considerations of Othello's tragic status as character must not ignore the implication that, given the culture in which the play was produced,

Othello's only real problem was that in this particular case, Desdemona's adultery, he was mistaken. Had he not been wrong, her death would have been, while not perhaps laudable, at least acceptable and justified within English culture.

7. How effective or widespread the use of this text was is difficult to determine, but if we use publication history as a guide, as Suzanne Hull suggests, then no devotional work was terrribly popular because none of the devotional books she surveys were printed more than once (91).

8. Bentley uses *Lampes* to mark divisions within in his text. The use of this word is most likely a dual reference to Matt. 5:15: "Nor do men light a lamp, and put it under the peck-measure, but on the lampstand; and it gives light to all who are in the house;" and the parable recorded in Matt. 25:1–13 about virgins being prepared with oil in their lamps for the coming of the groom.

9. As Mary Daly notes in *Gyn-Ecology*, the most effective form of repression is that administered by one's own community, so it would seem to be even more efficacious if one condemned oneself, even if using another's words.

10. This observation I owe to Judy Crowe, a graduate student at Illinois State University.

11. Puritans, when critiquing the perceived impurities in the Anglican Church, often accused them of still being Catholic, even though the Anglican Church was Protestant.

12. David Cressy has written a long, interesting, and useful essay on the churching ritual in early modern England. His basic argument is that some textual references suggest that women looked forward to churching because it was a female-centered ritual and was followed by a dinner or feast with female friends, at the expense of the husband. His point that we need to historically contextualize our information before making theoretical interpretations is well taken. However, I do not agree that just because women adapted themselves to a ritual and created a positive experience from it disallows a critical analysis. It is possible to critique the implications of the social ritual and the ways in which it is based on negative female stereotypes, and still recognize individual women's positive experiences of the churching ritual and the party that followed.

13. However, this perception of menstruation and childbirth did not go completely uncontested. Eucharius Roeslin, in *The Birth of Mankind, otherwise named The Woman's Book* (1545), argues that "they be greatly deceived and abused which call the terms the woman's purgation or the

cleansing of their blood, as who should say that it were the refuse, dross, and viler part of the other blood remaining in the body. . . . For undoubtedly this blood is even as pure and wholesome as all the rest of the blood in any part of the body else" (Klein 187).

14. See Nancy Tuana for a complete description of Classical and early modern definitions of the female, and the connections between them.

2

ROMANCE, FINANCE, AND THE MARKETABLE WOMAN: THE ECONOMICS OF FEMININITY IN LATE EIGHTEENTH- AND EARLY NINETEENTH-CENTURY ENGLISH NOVELS

Julie Shaffer

The eighteenth century saw great changes in England's economic and demographic organization, and these changes brought with them shifts in the distribution of power, with the bourgeois middle classes gaining strength that previously had belonged to the aristocracy and the landed gentry.[1] With these changes came greater possibility for movement across class lines than before, with the increasingly wealthy middle classes being able to live more like their "betters." These changes engendered conflicting attitudes about the future of the country's social structure and the traditional values that structure ensured. Conduct books, which arguably served as manuals instructing newly rising classes in behaviors proper to their new condition, proliferated and were consumed voraciously, suggesting that many felt the social structure would remain by and large the same, although with new people filling old roles.[2] Many felt that increased ability for movement across class lines, however, could lead only to utter social confusion.

The subject of women and their "natural"—hence proper—behaviors came to fill a central role in the belabored question of whether England's social structure and the values behind it could be maintained. Shifts in England's socioeconomic organization brought shifts in both sexes' roles, but the sheer number both of conduct books teaching women how to behave and heroine-centered novels offering their female readership similar models of behavior demonstrate that *women's* behavior in particular came most into question. As views toward women became less explicitly

misogynistic and women came to be seen to have a moralizing
influence,[3] the proper way for them to exercise their agency became
the topic implicitly addressed in conduct books and novels that
proliferated in the late eighteenth and early nineteenth centuries.
Although the issue was rarely stated as such, the textual treatment
of women in this era suggests strongly that there was a widely held
implicit belief that if women adopted desirable behaviors, treated in
many conduct books as natural to them, the social status quo and
traditional values might be preserved. All women needed do to work
this social influence was to exercise their agency in desired, prescribed ways. The period's heroine-centered fiction, especially,
reveals the extent to which the English imagined women and their
behavior as central to preserving the traditional social status quo.
What conduct books both prescribe and describe as natural to
women, this fiction shows in action and in plot lines in which
proper "natural" female behavior inevitably preserves traditional
values and the social status quo, and in which improper female
behavior equally inevitably is presented as so socially dangerous
that it threatens to invite complete social chaos.

While focussing on the agency granted to women and on the
results of the proper exercise of that agency, much of this fiction
masks the way women's worth remained defined via an older
paradigm in which they functioned largely as commodities embodied in human (female) form, desirable for displaying a family's
wealth and producing heirs; in this paradigm, women operated as
properties through which property was passed from man to man,
and they were valued to the extent that they were able reliably to
so function. Much heroine-centered fiction from this era focussing
on women's agency does not simply displace women's objectification; rather, it conflates the two ways of viewing women and
covers over the extent to which the old definition remained current. This fiction insistently avoids explicitly rooting women's
worth in their bodies and the proper deployment of them, suggesting that more significant is women's adherence to codes of
behavior that at first seem to have little to do with sexual behavior
or male property interests. These works reveal, however, that
female worth continued to be wrought with such issues.

To demonstrate that this is the case, I will first review how
marriage was approached in the periods leading up to the turn
from the eighteenth to the nineteenth century; these earlier views
of marriage most clearly treat females as commodities, as bodies to
be traded on a market in which property was exchanged between

males; here I will also describe conflicting imperatives that simultaneously required and forbade women from using their bodies to display their own marketability, class, or sexual appeal. I will then focus on ways one group of marriage-plot novels masks the period's insistence on viewing women as commodified bodies by presenting women's relationship to property as conflicted, and by presenting any awareness of women's relationship to property as knowledge which must remain hidden from women themselves if they are to be seen as moral at all. Then I will discuss Frances Burney's *Camilla*, a work that foregrounds what these others mask—that in the late eighteenth and early nineteenth centuries, properly exercised female agency ensures female marketability, and that where women are concerned, morality remains an economic issue tightly bound up with the protection of the social status quo.

As Lawrence Stone explains in *The Family, Sex, and Marriage*, over the course of the seventeenth and eighteenth centuries, definitions of the purpose of marriage underwent a change. The earlier definition presented it as a means of uniting two families to consolidate their strength; it subordinated individuals and their emotional interests to the political, economic, and social interests of family or kin. This view shifted to one in which the emotional interests of the individuals most immediately concerned—husband and wife—were paramount. Stone presents the relationship between these views in terms of a morally neutral historical shift, with marrying for family interest giving way to marrying for the individual's romantic interests, a shift he explains occurred over a long period of time and at different times in different social classes, with royalty, the aristocracy, and the laboring poor being the last to make the change (270–324).[4]

The earlier definition treated both bride and groom as pawns or commodities by which their families' interests might be served, but in fact females were more clearly the commodity than were males, in part because in England's patrilineal system, property was held, except in unusual cases, by males, and was passed from male to male. Women became, then, conduits of property between fathers and sons or sons-in-law; they worked as property themselves, given from a father to a husband—as property capable of transferring other property from man to man.[5] This system required that a woman remain faithful to her husband so he could be sure that his property would pass to his own sons rather than to those of his wife's lover. But a woman's remaining chaste was economically important not only to her husband but to her parents, too. A woman unchaste before marriage was considered unlikely to change later in a way that would protect a husband's interests and so compromised her parents' ability to bestow her in marriage to a man whose own economic or social attributes might aggrandize their property or social status.

A woman who indulged the unruliness of her body was problematic for husband and family not only in economic and social terms; because political power was based on inherited title and property possession, a sexually promiscuous woman threatened the structure of the culture *in toto*. An adulterous woman could pass a husband's estate and title not only out of his legitimate line but out of his class as well, scandalously blurring class lines. Because political institutions and the hierarchical class structure constituting British society as a whole relied upon authentic claims of paternity, it was vital to that structure that women remain physically chaste, and their being so formed the central element of their worth and of codes of behavior they were to follow.

By the end of the eighteenth century, however, discussions of proper female behavior rarely focused on either sexual chastity itself or on the economic and political necessity for strict control of women's bodies and, hence, the marketability of the controlled female body. The shift stemmed in part from changes in attitudes about what constituted human worth, changes that accompanied the middle classes' growth and growing influence. As Nancy Armstrong argues throughout *Desire and Domestic Fiction*, internal qualities of mind, feeling, and moral sense came to be valorized over accidents of birth such as the class into which one was born or the wealth one inherited. Worth in women was at least discursively revised from the surface inwards. What might be displayed on the surface became increasingly criticized, and displays of status and sexuality especially as signified by the body of the aristocratic woman or of those emulating her were attacked. An interest in appearance was insistently presented as revealing a trivial mind unable to focus on increasingly valued intangible qualities of mind (Thompson, *Between* 21–24). A woman preoccupied with her physical self-presentation revealed herself to be overly concerned with sexuality and status, as the aristocratic woman was imagined to be, signalling her sexuality through clothing and showing a desire to define her worth through class membership or through her wealth, both signifiable by clothing.[6] Women's perceived centrality in upholding or destroying Britain's class structure and traditional values is tied to a focus on *women's* concentration on appearances especially; women's imitating those in classes above them through emulative spending on dress, possessions for the home, and leisure was considered threatening to the class structure because it made it hard to ascertain through appearance or behavior who belonged to which class.[7]

It is precisely in regards to issues such as physical appearance that women received conflicting dictates. Whether a woman heeded her appearance or not, what she wore and where she appeared signalled her own and her family's status. And although women were taught that attention to appearance revealed a morally stunted mind, their reliance on marriage as their best option required recognition that physical attractiveness and clothes signalling some wealth increased a nubile woman's appeal and hence her chances on the marriage market (Thompson, *Between* 25–26). The commercialization of fashion and the social imperative to follow it prevented women from being able to ignore dress in any event, especially toward the end of the eighteenth century, when fashions changed and were disseminated quickly via the new English fashion doll and fashion plates in monthly magazines (McKendrick 40–51). Contradictory imperatives made attention to appearance "necessary, [but precisely therefore] demeaning" (Thompson, *Between* 31).

At this period, then, there is a displacement of the terms by which women had previously been judged; these became projected onto women's possible attitudes about themselves, and then denigrated. While women were previously viewed as bodies marketable to the extent that they were sexually controlled, women who remained aware of themselves either as sexualized bodies or as marketable through appearance and sexuality were judged undesirable for valuing physical, material surfaces over internal qualities. Women remained valued for and desired as wives precisely to the extent that they promised to be chaste. But attention to the body and its marketability was repressed and redirected onto behaviors that proved a woman's morality in less tangible terms, including modesty, self-effacement, and sympathy to others' needs and desires accompanied by a suppression of a woman's own such requirements.

While this code of behavior and morality has little outward to do with sexuality and economic worth, women's adherence to it in fact suggested they were likely to remain virgins until marriage and then to restrict sexual activity to marriage. The new code of behaviors, including tractability, passivity, and a responsive rather

than appetitive sexuality. These behaviors guaranteed and, ultimately, assured chastity and the correct passage of property
between men via the medium of woman's chaste body. But
mentioning a woman's bodily behavior and the economics of it
became virtually taboo. Women's bodily behavior slipped from
discursive view as female morality was cast in quite other terms,
yet that behavior and the economics and politics it affected
remained signified nonetheless.[8]

Just as changing views of human worth at first seemed to
validate female agency, covering the economics and body-rooted-
ness of female value, so too did ideas of marriage current at the
end of the eighteenth century. Defining marriage as an institution
based on two individuals' emotional desires seemingly values
women for their qualities of mind, emotion, and morality. Fiction of
the period constructed on the marriage plot, however, reveals the
extent to which means of judging women's agency and morality
continued to be based primarily on sexual behavior. While the
newer definition of marriage granted agency to both young men
and women by suggesting that both bride's and groom's desires
should be heeded, the way that the move toward marriage was
described in the period's fiction demonstrates very clearly that
women's newly granted agency was so defined to protect patriarchal interests by controlling women's bodies. When exercised
properly, that agency continued to guarantee the trustworthy
transfer of property between men and the preservation of lines
between classes that were kept clearly demarcated because
unthreatened by bastard offspring. This is especially clear in
heroine-centered fiction which, rather than treating the shift in
approaches to marriage as morally neutral and occurring over a
long period of time, presents it as a morally loaded synchronous
opposition. Here, marrying for love remains the valorized term, but
marrying for family interests gets replaced by a more selfish interest
in economic and social well-being: marrying for social and economic gains for oneself only, not for one's kin as well—marrying for
self-aggrandizement.

Much of this fiction proceeds through the story of a heroine
and her female foil, with the first marrying for love and the latter
marrying for self-aggrandizement; as the story progresses, it
becomes clear that the latter is utterly immoral. Her approach to
marriage generally proves to be only one in a series of steps that
proves her to be so thoroughly depraved that she takes the fatal
step into adultery that not only ruins her ability to realize her own

selfish ambitions, but also both blasts her reputation and compromises the welfare of her immediate and extended family. The way this body of novels proceeds appears at first to sever the connection between female morality and women's role as commodity because it appears to sever completely the connection between the moral female and economic interests. In fact, however, these novels simply mask there being no such severing in actuality; female morality remains as predicated in terms that protect the status quo of the social configuration as it did when female morality was seen more explicitly as a financial, social issue based on female chastity to ensure the trustworthy transfer of property between men.

One novel that proceeds through this paradigm is Susan Ferrier's *Marriage*. There, the moral Mary Douglas ignores her mother's advice that she marry for an establishment rather than for love. She rejects two titled and wealthy men, the Duke of Altamont and Lord Glenallan, as potential spouses, instead accepting as husband Colonel Henry Lennox, who has nothing but his person and personality to recommend him. By a plot twist near the novel's end, Lennox turns out to be heir to Castle Lochmarlie and so brings the virtuous Mary not only love and esteem but also estate, fortune, and status. On the other hand, her shallow, ambitious twin sister, Adelaide, marries the Duke of Altamont; in so doing, she gives up any chance for legal union with the man she really loves, her relatively fortuneless cousin Lord Lindore. Dissatisfied in her marriage despite the wealth and status it brings, Adelaide elopes with Lord Lindore within a year; she then finds herself not only relatively poor, but both banished from polite society and unloved by Lord Lindore, who marries her but remains indifferent to her.

Stories of characters like Adelaide Douglas make clear that a woman who marries when she doesn't love may lavish her love where she isn't married. But of course not all women have the option of marrying for love. Jane Austen's *Pride and Prejudice*, for instance, uses this same plot paradigm in modified form and makes this point especially clear. Charlotte Lucas may not marry for love, yet for financial security, she needs to marry even when she does not love, and, as Jane Bennet asserts, Charlotte's doing so need not be seen as immoral because the man she marries, Collins, is not immoral.[9] The same argument must extend to real women who have no more choice than Charlotte. But because books moving by this paradigm are rarely attentive to real economic constraints on women, they suggest that there are only two reasons for marrying—love or self-aggrandizement. By splitting these reasons between two female figures and focusing attention on the rewards that come to one and the punishments that come to the other, novels like *Marriage* prevent our recognizing that marrying for love is not always a realistic option; worse, they insist that those for whom this option is not available are damned to infamy. By presenting female characters who acknowledge the necessity of a husband who has property as greedy and mercenary, these novels present women who show awareness of their dependent financial state as irredeemably immoral.[10]

These novels, written in part to define proper, sanctioned femininity, treat women's awareness of the financial rewards of marriage as a moral issue. The texts illustrate the contrast between the heroine and her foil, the first of whom virtually embodies ideal femininity while the latter defines it negatively. The heroine is self-effacing where her foil is self-centered and self-interested; she is self-denying and modest where her foil is ambitious, proud, and desirous of public fame; she is emotionally vulnerable and tractable where her foil is heartless. Everything about the female foil suggests appetites indulged where they ought to be suppressed, which is why her ambitiousness so consistently leads to adultery—sexual appetite indulged to criminality.

By arguing that women's following greed and ambition leads only to utter depravity, these novels suggest that women will be best off if they not only turn away from but actively deny the desirability of property and position. But, ironically, these novels valorize the desirability of money, property, and social position by ensuring that their self-denying, unambitious heroines are richly rewarded not only with a husband's love—ostensibly what they have wanted all along—but, generally, with sumptuous estates and enviable social position as well. Austen's Elizabeth Bennet proves a case in point: she prefers remaining single over marrying Collins to ensure herself a financially secure establishment, but then gets not only a reformed and loving Darcy but Pemberley too. By valorizing wealth and position through the heroine's being rewarded with both, novels such as *Marriage* and *Pride and Prejudice* simultaneously acknowledge the desirability of those non-romantic elements of the heroine's reward, suggest that the only means of obtaining them is by acting as though one does not want them, and prevent any recognition of what it might mean for a woman *not* to have them.

These works mask the extent to which the period's definitions of female "worth" always conflate morality and economics.[11] Because they suggest that a properly moral woman not recognize the necessity of money, they imply that female morality and financial awareness are incompatible. But this articulation of the relation between female morality and financial awareness distracts attention from how thoroughly the issue of female morality in this period is, finally, economic. Those very qualities that make up the virtuous heroine, after all—modesty, self-effacement, self-denial, emotional tractability, and suppression of appetites—are precisely those that make up a woman most likely to be chaste. These qualities then guarantee that the woman possessing them can operate as a trustworthy conduit for the transferral of fathers' wealth to younger males legally related to them. Such a woman, then, best protects the particular configuration of property exchange that upheld her culture's political institutions and social structure.

The novels in which women who marry for the wrong reason end up in adulterous relationships do not make overt the fact that women's chastity was important precisely for these reasons, however, because these female characters end up banished before bearing children. By keeping "confusion of progeny" from becoming an issue, these novels mask the fact that the culture's construction of female morality was based in its need to see women as conduits of *others'* economic and social needs. They do so by relegating the issue to the subplot concerning the heroine's foil as well; in the main plot, the heroine's plot, the issue of female morality's relation to upholding the social structure is effaced, because the question of property is denied, repudiated throughout most of the plot, and brought in only at the end, as though an afterthought. Whenever these novels present female morality and economics as separate issues, they stray from views elsewhere recognized;[12] as soon as they reward the self-denying heroine with a marriage that brings her wealth and social position, however, they remind us that what they define specifically as female morality is wrought with more worldly concerns. These novels make clear that while female morality remains wrought with the issue of property, women themselves must relinquish control over their relationship to property, or get no reward at all. Behaving morally thus entails women's tacitly accepting their own status as property and conduit for the passage of other property; doing so enables women temporarily to enjoy the property they function to pass on while giving up more overtly agential control over that property.[13]

While novels proceeding by the above-described paradigm mask the conflation between (women's) morality and (men's) worldly interests at the base of their construction of sanctioned, rewardable female behavior, such is not the case with Burney's *Camilla*, a novel which tirelessly draws attention to the relation between the period's construction of female morality and questions of economics. Here, the blurring and reconfirmation of the relation between these two issues gets worked out through the heroine's marriage plot with Edgar Mandlebert, which revolves to a great extent around Mandlebert's attempts to judge Camilla's moral worth, but which is so intertwined with as to be inextricable from another story: that of the heroine's financial problems. In this *other* story, Camilla makes financial errors which make her appear less morally strict than she actually is, and which she sees as wholly at fault for her family's financial dire straits. Her errors not only undermine her ability both to represent her internal morality and to progress painlessly to her reward of her designated husband, they also appear to undermine her family's station in the world. By progressing thus, the novel demonstrates that in this period, female virtue is defined as being inextricably wrought with the financial and social welfare of the society in which women live.[14]

As the novel starts, the issue of economics gets raised and enmeshed in the heroine's marriage plot in a way that is quickly suppressed, or repressed; it continually returns in a displaced or rearticulated fashion, however, to disrupt her relationships with both Mandlebert and her parents. As it does so, it demonstrates that women remain judged by the extent to which they guarantee financial or social well-being to family and a potential spouse. The background for the way this occurs is a series of economic transactions affecting Camilla's family at the novel's outset; these begin when Camilla's wealthy uncle, Sir Hugh Tyrold, moves to an estate neighboring Camilla's family's own. He makes Camilla his heiress, disinheriting her cousins Indiana and Clermont Lynmere to do so, but soon disinherits her as well, making her sister Eugenia his heiress after she has been left scarred from accidents for which he blames himself. He then comes to believe that Edgar, heir to a neighboring estate, should marry the now disinherited Indiana to make up for Sir Hugh's having "robbed" her twice of her inheritance.[15]

This proposed match combines financial and romantic issues scandalously. Sir Hugh wishes for the match because he is unable to distinguish between the financial and emotional rewards that marriage or any family relationship should bring. And the same scandalous intermixing of worldly and emotional interests characterizes Camilla's situation. Edgar prefers Camilla to Indiana, and she develops an affection for him as well. But Camilla's financial situation parallels Indiana's; they both have been disinherited and are thus both are financially in need of a good match, with "good match" here used as conventionally defined by heroines' foils— good for the financial and social rather than the emotional rewards it brings. And our awareness of the existence and hence potential influence of economic needs in Camilla's romance plot prevents that plot from seeming as free from economic motivations as heroines' marriage plots are in the paradigm I have discussed above. Furthermore, Camilla's affection for Edgar is predicated from its onset not only as trespass against her affection for Sir Hugh, in its going against his wishes for the disposal of Edgar's hand and fortune, but also as trespass against Indiana's economic and social well-being: Camilla's love for Edgar gets viewed by Indiana and her governess, Mrs. Margland, as a theft of Indiana's worldly, rather than emotional, hopes. Affection, economics, social hopes, and love thus get alarmingly entangled in the heroine's connection to her male protagonist.

The scandal of our awareness that Camilla is as economically dependent on forming a good match as is Indiana, along with the confusion among motivations for relationships that derives from Sir Hugh's failure to distinguish between the economic and emotional rewards of avuncular and conjugal relationships, is suppressed as Edgar and Camilla grow close through sympathy of interests and sentiments, and as it becomes clear that Edgar will not marry Indiana. With this suppression, the definition of "good match" embraced by heroines' foils such as Indiana seems left behind. But from this point, the novel most clearly begins to show the relationship between female morality and issues of property and social standing.

The question of female morality gets raised first because Edgar's misogynistic tutor, Dr. Marchmont, advises Edgar to wait until Camilla shows her love for him and proves herself morally steady enough to be a good wife before proposing. Problems result almost immediately, because, according to the period's code for proper female behavior, for a woman to show her preference for a man before he declares his love for her would prove her forward and hence not morally strict enough to make a good wife; what Camilla thus needs to do to get Edgar to propose would also prove her unsuitable as a wife. Showing her love, in other words, should prevent him from proposing. This insoluble dilemma is the root of most of their problems, especially those that make Camilla appear less moral than she actually is. She must be passive, and, for the most part, silent; remaining so, however, leaves all her actions open to misinterpretation on Edgar's part, so remaining moral—following strictures on female behavior—prevents her from seeming as moral as she actually is.

Her problem is that of all women in this period: a woman's appearance was supposed to speak for her morality because speech itself from a woman was construed as suspect forwardness; a woman's body and face, along with the location in which she appeared and the company she kept, was supposed to work as sign for internal qualities. But in *Camilla*, as in other Burney novels, appearances mislead, and as long as the female body's manner of "speaking" intentions and morality is granted greater audience than a woman's explaining voice—as long as the voice itself must be silenced in order for the woman to seem moral at all—contingencies allow the body to contradict what a woman might otherwise say for herself.[16]

That the misleading speech of how and where Camilla physically appears is heeded more than what she would like to say verbally turns out to be the case in numerous episodes; I will limit my discussion to those in which the suppressed, or repressed issue of finances returns to complicate Camilla's ability to prove her morality. The issue returns primarily because of her brother Lionel's actions. He has squandered all his money and has been extorting funds from an uncle from whom he is to inherit money; he has also pressed Sir Hugh for so much money the he also leaves that uncle financially drained. He then imposes on Camilla's sisterly affection to get her to give him most of her money as well, but swears her to keep his debts secret.

In effect, Lionel continues the model set up by Sir Hugh: by playing on his sister's filial affections in a matter of money, Lionel mixes emotions and finance as scandalously as Sir Hugh had combined finance and romance. And by enjoining Camilla to silence, he reinforces the situation in which Camilla's body and its location alone must speak for her. Like a perpetrator of incest, however, he also reveals *his* knowledge that his actions are scandalous while forcing her beyond feeling simply complicitous for his abuse of her; finally, she sees herself alone as guilty for the aftermath of his wrongdoing. Sir Hugh's and Lionel's raising the issue of finance where typically we are aware only of affection ultimately contaminates all her relationships in which finances should play no overt part and makes her seem irresponsible and immoral when these other relationships develop problems. These begin both because Camilla has given her own money to her brother and because she, like all good heroines, is financially unaware; as a result, she outspends her ravaged funds and finds her*self* with financial problems. Unable to pay off her debts, she recognizes that she cannot ask her relatives for money, as they have all been drained not only by Lionel but by Clermont too. Her financial vulnerability, exacerbated by strictures on women that force Camilla to signify through physical, locational appearance only, leads to Edgar's judging her as morally fallen, hence unfit to be his wife.

This is demonstrated especially clearly after Lionel tries to coerce Camilla to ask Sir Hugh for money for him. When she finds she cannot do as Lionel asks, she leaves her rejected letters to Sir Hugh for her brother to find, but they are found instead by Sir Sedley Clarendel, one of her suitors. Seeing that she has written requesting money, he leaves her a draft for two hundred pounds sterling. The morally and economically bankrupt Lionel grabs this, heedless of problems that will of course occur from leaving his sister in debt to a man who is neither family nor accepted lover. When she goes to tell Sir Sedley she will repay the money as soon as possible, Mandlebert sees them together and misconstrues appearances, assuming that her meeting a professed lover alone means she has either agreed to marry the man, contradictory to what she has told Edgar, or worse, is involved in an illicit union with him. Camilla, verbally silenced for multiple reasons, cannot explain the situation to Edgar, so he misreads the financial situation as a sexual one and breaks with her.

While her financial difficulties here cause her to appear immoral, they must remain as unmentioned as finance is in the story of any good heroine: because an awareness of finances compromises any heroine's ability to appear moral, for Camilla to mention them would be as disastrous as for her to declare her love; either would compromise her ability to appear moral. But at the same time, speaking about these subjects is all that can save her reputation and relationship with Mandlebert. The situation is exacerbated by the fact that to clear her own name she must break her word to her brother; doing so would simultaneously clear and damn her, in precisely the same way as would her either declaring her love for Edgar or explaining that financial problems are her reason for meeting with Sir Sedley.

The particular way Mandlebert misreads Camilla's meeting with Sir Sedley highlights the connection between female morality and economics masked by other heroine-centered novels in the period. Edgar reads romance, sexuality, and morality where he should read finance only, but that all these terms become raised links them, foregrounding that economics are always at base in this period's constructions of female morality, especially in matters of young women's relationships with men. Because the issue of Camilla's relation to money appears within the marriage plot form, because the issue gets tied into questions about her relationship with Sir Sedley, and because Mandlebert suspects this relationship to be sexually illicit, the novel gestures to the demands of the patrilineal system, which requires that women remain chaste to ensure its smooth operation.

By having questions of finance impact the heroine's relationship to her parents and their welfare, the novel further demonstrates that women's morality was defined in this period according to their need to remain dependable and marketable commodities by which other property could be transferred between men. As Camilla's financial matters are misconstrued into sexual ones, they not only harm her relationship with Edgar, they threaten to ruin her parents and her relationship with them as well, by exacerbating the drain on their finances and by making her seem less moral than they would wish. They have told her that as Lionel has proven profligate, all their expectations are on her to redeem their belief in their children. Feeling that her own financial improprieties are as bad as Lionel's, she concludes she has injured her parents in every way. When her father gets thrown into jail for debts she has incurred, Camilla sees the fault as entirely her own, not recognizing that her own debts would have been inconsequential, had Lionel's more massive debts not drained their parents long before.

Camilla's drain on her family's funds, insignificant as it might have been had Lionel not devastated those funds first, stands in for the damage any appetitive woman could wreak on her family: not only does she consume their stock the way an unmarriageable daughter might be feared to do while living out her life at home, she also undermines their ability to preserve or augment their economic status through her marriage to a man who might stabilize or improve their situation through his own economic resources. A match with Edgar had been presented as desirable for Indiana for the material boons it would bring, after all, and, as I have argued, it must be seen as desirable for Camilla for the same reasons. That the marriage gets (temporarily) called off for reasons that conflate finance and (sexual) morality highlights the fact that a woman's morality in this period was tied to her ability to preserve or augment the property primarily of the men in her life: father, husband, and, eventually, sons. By forcing the issue of a woman's relationship to money and property into an exploration of others' judgment of that woman's morality, *Camilla* foregrounds the extent to which economy and female morality are always intertwined, no matter how thoroughly other texts mask and so suppress that fact. By reminding us that an otherwise adequately moral woman's financial problems may cause a man to see her as immoral and hence prevent his marrying her, *Camilla* recovers the suppressed and forces us to face it.

The situation is even clearer in the case of Camilla's beliefs about her dire effect on her parents' social and financial standing. Camilla is wrong to conclude that her own debts have "ruined" her family, but her doing so is understandable: the period's primarily unstated view of women as commodities and conduits of property makes it so difficult to sever the connection between women's morality and parents' welfare that it does not occur to her that the fault lies elsewhere. Unable to recognize that her brother has caused the family woes, her self-judgment makes clear an assumption that the book demands we interrogate: men's wasting of family resources is expected, if not sanctioned, but a woman's morality, her value, is defined otherwise: it is a(n economic) resource for her family, her immorality a catastrophic drain on both their coffers and their respectability.

Through its treatment of problems that disrupt maritally directed relationships and family welfare, *Camilla* alerts us to the financial issues anchoring the period's emphasis on and definition of female morality. The novel thereby reminds us that when the interrelation between morality, physical chastity, and property remains unstated, that interrelation and the stakes behind it remain unavailable not only to the consciousness of the innocent and rewardable heroine. They remain unavailable to the consciousness of the reader as well, who conventionally has been led away from an awareness of women's persistent status as volatile property whose bodily (sexual) behavior could make or break the social order. This awareness becomes the clearer when we heed novels like Burney's and recognize the vital role of finance in the romance of the properly, morally—physically and economically controlled—"feminine" female.

Notes

1. The middle classes did not gain overt political power until the vote was extended to middle-class males in 1832 and, according to John Rule, until around 1815, they supported aristocratic control rather than articulating their interests as separate. They could do so, however, because aristocratic rule protected their interests, which increasingly drove national policy; as Rule points out, wars during the eighteenth century were fought for trade rather than ideology, showing governmental recognition of the national importance of middle-class concerns (31–32, 91–92, 99).

2. For a more detailed discussion of conduct books and the role they played in working out some of the issues I explore in this essay, see Armstrong, and Armstrong and Tennenhouse.

3. For ways this shift was brought about by conservative and radical reformers in conduct books and fiction at the end of the eighteenth century, see Myers.

4. Because Stone treats the nuclear family based on companionate marriage as the goal toward which western history has quite properly tended, his view of the shift away from marriage as a primarily economic or political institution is hardly objective; while treating it as morally neutral, it is nonetheless a positive shift in his system. While this slant is problematic, Stone's work remains useful as an overview of shifts in definitions of marriage over the course of the period about which I am writing here. For an overview of critical responses to Stone, see Yeazell (248–49).

5. Throughout "The Traffic in Women," Gail Rubin discusses this function of women in patrilineal societies in general; in "The Double Standard," Keith Thomas makes it clear that in eighteenth-century English society (and in other periods as well), women's sexuality was presented in the terms I use here, while highlighting contradictions in such beliefs (209–16).

6. On the construction of women's sexuality as suppressed and tractable, see Poovey (15-30); on women's need to keep from signalling sexuality through their dress and ways this could be manipulated so that modest dress too was presented as beneficial precisely because it was sexually alluring, see Poovey (21–23) and Yeazell (5–11).

7. Jane West argued, for instance, that those from the lower classes should dress according to their station, as otherwise it becomes almost impossible to know from the semiotic system of clothing alone which people filled which roles (I:164–66). Throughout her 1806 *Letters to a*

Young Lady, West arraigns movement across class lines as an insult to Providence and as leading to depravity and the decay of all that for which England might be proud. McKendrick cites writers railing throughout the eighteenth century and into the nineteenth on emulative spending on clothing, possessions, and leisure (18, 27–29, 50–54, 95) as does Rule (57, 85–88), who points out that such emulation was considered to lead to social and national decay through "leading the middle classes to neglect their businesses and the lower classes into a crime-supported idleness" (44).

8. On these issues, see Yeazell (3–80) and Poovey (15–30).

9. *Pride and Prejudice* departs from the convention precisely because it recognizes that contingencies of women like Charlotte should prevent our judging them as immoral. While Charlotte marries where she does not love, she is not portrayed as experiencing the plotline of personal compromise and destruction that plagues other female figures who do not love the men they marry. The plotline of Julia Bertram in Austen's *Mansfield Park* follows the paradigm more closely; she marries for money and position, rather than for something closer to love, and she, like other heroines who choose incorrectly, ends up immorally adulterous and then banished from society.

10. Other novels drawing on this paradigm include *Pride and Prejudice*, in its treatment of Lydia (although she is somewhat recuperated through marrying Wickham, with whom she first has a premaritally sexual relationship); Ferrier's 1824 *The Inheritance*; and Ann Howell's 1796 *Georgina* and Mary Charlton's 1803 *The Wife and the Mistress*, both of which contain the paradigm appears in rather complex form. Novels working on variations on the theme, linking women who desire to marry for fortune or vanity with immorality and adultery without pairing these characters to more upright heroines, include Maria Edgeworth's 1813–14 *Vivian* and 1812 *The Absentee*, along with Defoe's 1722 *Moll Flanders*.

11. Newton develops this idea more fully by arguing that while *Pride and Prejudice* allows readers to see that most female characters in this novel are financially dependent in a way the male characters are not, the novel does not finally force us to heed this fact fully or to dwell on it (55–85). Thompson argues with Austen, however, and much depends on where one directs one's attention, because Austen raises issues at her novels' outsets but then moves on to moral issues; as such, she "reveal[s] a world of commodity while distancing it with moral ideas, at once announc[ing] and den[ying] the presence of economic determinism," leaving her works from one side seeming materialist, from the other idealist (*Between* 43).

12. They are so recognized by Samuel Johnson, for instance, who explained that "'Confusion of progeny constitutes the essence of the crime [of adultery] . . .'" (qtd in Thomas 209); "'The unchastity of a woman transfers [property] from the rightful owner'" (qtd in Poovey 5–6).

13. That the impropriety of women's possessing property is presented in Burney's work is suggestively outlined in Catherine Gallagher's discussion of Burney's *Cecilia* in *Nobody's Story* (203–56) and in James Thompson's discussion of *Camilla* in his chapter "Burney and Debt" in *Models of Value*. Thompson asserts that women's incapacity to handle money responsibly in *Camilla* works ideologically to argue for the separation of spheres by suggesting that women are so lacking in control over money that they ought to be ejected from the public (economic) sphere to become protected in the home, relinquishing finance to men's more capable hands.

14. Most of Burney's novels explore the thoroughness with which female morality, or means of judging it, gets caught up with women's relation to property. Such is the case with both *The Wanderer* and *Cecilia*, in the latter of which the heroine's worth is judged by others by the extent to which she cannot only convey wealth in marriage but also control her own expenditures responsibly.

15. The process by which Sir Hugh disinherits his nieces and nephews is more complex than my summary here may suggest, but it ultimately leaves all but Eugenia completely disinherited. Although the match between Indiana and Edgar is not explicitly discussed in the terms I have used, we are led to recognize that Sir Hugh may desire it for its ability to give restitution to the disinherited Indiana, because he wishes for a match between Eugenia and Indiana's disinherited brother Clermont for the ability of *that* match to provide restitution for Clermont. The parallel between what the matches can provide the disinherited siblings, along with Sir Hugh's guilt for disinheriting the two, invites us to see him desiring these matches for the same reason.

16. For a discussion of the ways women's appearance was treated in this period as adequately "speaking" their internal moral or mental qualities, see Poovey (24); to see ways the issue is problematized in Burney's *Evelina*, see my "The High Cost of Female Virtue," especially 119–29.

II

THE BODY BEAUTIFUL

3

MOLDING WOMEN'S BODIES:
THE SURGEON AS SCULPTOR

Alice E. Adams

Human imagination and fantasy have no limits.

—Ricardo Baroudi, *Aesthetic Surgery of the Breast*

Dr. James Burt, a prominent Dayton, Ohio, gynecologist, was forced to surrender his license in 1989 after several of his former patients filed suit for malpractice. For many years, he had been performing operations on women which he claimed would help them achieve orgasms during intercourse. In 1975 he self-published a book entitled *Surgery of Love* in which he stated that he had been performing "love surgery" on women without their consent while they were in the hospital for one of his "painless" childbirths or for other gynecological surgery. The basic operation involved realigning the vagina and removing the skin covering the clitoris, but over a thirty-year period Burt's "reconstructive" procedure evolved, becoming gradually more complex and invasive. The women Burt operated on were often dismayed to find themselves sexually crippled. They were left with so much sensitivity, pain, or scar tissue that they could not endure, let alone enjoy, intercourse. Some developed chronic urinary infections and incontinence.

My first response to the news of Burt's downfall was a shudder of horror and relief. I had followed his career through accounts in the popular press. Most coverage was concerned with a single question: Could Burt's "love surgery" make women have orgasms during intercourse? Until some of his former patients filed malpractice suits, I had never heard about the disabling effects of the surgery.[1] I found especially chilling the fact that Burt was in practice for decades without any protest from his colleagues, who had seen and sometimes tried to repair the results of his surgery. If the women he had operated on had not, at last, joined forces against him, his own colleagues would have allowed him to go on forever. The success of Burt's career means that his practices were well within the bounds of what is permitted in the specialty. St. Elizabeth's, the Dayton hospital where Burt performed surgery, stated that the surgery "is a combination of recognized gyneco- logical procedures."[2] Though an extremist, Burt was not an aberra- tion. I view James Burt as a connecting line that delineates a constellation of issues regarding the representational and surgical treatment of women's bodies in gynecology and cosmetic surgery. Many contemporary gynecological surgeries, including the common episiotomy (an incision in the vagina made just before the birth of the baby's head), partake of a surgical aesthetic of women's bodies that has been evolving since the dawn of modern American gyne- cology in the nineteenth century. By "surgical aesthetic" I mean the theory and practice that deals with the surgical transformation of women's bodies from a "natural" state of inadequacy and ugliness into a potentially "ideal" state of beauty and perfect functioning. Plastic surgeon Robert Goldwyn writes that in pursuing his profes- sion, "I can easily push my 'aesthetic' button. It takes little for a male surgeon to appreciate female beauty. But to go beyond lust, to define physical beauty, and to struggle to bring it forth through operation, is a different matter, requiring study and training."[3]

The aesthetic and the lust to create that motivates Goldwyn is not peculiar to plastic surgeons. It is also evident in the "combi- nation of recognized gynecological procedures" that made up Burt's favorite surgery, and it is evident in the more common gyne- cological procedures discussed below.

I cannot identify an essentially "natural" aspect in my body that I must shield from unnatural manipulations, so I will not urge a total abolition of genital or other cosmetic surgery. In the writings and images I will consider in this essay, the division between natural and artificial bodies quickly loses its clarity, but it is still important to analyze the ways in which surgeons, women under- going surgery, and feminist critics use the natural/artificial oppo- sition to structure their thinking about gynecological and cosmetic surgery. The vital questions—questions of who designs the trans- formed body, who suffers, and who derives pleasure in the trans- formation—can only be answered by referring to the oppositional philosophy that differentiates between a natural and artificial body.

Dr. Burt's writings and practice demonstrate how elusive the natural/artificial division is. Burt, a modern-day Pygmalion, held that a woman in her natural (i.e., pre-surgery) state is fundamentally flawed. Burt wrote that women's vaginas are "structurally inadequate for intercourse. This is a pathological condition amenable to surgery."[4] The post-surgery body, its natural pathology cured, will better match an ideal image. That ideal is so familiar it seems natural. A woman who has orgasms during intercourse with a man, according to an old but still influential version of psychoanalysis, is more mature and more healthy than other women.

In this essay, I analyze textual and visual material from gynecology journals, histories of gynecology, and fiction, demonstrating how the philosophy that opposes the natural and artificial body influences gynecological and cosmetic surgery. I am especially concerned with how factors of gender, class, and race influence the development and practice of aesthetic gynecological surgery and their impact on the rhetoric of the natural body. In the case of Burt and other surgeons I will discuss, women often have not given their consent—informed or otherwise—to the surgical modifications they undergo, an ethical problem that is linked directly to the sexual, social, economic, and racial differences between gynecologists and their patients.

Fathers of Gynecology

To provide a historical context for understanding the phenomenon of Dr. Burt, I will bracket him with two famous early gynecologists, J. Marion Sims and Baker Brown, whose practices present a similar aesthetic and similar ethical concerns. The century that intervenes between Sims and Burt has produced an amazing array of technologies and procedures that have altered thinking about how modifiable women's bodies are, but the basic idea that gynecological surgery provides a means for women to achieve a closer approximation of an ideal feminine beauty and virtue has not changed.

Sims, often identified as the father of gynecology, performed a series of experimental surgeries for vesico-vaginal fistula on slaves in the South during the 1840s.[5] It would have been difficult for Sims to perform repeated experimental surgeries on the white women he eventually intended to treat, although he did operate on indigent white women when he moved north. In her study of Sims' career, historian Deborah Kuhn McGregor points out that women under slavery, because they were often poorly nourished, were more susceptible to the kinds of birth injuries Sims operated for.[6] The procedure Sims eventually developed relieved some of their physical suffering, but their original injuries were caused by the system of slavery that weakened their bodies, forced them to reproduce, and then made them available for Sims's use. A complex network of factors, including the development of surgical technique and the availability of a group of physically vulnerable women, established the context for Sims's successful career.

With Sims, the "surgical aesthetic" is already in place. Of his research into surgical cures for vesico-vaginal fistula, Sims wrote that he wanted to relieve "the loveliest of all God's creations of one of the most loathsome maladies that can possibly befall poor human nature."[7] It is, then, "human nature" that is diseased when a woman suffers a vesico-vaginal fistula. But this specifically female "human nature" is diseased even before the injury. Ann Dally quotes J. Marion Sims on his original reluctance to specialize in gynecological surgery: "If there was anything I hated, it was investigating the organs of the female pelvis." Dally reports that Sims's aversion is shared by many of his modern professional descendants. Medical students have trouble adapting to gynecology "due to the unaccustomed exposure of the female organs, the contact with women so exposed, the sexual connotations, and their suppression in the mind, and last but not least, the characteristic smell, which many find unpleasant or disturbing."[8]

According to Dally, this initial tendency to feel disgust is, in fact, a sign of moral health, since "[o]ne might even suspect the motives and fantasies of a student who felt comfortable with gynaecology from the start." I doubt that many women would feel confident in their gynecologist's decision to perform a hysterectomy if they suspected that he (Dally does not seem to take women physicians into account) was disgusted by women's genitals. At least as much as the desire of which Dally disapproves, disgust can produce equally powerful and destructive "motives and fantasies." Burt's contention that women's genital structure "is a pathological condition amenable to surgery" suggests a high degree of anxiety about women's genitals, but it does not suggest moral health.[9] The disgust that Sims and Burt felt was masked in the expression of compassion. Like Sims, Burt avowed his dedication to women's concerns, telling a reporter after news of his practices became public, "I care about women. I have more compassion for women and their problems than I've ever had."[10]

Because of Sims's "normal" disgust for "the organs of the female pelvis," and because of his dedication to women, Dally thinks that contemporary feminists, including Barbara Ehrenreich, Deirdre English, G. J. Barker-Benfield, and Mary Daly, are wrong to condemn Sims. Dally's defense of Sims hinges on the willingness of his slave "patients" to go ahead with surgery. Dally says that "many slave patients were keen to cooperate and were delighted when the operations succeeded."[11] The issue of informed consent is as pertinent to Sims's use of slave women as it is to Burt's "love surgery," though for different reasons. The slaves Sims experimented on could neither give informed consent nor refuse treatment. Dally's interpretation rests its authority on the claims Sims makes on the women's behalf. Dally accepts without question Sims's claim that he operated on slave women solely because he was moved by their pleas for help. They may have been, as he says, "clamorous" for his operations; certainly they were suffering unimaginable physical misery, and the repeated surgeries at least offered some small hope of recovery. But it is not possible to think of them as self-selected experimental subjects who freely chose their involvement; nor is it possible to see Sims as a selfless philanthropist. The women's affliction rendered them unable to work. Besides benefiting their owners' pocketbooks, the operations they endured benefited Sims and his future patients (among whom was Princess Eugenie of France, whose fistula was repaired in a single operation performed under chloroform).

The situation in which these women found themselves differs in many respects from that faced by most women who contemplate gynecological surgery today. However, poor women, especially black women and other women of color in the United States, still face many hazards when they seek obstetric and gynecological care, including coerced sterilization and unnecessary procedures performed by doctors in training. Burt's practice shows that relatively privileged white women are also vulnerable to abuse. Many of the issues involved in Sims's experiments, especially the thorny question of informed consent, are still relevant in women's medicine today, not only in experimental fields such as infertility therapy, but also in standard gynecological and obstetric surgery.

Cures for Desire

Sims's procedure provided a cure for a clearly definable disorder, but other surgeons, working from a similar assumption of women's natural pathology, developed procedures that cured illusory diseases.[12] In a strangely fitting precedent for Burt's mutilating surgeries, surgeons in nineteenth-century Britain and the United States performed clitoridectomies on women who masturbated, showed pronounced sexual desire, or had large clitorises. Baker Brown, a British physician who attempted to popularize the operation in his home country in the 1860s, aroused strong opposition among his colleagues because he often either failed to get his patient's consent or obtained consent by manipulation and coercion (Dally 179). Following his dismissal from the Obstetrical Society, Brown went to the United States, where his procedure was greeted with more enthusiasm.[13]

Although the operations promoted by Baker Brown and his professional descendent, James Burt, reflect changing attitudes toward women's sexuality, their practices are complementary. Brown operated to "cure" women of their desire for clitoral stimulation (among other things); Burt operated to "cure" women of their lack of enjoyment of intercourse. Both operated to make women conform to traditional heterosexual values, and both believed that women suffer from a natural sexual pathology. Thus, heterosexuality and the view that women are sexually abnormal are inextricably linked, in that male sexual functioning is posited as the norm and female sexual functioning as the deviant.

Considering the character and purpose of the procedures advocated by Brown and Burt, two influential Western surgeons, the tendency of Westerners to dismiss as a foreign barbarity the practice of clitoridectomy, genital excision and infibulation in some Muslim societies is misplaced.[14] Plastic surgeons in the U.S. have recently performed similar, though less invasive, procedures to alter the appearance and functioning of women's genitals. Two women who considered their labia too large turned to plastic surgeons, who diagnosed hypertrophic labia and agreed to perform surgery. A case report appearing in *Plastic and Reconstructive Surgery* recounted the history of one of the women who underwent labial reduction.[15] The woman told her surgeon that she was unable to achieve orgasm because she was so embarrassed by the size of her labia minora. The report includes before and after photographs (see figs. 3.1 and 3.2). In the post-surgery photograph, three months later, the labia appear like those of a child, an effect reinforced by the shaven pubis. Her surgeon reports that her genitals are now "normal-appearing" and she is fully orgasmic.[16]

FIGURE 3.1

Preoperative appearance of objectionably long labia minora

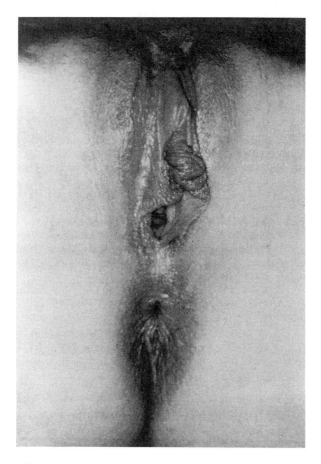

From Darrill Hodgkinson, M.D., and Glen Hait, M.D., "Plastic Vaginal Labioplasty" in *Plastic and Reconstructive Surgery* (September 1984). © Williams and Wilkins, A Waverly Company. Used by permission.

Darryl Hodgkinson, a plastic surgeon in the U.S., wrote a case report on labial reduction in which he describes female circumcision in Islamic countries. By using "female circumcision" as background for his case study of labial reduction, Hodgkinson implies a link. Particularly significant is his mention that one of the primary motivations for circumcision is the "belief that uncir-

FIGURE 3.2

Appearance three months after reduction vaginal labioplasty

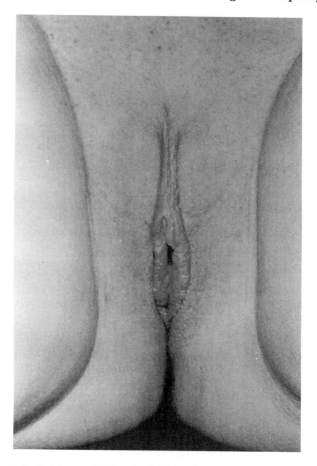

From Darrill Hodgkinson, M.D., and Glen Hait, M.D., "Plastic Vaginal Labioplasty" in *Plastic and Reconstructive Surgery* (September 1984). © Williams and Wilkins, A Waverly Company. Used by permission.

cumcised women retain male characteristics that render them unfit for marriage."[17] If we consider our own history and present practice, it is apparent that female genital surgery in the West has been influenced by some of the same factors that influence Muslim practices. Nineteenth-century clitoridectomy in Britain and the United States was intended to make sexually passive, God-fearing

Christian wives and mothers out of women who might otherwise be promiscuous and unruly; psychoanalysis described the clitoris as an inferior but masculine organ that must be abandoned if a woman is to achieve full feminine sexuality.

The religious motive, still extremely important in Muslim excision, has faded from contemporary practices in the West.[18] However, Burt's "love surgery," in common with certain common obstetric procedures described below and plastic surgery of the breasts, thighs, stomach, and buttocks, are all intended to make women's bodies conform to a heterosexual ideal. Dr. Goldwyn points out that women's magazines advise women to "improve your looks so that you can be wanted by a man"(Goldwyn 49). Although he realizes that, as a plastic surgeon, he is "reinforcing this situation," he evidently does not plan to stop contributing to the problem. He claims that "women are being betrayed by women," an argument that has also been advanced in regard to Islamic "female circumcision," which is usually performed by women. An American women's magazine, ironically titled *For Women First*, recently demonstrated the validity of Goldwyn's argument about women's betrayal when they published an anonymously authored article titled "Intimate Surgery" advocating that women who don't have orgasms during intercourse consider a version of James Burt's genital surgery. This appeared long after Burt's mutilating practice became public knowledge; the article further recommended "hymen reconstruction" for women who want to "be virgins in every sense of the word" and C-section deliveries to prevent vaginal sagging.[19]

The tendency in the West for women to try to construct a body that will be attractive to men speaks not only to their desire for emotional and sexual fulfillment, but to economic and social factors that are even more important in excision. Muslim women in the Sudan, for instance, cannot find husbands or be accepted as social adults unless they have undergone excision. The differences between Muslim excision and Western genital and cosmetic surgery are complex, but the tendency of some westerners to dismiss female circumcision as an incomprehensibly alien custom is at odds with our own history and present practice.

Episiotomy: Reconstructing the "Natural" Vagina

Dr. Burt's genital surgery was unusually extensive, but it is related to common obstetric procedures. It was while repairing episiotomies that Dr. Burt began to develop his personal brand of "love surgery." Episiotomy, an incision made in the vagina just before the birth, is "the most common surgical procedure carried out on women" and is often done without their "knowledge or consent."[20] The putative benefits of episiotomy include preventing cerebral damage to the baby, facilitating delivery, and preventing perineal tears (Simpson 9). Stephen Thacker, in a comprehensive review of eighty years of literature on episiotomy, concludes that "if [women] were fully informed as to the evidence for benefit . . . in the face of demonstrable risks, it is unlikely that women would readily consent to having routine episiotomies. As with any procedure, we believe the ethical course is to present to women the opportunity to make the choice."[21]

Many women do not question the need for an episiotomy during delivery. Many obstetricians do not even consult with the laboring woman about the incision or its repair. Given the lack of solid evidence for the benefits of episiotomy, the increased postpartum pain and longer recovery time it causes, and problems with "unsatisfactory anatomic results," obstetricians must look to custom and personal conviction to justify the procedure (Thacker, 333). One doctor's uncertainty about the value of the episiotomy led him to write to an obstetrics and gynecology journal, asking his colleagues if there have been any studies to prove "the old wives' tale" that episiotomies prevent vaginal prolapse.[22] According to one respondent, the question of efficacy is not as important as the doctor's personal desires. "[H]ow you feel about episiotomy is probably one of the most important determining factors. . . . You must have control over your practice and not defer to . . . fads and gimmicks currently being advocated by the fringes of consumers."[23]

None of the respondents could cite studies to prove or disprove the contention, but the doctors' outspoken opinions reveal some anxiety at the thought of allowing their patients' perineums to sag. One doctor lists among his reasons for performing episiotomies the preservation of the "appearance of the introitus. Episiotomy may be considered a plastic surgical procedure designed to preserve the appearance and sexual functioning of the introitus and vagina." He goes on to remind his colleagues that "with current sexual practices vulvar appearance takes on increased importance."[24] Another doctor, calling on obstetricians everywhere to "preserve the integrity of one of nature's miracles" (referring to women's vaginas) looks forward to the day when "Ob/gyn residents will again sharpen their skills on the female perineum."[25]

Like Sims and Burt—and in common with some proponents of excision and infibulation in Muslim societies—these obstetricians configure their relationship to their patient's genitals in terms of disgust for women's pre-surgical genitals and reverence for the heterosexual ideal of the tight vagina. The obstetrician reasons that, without his surgical intervention, the woman's vagina will be stretched and unattractive to her male lover. He contrasts the ideal "natural" woman, represented in the tight vagina ("one of nature's miracles"), with this flawed woman. However, the real woman will never precisely embody the ideal that possesses the surgeon's imagination. Brown and Burt operated compulsively; Burt proudly claims to have performed "love surgery" on thousands of women. The compulsion that continually sent him back to the operating room to try out new, more invasive techniques attests to his failure to achieve the ideal.

The uneasy conjunction of the real and ideal evident in medical representations of women's genitals finds an appropriate counterpart in the only other medium in which women's genitalia are commonly on display, men's magazines such as *Penthouse*, *Playboy*, and *Hustler*. Laura Kipnis offers a class-based reading of the images of women's bodies offered in these men's magazines, making the point that in *Penthouse* and *Playboy*, the upscale magazines, women's bodies are romanticized.[26] She mentions "the airbrushed top-heavy fantasy body of *Playboy*" and "the ersatz opulence, the lingeried and sensitive crotch shots of *Penthouse*, transforming the female genitals into objets d'art." However, in *Hustler*, the raunchy, downscale version of the genre,

> It's a body, not a surface or a suntan: insistently material, defiantly vulgar, corporeal. In fact, the *Hustler* body is often a gaseous, fluid-emitting, embarrassing body, one continually defying the strictures of bourgeois manners and mores and instead governed by its lower intestinal tract—a body threatening to erupt at any moment (Kipnis 375).

Such a body is a marked contrast to the ideal, the sleek, smooth bodies of models unmarked by childbearing or age. The ideal is still evident in *Hustler*, as it is still evident in representations of women's bodies in gynecology journals. But in *Hustler*'s photo spreads, this body is the frame for vagina and anus, often shaved and held open for deeper viewing, represented in a clinical clarity greater than that achieved in many gynecology journals.

According to Kipnis, the history of *Hustler* pictorials is a competition for explicitness in which the other men's magazines were soon outpaced. *Hustler* presented pictorials of anatomic variations: the genitals of pregnant women, older women, hermaphrodites, and transsexuals: a clinical array of "oddities" that would never make it into *Penthouse*. This interest in the "gross"—the implicit acknowledgment that both disgust and desire attend the viewing of women's sexual organs—marks the magazine as downscale.

Ob/gyns daily face the "gaseous, fluid-emitting, embarrassing body" that *Hustler* presents, and they carry the complementary ideal in their imaginations. Dally's observations about the sexual connotations of vaginal exams, and the coincidence of sexual feeling with disgust, is reinforced in Diane Scully's reports of interviews with ob/gyn residents, one of whom, when asked about the conduct of pelvic exams, replied that "[i]f you don't wear gloves, it is much more provocative." When Scully asked about the danger of infection to the woman if he refuses to wear gloves, he answered, "The vagina is a dirty part of the body; what are you going to infect?"[27]

If this dirty, smelly, messy body—a body, as Kipnis describes it, "threatening to erupt at any moment"—is uncovered in both the pornographic and the medical arenas, it is also apparent in women's descriptions of female bodies. Simone De Beauvoir's famous description of "feminine sex desire" views a woman's sex organs as threatening even to herself: "Woman lies in wait like the carnivorous plant, the bog, in which insects and children are swallowed up. She is absorption, suction, humus, pitch and glue, a passive influx, insinuating and viscous: thus, at least, she vaguely feels herself to be."[28]

Whereas De Beauvoir, in a practice now discredited among most feminist scholars, constructs a conveniently universal "woman" to validate a personal perception, Emily Martin studies class differences to account for women's variable perceptions of their reproductive bodies. Nevertheless there are points of comparison between the results of Martin's study and De Beauvoir's effusive disgust for women's genitals. In discussing menstruation, middle-class women tend to employ metaphors of "failed production" borrowed from medical discourse. They describe menstruation in terms of "sloughing," "degeneration," and "waste matter."[29] Although only middle-class women tend to adopt metaphors from medicine, a sense of disgust is apparent in descriptions of menstruation offered by women at various class levels. Martin quotes a working-class woman: "your period makes me sick because the blood, it ain't got the best odor in the world . . ." (Martin 108). In spite of the affective similarities across classes, Martin implies that middle-class women would benefit from participating in the working-class women's "phenomenological" (i.e., experiential and personal) descriptions of menstruation. Both Kipnis and Martin suggest that working-class representations of women's bodies are sites of resistance to middle-class hegemony, but the representations they analyze do not resist dominant perceptions of women's genitals as disturbing and dirty. I would locate both the dividing line and the bridge between the lower-class and middle-class body at the site where medicine intervenes to offer a practice of transformation, because surgical "cures" for women's generally agreed-upon original ugliness and natural pathology is only available to those who can pay. In the Fay Weldon novel I analyze in the section following, surgical transformations coincide with upward mobility.

A Body with Class

Fay Weldon's 1983 novel *Life and Loves of a She-Devil* posits a woman's body as the site of class struggle.[30] In the novel, Ruth, a typist, hoists herself up the social and economic ladder through a combination of financial manipulations and plastic surgery. In her original physical form, Ruth presents the image of the coarse, lower-class drudge. She is heavy-boned, stands over six feet tall, weighs more than two hundred pounds, and possesses a mouth full of crooked teeth. But when her husband dumps her for his rich, glamorous mistress Mary Fisher, Ruth decides to recreate herself in her enemy's image. She undergoes dental torture to restructure her teeth and jaw, loses forty pounds, has her legs and arms shortened, her breasts made smaller, and her belly and buttocks lifted. A gynecologist restructures her genitalia à la James Burt. Many surgeries are needed to remake her face to match Mary Fisher's conventional prettiness. Meanwhile she ruins her husband Bobbo and his mistress, who eventually dies of cancer, the degenerative complement to Ruth's construction. When the reversal is complete, Ruth picks Bobbo up from the rubbish heap and transforms him into her willing slave. Now he loves her, says Ruth, because "He has us both in the one flesh: the one he discarded, and the one he never needed after all" (Weldon 240).

Not wanting their star patient to look "like all the others," Ruth's surgeons balk at the conventional body and face Ruth has chosen. When Ruth chooses "love surgery," one of her surgeons complains that this "seems an interference with the essential self" (Weldon 220). But Ruth has no "essential self." In her "original ugliness" and at every point of her construction, Ruth reflects back only the desires and fears of her culture. *Lives and Loves of a She-Devil* does not recount the degradation of an essential, natural self into an ersatz copy. Nor does the novel describe the transformation of a valueless, ugly working-class body into a valuable, beautiful, elite body. Ruth is always a parody of feminine beauty and fragility; the only interesting question is who has control over her construction. She is neither the innocent victim of a "beauty myth" nor the triumphant creator of a new, more authentic, self.

"Original Ugliness"

Although some concern has arisen in recent years about "scalpel slaves" whose distorted body image leads them to seek repeated plastic surgeries that destroy their health and, ironically, their looks, cosmetic surgery is usually presented as a reasonable solution for healthy women who would simply like to improve their appearance. An article in *Psychology Today* offers examples of healthy and unhealthy patient responses to the surgeon's initial interview questions; supposedly healthy responses all reveal that the patient possesses a very specific image she is trying to achieve.[31] The desire for specificity implies that the favored patient possesses a vision of the ideal and is deeply committed to her own transformation.

In fact, her ideal vision may be formed according to standards more exacting than her surgeon's. "The Beauty System," an essay by Dean and Juliet Flower MacCannell, describes the rigidity and scope of current paradigms: "Beauty standards apply to face paint color, body size and weight, breast shape, upper arm measurement, head and body hair texture, color and visibility, facial expression, garment and accessory selection and co-ordination."[32] The professional beauties whose beauty books the authors analyze often begin with a confession of "original ugliness." Viewed in the context of the split image of woman found in medicine and literature, their innate physical inadequacy forms the basis for a lifelong battle between ideal vision and gross physical reality.

If ugliness is women's original, and hence "natural," state, it is equally natural for them to attempt to merge with the ideal. Diana Dull and Candace West, in a study of how cosmetic surgeons and patients account for their respective roles, found that women often "described their desires for [cosmetic] surgery as 'normal' and 'natural,' explicitly comparing their inclination to buying makeup and having their hair done."[33] Their surgeons described cosmetic surgery in similar terms, speaking of a "natural order" to cosmetic alterations, so that a woman would "normally" have her breasts augmented at twenty-five and her face lifted at fifty-five. Surgeons say women's desire to look their best with the help of cosmetic surgery is "essential to their nature as women" (Dull 64). Both patients and surgeons pointed specifically to certain ethnic features as appropriate sites for surgery. The "original ugliness" from which women can be saved by surgery includes not only small breasts or sagging eyelids, but "Jewish noses" and "Negroid lips" (Dull 58). The Caucasian face joins large breasts, tight skin, and slim hips as an aspect of the ideal image. Having identified the narrowly defined ideal as "natural," it follows that the pre-surgical nose, breasts or genitals—the raw resource—is deformed. Bernice Hausmann's work on the history of plastic surgery pinpoints the moment in 1950 when the small breast was defined as a "deformity" by plastic surgeons.[34] Thereafter, the small-breasted woman suffered from "hypomastia." A recent textbook, *Aesthetic Surgery of the Breast*, contains a chapter defining in precise detail, using geometric calculations, the size, position, nipple placement, and proportion of the perfect breast.[35]

The agreement of surgeon and female patient that her body suffers from an inherent pathology preventing it from achieving "natural" beauty means that neither party need question the content of the cultural construction. The constructed body is as "natural" as the base resource from which it is built, as long as it is constructed in accordance with a conventional ideal of feminine beauty. According to this logic, we are composed at once of natural and technological aspects; our natural aspect is a crude resource, made valuable in the process of surgical transformation. Kathryn Morgan contends that "we have arrived at the stage of regarding ourselves as both technological subject and object, transformable and literally creatable through biological engineering. . . . I interpret the spectacular rise of cosmetic surgery as a form of biotechnology that fits this dialectical picture of modern technology."[36]

The technological "dialectic" occurs not only between the woman and her surgeon, with the woman serving as the resource and the surgeon as the engineer; it occurs within the woman herself. And it becomes much harder, when considering the internal dialectic, to distinguish the natural from the technological, the resource from the product. Further, in a dialectical model, the abuser/victim dichotomy is meaningless.

Morgan makes the important point that feminists have, to date, largely ignored the issues involved in cosmetic surgery: "In the face of a growing market and demand for surgical interventions in women's bodies that can and do result in infection, bleeding, embolisms, pulmonary edema, facial nerve injury, unfavorable scar formations, skin loss, blindness, crippling, and death, our silence becomes a culpable one" (Morgan 28). She identifies the context for cosmetic surgery as patriarchal, Eurocentric, and white suprema-cist. In the pursuit of an effective activism, Morgan suggests that feminists participate "in the fleshly mutations needed to produce what the culture constitutes as 'ugly' so as to destabilize the 'beautiful' and expose its technologically and culturally constitutive origin and its political consequences"(Morgan 46). She sees her suggestions as "utopian;" she is not, in other words, entirely serious in advocating "actual participation in . . . fleshly mutila-tions," but I see this tactic as rhetorically, as well as practically, problematic. If we shrink from this challenge, she suggests, it is because we are caught up in the "beauty imperative." I sense in her challenge a rebuke to "beauty-conscious" feminists, suggesting that feminists are to blame when they participate in mainstream culture.

Conclusion

I have chosen in this essay to explore connections among cultural practices that are not usually considered comparable. A porn magazine such as *Hustler* is a very different venue for negotiating an aesthetic of women's sexual and reproductive bodies than obstetric and gynecology journals (on the one hand) or feminist writings (on the other). It is not my intention to conflate them in terms of their purposes or effects, but none of them occurs in isolation. In several case studies printed in *Aesthetic Surgery of the Breast*, the authors explain that the women whose before-and-after breasts they have photographed sought breast augmentation to enhance their careers as models or exotic dancers.

The stark black-and-white photographs of topless models' breasts appearing in the medical text conform to the conventions of medical representation, but the link to pornographic representation is evident in the text and in the images themselves. The businesslike pornography of medical photographs illustrates Robert Goldwyn's statement that the task of the cosmetic surgeon is "to go beyond lust, to define physical beauty, and to struggle to bring it forth through operation. . . ."[37] The combination of sexual desire, surgical prowess, and aesthetic pleasure evident in the practice of cosmetic surgery is also at work in gynecological and obstetric procedures such as "love surgery," episiotomy, and labial reduction.

One of the most important goals of cosmetic surgery, including genital surgery, is to create an organ that appears "natural." But the nature the surgeon seeks is an ideal. In view of this, Kathryn Morgan's tongue-in-cheek suggestion that feminists use mutilation to destabilize notions of feminine beauty suggests one painful way of overturning the natural/artificial divide that structures our rigid notions of beauty. Surgical mutilations would not result in a representation of the "natural," since the point of performing mutilations would be to advertise their origins on the operating table. Mutilations would, instead, actively valorize the "artificial" (Michael Jackson's progressive surgical transformations demonstrate that such a practice is already possible.) The interesting question is not whether a woman should undertake dangerous procedures to alter the appearance and functioning of her body, but whether she should conceal those alterations under the mask of the "natural." A body that flaunts marks of surgery breaks down the natural/artificial opposition (and defies the taboo against the public revelation of traditionally private aspects of the body) by removing the mask of the natural to reveal the artificial. Public acknowledgments and representations of the results and scars of cosmetic or sexual surgery would have political rewards similar to those advocated by Suzanne Santoro in describing her use of images of vaginas in her art: "For most feminists vaginal imagery . . . attacks the idea of women's genitals as mysterious, hidden, and threatening, and attempts to throw off the resulting shame and secrecy."[38]

However, lifting the taboo against public acknowledgment or display of the altered organ would not be enough to ensure that women would always be able to make their own choices about genital or cosmetic surgery. "Female circumcision" in Islamic cultures is a ritual in which the family and community participate, and the purposes of the surgery are publicly acknowledged. Nevertheless girls and women have even less power to refuse "female circumcision" than women in the United States have to refuse episiotomy. In his report on clitoridectomy among the Kikuyu in Kenya, Dallas L. Browne asserts that "circumcision remains a central feature of Kikuyu identity. Its abolition could lead to a total breakdown of Kikuyu culture."[39] Browne makes this claim to support his argument that arrogant Westerners, who know little about the social significance of clitoridectomy, should not criticize the practice. But his claim for the social significance of clitoridectomy is also applicable to the range of Western practices I have discussed in this essay. As a history of Western gynecology suggested, "the sexual and reproductive organs of women . . . acquire emotional and social meanings" that extend beyond a woman's individual life.[40] The social meanings extend to the aesthetic, sexual, and economic interests of men. The only way to begin to define women's interests in genital and cosmetic surgery is to insist on full participation in our own reconstructions. I have in mind here not only women's agency in performing them, for women do perform physically and emotionally devastating transformations on their own and other women's bodies. We must also continually challenge the purpose and value of such reconstructions. It is particularly difficult to separate the interests of heterosexual women from those of men, not only in societies where clitoridectomy is one of the prices women pay for the privilege of being considered marriageable, but also in the United States, where the catalogue of potentially mutilating practices is limited only by money and where an approach to whole-body perfection, through dieting, exercise, and surgery, makes some women far more competitive than others on the heterosexual market. At a minimum, women's right to informed consent and informed refusal must be enacted. Only by inserting ourselves fully into the reconstructive process can we begin to direct it and change not only its "emotional and social meanings," but its literal effects on our health and sexuality.

Notes

1. Accounts of the malpractice suits and the end of Burt's career appeared in newspapers and popular magazines. See Julia Helgason, "He Hurt Us, Physically and Emotionally, Burt's Ex-Patients Say." *Dayton* (Ohio) *Daily News/Journal Herald* (November 6, 1988) 311:G1–G2; Isabel

Wilkerson, "Charges Against Doctor Bring Ire and Questions," *New York Times* National (December 11, 1988); Montgomery Brower and Giovanna Breu, "James Burt's 'Love Surgery' was supposed to boost pleasure, but some patients say it brought pain." *People* (March 27, 1989); Gerry Harness, "My Gynecologist Butchered Me!" *Redbook* (July, 1989) 22, 26.

2. Julia Helgason. "He Hurt Us, Physically and Emotionally, Burt's Ex-Patients Say." *Dayton Daily News* (November 6, 1988): G1–G2.

3. Robert Goldwyn, *Beyond Appearance: Reflections of a Plastic Surgeon* (New York: Dodd, Mead & Co., 1986) 10.

4. Quoted by Isabel Wilkerson. "Charges Against Doctor Bring Ire and Questions." *New York Times* National (Sunday, December 11, 1988).

5. A vesico-vaginal fistula is a tear in the tissues separating vagina and bladder, sometimes resulting from an injury suffered during childbirth.

6. The difficulties African American slaves experienced in childbirth may be, according to some researchers, ultimately traceable to a lack of digestible calcium in their diets, which may have led to pelvic deformities. Deborah Kuhn McGregor, *Sexual Surgery and the Origins of Gynecology: J. Marion Sims, His Hospital, and His Patients* (New York: Garland Publishing, 1989) 71–72. Judith Leavitt reports that, at the turn of the century, 10.8 percent of black women delivering at Johns Hopkins Hospital suffered rachitic pelvises, as opposed to 0.8 percent of white women. *Brought To Bed: Childbearing in America, 1750-1950* (New York: Oxford University Press, 1986) 69.

7. James Ricci. *One Hundred Years of Gynaecology 1800–1900* (Philadelphia: Williams & Wilkins, 1945) 127.

8. Ann Dally. *Women Under the Knife: A History of Surgery* (New York: Routledge, 1991) 21.

9. Quoted by Isabel Wilkerson. "Charges Against Doctor Bring Ire and Questions." *New York Times* National (Sunday, December 11, 1988).

10. Quoted in Julia Helgason and Dave Davis, "'Media Has Accepted Lies as Truth,' Says Burt." *Dayton Daily News/Journal Herald* (November 20, 1988). A colleague said that Burt "believed . . . that his mission on earth was to improve the lot of women." Helgason (November 20, 1988).

11. Dally 8. Of Sims's initial surgical experiments for vesico-vaginal fistula, she writes that he "soon had seven young black women, all of them slaves and apparently all longing to be free of their affliction and prepared to suffer for it" (28).

12. Barbara Ehrenreich and Deirdre English recount the long history of useless and debilitating gynecological and psychiatric treatments for women's supposed disorders in *For Her Own Good: 150 Years of the Experts' Advice to Women* (Garden City: Anchor Books, 1979).

13. After he died, a post-mortem exam revealed "extensive softening and degeneration of the brain" an indication that Brown was mentally ill when he became the zealous champion of clitoridectomy (Dally 184).

14. Clitoridectomy involves excision of the clitoral hood and part or all of the clitoris. Excision and infibulation, the more radical version of "female circumcision," involves clitoridectomy, excision of the labia minora, and sewing the labia majora together. For more information on female genital surgery in Islamic cultures, see Efua Dorkenoo, *Female Genital Mutilation: Proposals for Change* (London: Minority Rights Group, 1992); Hanny Lightfoot-Klein, *Prisoners of Ritual: An Odyssey into Female Genital Circumcision in Africa* (New York: Haworth Press, 1989); and Fran Hosken, *The Hosken Report: Genital and Sexual Mutilation of Females* (Lexington, Mass: Women's International Network News, 1982).

15. Darryl J. Hodgkinson, M.D. and Glen Hait, M.D. "Aesthetic Vaginal Labioplasty," *Plastic and Reconstructive Surgery* (September, 1984), 414–16.

16. Similarly, Marcia Goin mentions in "Psychologic Aspects of Aesthetic Surgery of the Breast" that some women become orgasmic only after undergoing breast augmentation. *Aesthetic Surgery of the Breast* 20.

17. Darryl Hodgkinson, *Plastic and Reconstructive Surgery* 414.

18. However, as late as 1923, a New York physician complained about surgeons performing genital surgery, including clitoridectomy, as a means of improving a woman's spiritual life. John F. W. Meagher, M.D., "Quackery de Luxe: A Form of Medical Charlatanism Known as Orificial or Constructive Surgery." *New York Medical Journal and Medical Record* (February 21, 1923) 224–30.

19. "Intimate Surgery" *For Women First* (August 1, 1994) 46–50. A one-column sidebar to this four-page article recommends several procedures to enlarge men's penises, but Douglas Whitehead, M.D., who directs a program for male sexual dysfunction, significantly concludes that "ninety-nine percent of the men who want this surgery have a normal penis (five to seven inches when erect)" (50). No similar observation that most of the women who have "love surgery" have normal genitals is offered.

20. D. Simpson, "Examining the Episiotomy Argument." *Midwife, Health Visitor and Community Nurse* 24:1 (Jan/Feb 1988) after Kitzinger (1981) 9.

21. Stephen B. Thacker and H. David Banta. "Benefits and Risks of Episiotomy: An Interpretative Review of the English Language Literature, 1860–1980." *Obstetrical and Gynecological Survey* 38:6 (1983) 334.

22. *Collected Letters of the International Correspondence Society of Obstetrics and Gynecology.* 23:1 (January 1982): 1–8.

23. Philip Alberts, M.D. *Collected Letters* 3.

24. Robert J. Sokal, M.D. *Collected Letters* 2.

25. Cruikshank, M.D. *Collected Letters* 3.

26. Laura Kipnis, "(Male) Desire and (Female) Disgust: Reading Hustler." *Cultural Studies* Lawrence Grossberg, Cary Nelson, and Paula Treichler, eds. (New York: Routledge, 1992) 373–91.

27. Diana Scully, *Men Who Control Women's Health: The Miseducation of Obstetricians and Gynecologists* (Boston: Houghton Mifflin, 1980) 115.

28. Simone De Beauvoir. *The Second Sex* 1952 (New York: Vintage Books, 1974) 432.

29. Emily Martin, *The Woman in the Body: A Cultural Analysis of Reproduction* (Boston: Beacon Press, 1987).

30. (New York: Pantheon, 1983).

31. See Jennet Conant, "Scalpel Slaves Just Can't Quit," *Newsweek* (January 11, 1988): 58–59; and Annette Hamburger, "Beauty Quest," *Psychology Today* (May 1988): 28–32 (31).

32. *The Ideology of Conduct* (New York: Methuen, 1978) 208.

33. Diana Dull and Candace West. "Accounting for Cosmetic Surgery: The Accomplishment of Gender." *Social Problems* 38:1 (February, 1991) 56.

34. Bernice Hausmann. "Beauty and Behavior: Plastic Surgery and Theories of Human Personality, 1920–1960." Paper delivered at Drake University, Des Moines, Iowa, 1992.

35. "The ideal breast has basically a conical shape with the nipple-areola complex located in the vertex. It is divided in two upper and two lower quadrants, with medial and lateral aspects. . . . The ideal volume of the breasts is difficult to estimate. Within the normal aesthetic limits they should be proportional to the lower segment of the trunk. In general, the circumference of the chest should be the same as that of the hips." Ricardo Baroudi, "Preoperative Evaluation for Breast Surgery,"

Aesthetic Surgery of the Breast. Edited by Nicholas G. Georgiade, Gregory S. Georgiade, and Ronald Riefkohl. (Philadelphia: Saunders, 1990) 19.

36. Kathryn Pauly Morgan. "Women and the Knife: Cosmetic Surgery and the Colonization of Women's Bodies." *Hypatia* 6:3 (Fall 1991) 30.

37. Robert Goldwyn, *Beyond Appearance: Reflections of a Plastic Surgeon* (New York: Dodd, Mead & Co., 1986) 10.

38. Shirley Ardener, "A Note on Gender Iconography: The Vagina." *The Cultural Construction of Sexuality* ed. Pat Caplan (London: Tavistock Publications, 1987) 129.

39. Dallas Browne, "The Kikuyu Clitoridectomy Controversy," *The Politics of Culture* Brett Williams, ed. (Washington: Smithsonian Institution Press, 1991) 250. Browne includes a section titled "Clitoridectomy in the United States," in which he confuses clitoridectomy (removal of all or part of the clitoris) with labial reduction as practiced by his source, Darryl Hodgkinson. As a result of this confusion, he writes that clitoridectomy may actually improve a woman's sexual pleasure: "Although many authors have argued that clitoridectomies provide a one-way ticket to the loss of sexual pleasure, this report suggests that an improved self-image can increase sexual enjoyment"(262–63).

40. "Gynecology: Duty or Service?"

4

THE "ASSEMBLY-LINE LOVE GODDESS": WOMEN AND THE MACHINE AESTHETIC IN FASHION PHOTOGRAPHY, 1918–1940

Christine Moneera Laennec

Fashion photography is in its own way a particularly revealing manifestation of popular culture, since it does not represent the reality of a given time and society—far from it—but an ideal image that society has of itself, and a reflection of its preoccupations and anxieties.[1] This ideal image acts both as a confirmation of the fondest desires of its public and as a force that shapes those desires, shifting constantly in the process. A growing area of scholarly research has focused on fashion as an important cultural signifier. As Kaja Silverman has written, "every transformation within a society's vestimentary code implies some kind of shift within its ways of articulating subjectivity." (149)[2] This changing outlook manifests itself not only in terms of changes in clothes design, but equally as changes in fashions of the body itself. In the Western world at least, "[b]odies are regarded . . . as a barrier separating the inner self from the outer world, a relationship articulated through clothes and modes of wearing them" (Craik 12).

The early twentieth century saw a fascination with machines and mechanization, which Susan Fillin-Yeh has termed the "machine aesthetic."[3] The machine aesthetic affected the world of fashion as well as art, and in the fashion photography of the time, we can see that it also influenced how the (fashionable or desirable) body was being defined. Artists and critics writing in the twenties and thirties continually posited an affinity between women and machines, and in looking at the fashion photography of the period between World War I and World War II—a period that witnessed sweeping changes in society, and thus in fashion and art—it soon becomes apparent that women were indeed being portrayed in relation to images of machines and mechanization. In speaking about these images, I borrow Marshall McLuhan's phrase "assembly-line love goddess" (93): although McLuhan's work has in many respects been superseded by contemporary feminist commentary—or perhaps because McLuhan, writing in the late fifties, was himself closer in time and perspective to the photography that is the subject of this study—his formulation, it seems to me, perfectly expresses what happens (from a feminist point of view) when the machine aesthetic and the world of fashion come together. In many ways the Second World War disrupted the influence of the machine aesthetic on fashion: the post-war female ideal for several decades was soft, dependent, and domesticated, before fashions again changed to the current ideal of an engineered, reproducible, "hard" body. However, this early preoccupation with mechanization, as its presence in fashion photography during this period suggests, actually provides us with an early precursor to the fashionable techno-body of the late twentieth century.

The Machine Aesthetic

As industrialization picked up speed in America at the beginning of this century, the machine aesthetic began to be discussed in various artistic circles, such as the avant-garde and Surrealist movements, and Alfred Stieglitz's 291 group. The connection between photography and the machine aesthetic was not coincidental, for it was in these years that the mechanical process of capturing and creating images became recognized as an art form (see for example Walter Benjamin's "The Work of Art in the Age of Mechanical Reproduction"). The machine aesthetic later worked its way into popular culture: consumer-oriented industrial design, "streamlining" and a preoccupation with function continued throughout the thirties, forties and fifties. The discussion of a connection between women and machines can be seen as early as 1900, when Henry Adams, in his essay "The Virgin and the Dynamo," puzzled over how man could incorporate the super-human power of the machine into his life and his understanding of the world (379–90). Francis Picabia's *"Portrait d'une jeune fille américaine dans l'état de nudité"* (1915), is perhaps the most striking example of what other artists were working through on less explicit levels. The young nude American girl is a Forever spark plug.[4]

The theme of the energy implicit in both female sexuality and machines (as Henry Adams put it, "two kingdoms of force which had nothing in common but attraction" [245]) underlies a collaborative piece by Marius de Zayas and Agnes Meyer in *291* entitled "Mental Reactions." This story of a meeting between a man and a woman is recounted by the woman, with the type presented amidst mechanical geometric forms. The fragmented narrative ends: "I feel him making a mental note: 'Experiment No. 987. Reaction perfect.'"[5] The implication is that the woman finds herself unwittingly reacting in a predictable, mechanized way during a sexual confrontation. Just as with the woman's automatic flashing smile in Fernand Leger's film *Ballet mécanique* (1924), the woman's natural response becomes somehow transformed into a mechanical (unhuman and unnatural) process. A statement made by Paul Haviland in 1915, also in the pages of *291*, indicates that perhaps what is really at stake in this recurrent juxtaposition of women and machines, what man is really trying to comprehend, is not the Dynamo at all but the Virgin. He writes,

Man made the machine in his own image . . . the machine is his "daughter born without a mother." That is why he loves her. He has made the machine superior to himself. That is why he admires her. . . . After making the machine in his own image he has made his human ideal machinomorphic.[6]

In this version of the Creation myth it is once again man who is the creator, and the machine/woman who is the "created"—in his image, only perfected. The idea of woman as a mechanical (and thus reproducible) realization of man's desires remained merely implicit in fashion photography, which functioned much more intuitively in conveying an image of what was up-to-date, glamorous and modern. Fashion photography cannot afford to operate as overtly as Picabia or Haviland in equating women with machines. But, in its own way it reflects what one of *Vogue*'s illustrators reported to Condé Nast from the 1925 Paris Exposition of Decorative and Industrial Arts: "Modern aesthetics can be explained in one word: machinery" (Seebohm 227).

Movement, Energy and Anonymity

The most striking characteristic of the photographs from the twenties and thirties is their sense of potential movement, like that conveyed by Picabia's Forever spark plug. Fashion photography from just after the First World War shows little implied movement. Baron De Meyer's dreamy, soft-focus photographs illustrate beautifully the sort of static image that would soon become passé with the advent of such photographers as Steichen, Hoyningen-Huene, and Horst. The women photographed by De Meyer were all well-known, recognizable personalities—far from being models in the contemporary sense of the word, they wore their own clothes rather than a marketed product that the readers of a fashion magazine could buy for themselves. They are shown in softly-lit, elegant poses, exemplifying the role of aesthetic objects that women of their class were expected to fill.[7] They seem very reflective and closed in on themselves, as if conscious of the fact that they have no other function than that of being perfectly decorative. De Meyer's photographs from the years following the Great War show the sort of staticity which was to disappear in the fashion photographs of the twenties. In his photograph of Jeanne Eagels (1920), for example we see her seated quietly in a chair, languidly motionless: she does not look out of the photograph to meet the viewer's gaze. In another photograph by De Meyer from 1919, Ann Andrews is looking into a mirror but it is held so that there is no reflection.[8] As in the photograph of Jeanne Eagels, Ann Andrews does not look directly at the viewer. Furthermore, she is not even able to look at herself: the absence of any reflection in the mirror could be read not only as an elision of her position as viewing subject, but also as suggestive of a denial of her very being. The static quality of these photographs would disappear in the fashion photography of the following decade.

By the twenties, women had begun to lead more active lives, and their clothes reflected that change. In the space of ten years women went from being encased in corsets and floor-length gowns to wearing knee-length dresses over a minimum of underpinnings. In the flurry of activity during the First World War they had even worn trousers and coveralls, a fact whose shocking implications the rest of the world was at the time too busy to dwell on for long, but which in fact signalled an independence for women that did not disappear after the war. The new energy and freedom that women had achieved by the twenties is apparent in two photographs by Edward Steichen of Marion Morehouse in 1927, and Gertrude Lawrence in 1928. In both photographs the women seem to be responding directly to the camera; in the case of Marion Morehouse, casually advancing toward it [Figure 4.1]. This dynamic

FIGURE 4.1

Marion Morehouse modelling Cheruit gown, Steichen, 1927

From *A Life in Photography*, by Edward Steichen. Copyright © 1963 by Edward Steichen. Used by permission of Doubleday, a division of Bantam Doubleday Dell Publishing Group, Inc.

quality is noticeably absent in De Meyer's photographs from only a few years before. The women in Steichen's photographs activate the space around them. While in the pre-war heyday of De Meyer's photographs, beautiful women were considered desirable because of things exterior to them (their family, their husband's name and wealth), by 1928 the idea of a beautiful woman had much more to do with an active rather than passive participation in life. Though Morehouse and Lawrence (like Andrews and Eagels) were well-known women, their reputations are anchored more by their accomplishments as artists and intellectuals than by any status as a wife (however, in the caption, Marion Morehouse is also identified as "Mrs. e. e. cummings"). They are far from passive objects for aesthetic consumption: they actively command the viewer's attention.

The same kind of visual dynamic can be seen in a completely different way in Steichen's 1925 photograph of abstract fashions [Figure 4.2]. It is a very successful representation of all that was up-to-date in 1925, and reminds one of Sonia Delaunay's "simultaneous" clothing designs that were a huge hit at the 1925 Paris Exposition of Decorative and Industrial Arts (Morano 21).[9] There is explosive movement in this photograph, but it is movement created not by the woman herself, but by the composition's use of diagonals and abstract forms. Also, here the woman modelling the clothes is anonymous: a practice that would soon become the predominantly accepted one for fashion photography. She is turned away from the viewer, and—importantly—only her head differentiates her body from the background. She is literally an abstracted form. A similar obliqueness works to convey the dynamic within the static in Steichen's July 1932 *Vogue* cover [Figure 4.3]. Here a sense of movement is even stronger than in the photographs so far considered, perhaps because it is more potential. The position of the woman indicates that she is on the verge of throwing the ball down. Her face is hidden completely from us in shadows, thus her energy, unlike Marion Morehouse's, is a completely anonymous one. The increasingly popular use of models who were not personalities known to the public reflected the revolutionary changes that were taking place in the fashion industry (and in the mechanization of the world in general). Things had changed enormously since the days of Ann Andrews' no doubt handmade and personally commissioned dress, for the standard of beauty had become one much more of uniformity. By the thirties, the ideal American girl was both anonymous and ubiquitous, and above all

FIGURE 4.2

American *Vogue*, Steichen, June 1, 1925

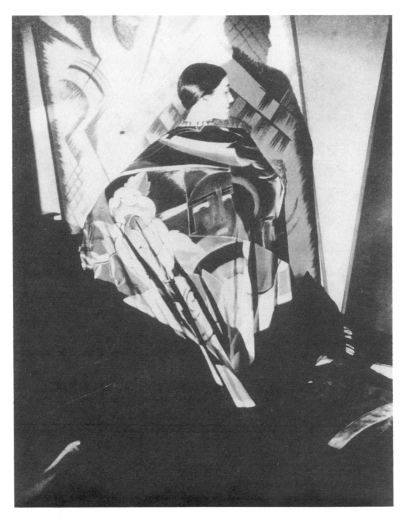

Edward Steichen. Courtesy *Vogue*. Copyright © 1925. (renewed 1953)
by the Conde Nast Publications, Inc.

FIGURE 4.3

Vogue Cover, Steichen, July 1, 1932

Edward Steichen. © British *Vogue*, The Conde Nast Publications Ltd.

(as Haviland hints), reproducible. She was beautiful not by virtue of her station in life, but through careful dieting and exercise, and she could be found everywhere. Similarly, the bathing suit worn by the girl on the cover is one that the reader of *Vogue* can go out and buy herself.

Mechanization: The Assembly Line

As fashion photography continued to evolve, it did in fact achieve a truly dynamic movement towards the late thirites, and this development can be seen occurring at the same time as a preponderance of images involving fragmentation and repetition. While these are not explicitly mechanical images, they work in such a way as to evoke various mechanized processes, not the least of which was the mass production and commercialism that by this time had become central to the fashion industry.[10] One of the most characteristically "modern" uses of fragmentation which we can begin to see in the fashion photography of the twenties is the use of synecdoche (using a part to indicate the whole) in representations of the human body. When in 1926 Steichen photographed a pair of feet (to sell McAffe Oxfords), he did it in such a way as to indicate not only the rest of the body but an entire way of life. In the center of the photograph we see a pair of (well-heeled) women's feet, spotlighted by a flashlight held by an usherette.[11] There is a lot of sublimated information in the semi-darkness at the edges of this photograph which tells us about the owner of these shoes: the fact that she is going to the theater is indicated not only by the flashlight but by the playbill in her male companion's hand; they are both wearing elegant evening attire: he has white gloves and a cane, and the hem of her wrap is of beautiful embroidered velvet. It doesn't matter what the faces belonging to these feet are; it could be anyone, it could be everyone (it could even be you!).

One of the implications of thus fragmenting the body is a loss of personal identity.[12] Another is that the models in these photographs become interchangeable idealized forms; they are no one in particular and everyone. From interchangeablity, the reproducible woman is only a few steps away. Interestingly enough, at the same time that the fragmentation of the body becomes a recurrent theme of fashion photography, repetitive images also begin to appear. Repetition—implying an infinite succession of objects— implies uniformity and suggests the assembly line. Images of

FIGURE 4.4

American *Vogue*, Hoyningen-Huene, July 5, 1930

George Hoyningen-Huene. Courtesy *Vogue*. Copyright © 1930 (renewed 1958) by the Conde Nast Publications, Inc.

seemingly endless, identical or nearly identical elements are reflective of just the sort of reproducibility in standards of fashion and elegance at this time that I have been discussing. Two photographs of beach fashions from 1929 and 1930, the first by Martin Munkasci and the second by Hoyningen-Huene, both illustrate repetition and uniformity reminiscent of assembly-line beauty. Hoyningen-Huene photographs six people in such a way that one has the impression that they are on a crowded beach [Figure 4.4]. The edges of the photograph only slightly crop their figures, and the angular disposition of the bodies conveys the idea of a greater expanse of repeating forms. In Munkasci's photograph (which we were unfortunately unable to reproduce here) we see the tops of identical parasols carried by what seems to be a troop of women in identical bathing suits marching in formation along the beach.[13] Munkasci's photograph uses the same angled duplication of figures as Hoyningen-Huene's, but the cropping is much more severe. No body is completely represented, and of the six (faceless) figures the most we see are the legs of only one. The parasols stand in for the figures who are carrying them. Because the photograph is so much more cropped than is Hoyningen-Huene's, the impression given is of an infinite number of identical young women marching along.

The military implication was perhaps not too far from Munkasci's thoughts at the time, and the sexual connotations implicit in an image of identical women moving in precise formation are very strong as well. Rather than being Adam's virgin of 1900, an immaculate conceiver and reproducer, the machine was now identified as a powerful female sexual force. In *The Mechanical Bride*, McLuhan analyzes advertisements that depict women's bodies in an assembly-line manner in terms of "the interfusion of sex and technology," focussing in particular on the chorus line as a variant of the assembly line (94). He argues that the chorus line seduces through its "smooth, clicking routines" (94) quoting Gilbert Seldes's remark that "[t]he revue corresponds to those de luxe railway trains which are always exactly on time, to the millions of spare parts that always fit." McLuhan concludes:

Thus, one answer to the ad's query: "What makes a gal a good number?" is simply "looking like a number of other gals"; to the query, "What's the trick that makes her click?" the answer is "being a replaceable part." . . . To be seen in public with these numbers is a sure sign that you are clicking on all cylinders. Any interest that they have in themselves is incidental. (96)

Here the dark side of the "machinomorphic woman" is brought out in all its horror. The hostility evident in the remark that women's sexual charms lie in their being "replaceable part[s]" invites us to reflect on the threat (i.e., the threat to patriarchal society which reveres machines) implicit in the idea of a machine woman. This power is often a potential one only (as in the swimmer who is about to throw the ball). But if one considers the social reality for women, who had so quickly moved out of their parlors and into the munitions factories during the First World War, and who truly did "wear the pants" while the men were off fighting, the potential movement portrayed in fashion photography could well also reflect a true coming into power by real women. The need, therefore, to harness this power can be seen in the fashion industry's (and society's) message to women that they were most desirable when their individuality was submerged, when they all looked alike. It is surely not coincidental that images of repetition in these photographs all involve fragmentation and mutilation. The ideal of an endless procession of identical women "clicking on all cylinders" (as we see in the Rockettes or any beauty pageant) is indeed an effective way of reducing individual female identity so that no one element herself has any interest or power whatsoever.

However, in implicitly promoting the ideal of the assembly-line love goddess, fashion magazines were treading on thin ice. If being beautiful because one looks exactly like the current ideal is one thing, being replaceable is really quite another, and the fashion press narrowly avoided bringing this argument to its logical conclusion. It is interesting that by the late thirties, assembly-line and mechanical imagery became explicit not only in fashion photography but even in fashion magazine copy. What Henry Adams had begun by suggesting in 1900 had, almost forty years later, been embraced by the fashion industry itself. In February 1938, *Vogue* enthused, "We talk about American looks with the same unaffected pride as we do our American highways or schools systems" (Devlin 119). The introductory section of *Vogue*'s 1939 piece on the Woman of Tomorrow talks about her in terms of an assembly line, but in a more ambivalent way. Here the machine as an ideal is differentiated from the assembly-line product: "However, this is how we like to think of the American Woman of Tomorrow: That her face will be beautiful, but that beauty will not be merely an assembly-line product. That her body will be a perfectly-working machine, unencumbered with pain . . . That her mind will work clearly, unfogged; with cold logic and warm sympathy" (Feb. 1, 1939: 61). While uniformity is desirable, then, complete replaceability and loss of identity is not. However, the fashion photography of this period continues to portray an ideal of uniformity and in very subliminal ways does present a "love-goddess assembly line."

One of the most interesting ways in which fashion photography touches on the problem of reduplication is in the use of mirrors. Two photographs by Steichen from January 1935 are especially provocative examples. The first, shows a woman reflected in a mirror, but the mirror image seems to be a photographic duplication of the same side of the woman's face which is turned towards the camera.[14] This photograph is reminiscent of Man Ray's surrealist portrait of Jean Cocteau, where we see the back of Cocteau's head as he looks in the mirror, and in the mirror, the back of his head again. The second, of a woman in a mirrored stairwell, is even more interesting [Figure 4.5]. Her image is repeated at least seven times, and each frame of the mirror shows her at a different angle. Furthermore, in none of the mirror-images does she meet her own gaze. One has the impression both of reduplication and of difference: a neat solution to the problem of replaceability. We are looking at eight slightly different versions of the same ideal, and just barely avoiding implications along the lines of the mechanical smile in *Ballet mécanique* or of "Reaction perfect" in Agnes Meyer and Marius De Zayas's "Mental Reaction." In these cases, mechanization is inseparable from the notion of sexual function. The implication of a robotic ideal of female sexuality—as in the 1970s film *The Stepford Wives* where a community of men gradually replace their wives with robot women who give them outstanding sexual service—is that real women leave much to be desired in their natural state. (This of course is the premise of all fashion magazines.) In the fashion photographs and magazine articles of the 1930s, beautiful women are considered beautiful to the extent that they conform to a code of uniformity, but without going as far as actually all being identical: beautiful women are still not machines, but human beings. The seduction of mechanization and reduplication must be seen to be ultimately a human seduction. The machine-woman is not a robot woman, but a "new, improved" (i.e., perfected) real woman.[15]

FIGURE 4.5

Mary Taylor dress, Steichen, 1935

Edward Steichen. Courtesy *Vogue*. Copyright © 1935 (renewed 1963)
by the Conde Nast Publications Inc.

FIGURE 4.6

American *Vogue*, Hoyningen-Huene, July 5, 1930

George Hoyningen-Huene. Courtesy *Vogue*. Copyright © 1930 (renewed 1958) by the Conde Naste Publications, Inc.

Women Inside (Mechanical and Social) Structures

Another manifestation of the machine aesthetic in fashion photography which becomes apparent during the thirties is the recurrent image of women in—if not actual machines—structures that imply mechanization and function. As in Steichen's staircase photograph, which depicts a woman encircled by metal bannisters, women are often shown inside, or interacting with, some kind of structure or mechanism which by its very nature implies movement, such as wheels, ladders, staircases, and coils. Hoyningen-Huene's 1930 photograph of a girl in a hoop is a good example of this. It is difficult for the viewer to determine whether the girl is in control of the hoop, or whether she is caught within it. The effect of her body being positioned off-balance suggests that she is about to roll forward (or perhaps even backward). This thought is more than a little disturbing, because her head would be injured if she did so. There is even an implication of decapitation in the photograph, with the hoop bisecting her neck [Figure 4.6].

Nowadays not only do we associate physical vitality and sexiness, but we consider them to be synonymous. However, as we have seen, in 1928 the idea of a beautiful woman being beautiful because she was in motion was a fairly new idea. That the link between dynamism and feminine beauty should be repeatedly expressed with images of mechanized movement is understandable if taken in terms of a general endorsement of speed, streamlining and clean lines which signified glamour at the time. But what about the implications of the human (female) body within mechanical structures? To what extent is the girl in the hoop in control? How optimistic should we be about her possible decapitation? The ominous side of the connection between women and machinery is evident in a surrealistic photograph (labeled as such) by Andre Durst from 1936, in which a woman is surrounded by a coil or lasso [Figure 4.7]. The disturbing element of this image is reinforced by the fact that the woman thus encircled is wearing a blindfold. We might well ask the same sorts of questions as we did of the Steichen photograph of the girl mirrored in the stairwell. Is she trapped by the railing and mirrors, or is she in control? Once again we see implicit violence and the threat posed by women—and mechanical forms with them—going out of control.

By the late thirties, interest in the machine aesthetic had become explicit and more intellectualized. At the same time, fashion photography began to move outside of the studio and

FIGURE 4.7

"Surrealist Fashions," Durst, 1936

Andre Durst, © British *Vogue*, The Conde Nast Publications Ltd.

FIGURE 4.8

Model in front of Henry Dreyfuss's locomotive, Frissell, 1939

Toni Frissell. © British *Vogue*, The Conde Nast Publications Ltd.

images of women in mechanical structures continued to appear, with messages that are as ambivalent as the more posed studio photographs. One example is Blumenfeld's 1938 photograph of Lisa Fonssegrives perilously perched on the Eiffel Tower. She is wearing an evening dress, has one arm around the Eiffel Tower's curved girders, the other holding her gown out to flutter in the strong wind. She is looking away from the camera and down over the city of Paris, which is stretched out at a vertiginous distance far below her.[16] Another example is Toni Frissell's 1939 photograph of a model in front of Henry Dreyfuss's newly-designed locomotive [Figure 4.8]. The association of (idealized) women with industrial design was wholeheartedly embraced, and Henry Dreyfuss's train signified to the readers of *Vogue* all that was modern, and even one step ahead. But in both of these photographs we find the same rather frightening qualities as in Hoyningen-Heune's girl in the hoop, as in Durst's photograph, and Steichen's staircase girl. What will happen to the blindfolded woman in the coil? Is Lisa Fonssegrives going to fall, or even jump to her death? Is the model being run down by Dreyfuss' locomotive?

We may well ask: what happened? When did the romance with the machine turn nasty? Suddenly instead of being on top of the glamorous skyscraper thirties world, we find ourselves faced with looming machines and structures that will almost bear down on us if we don't quickly turn the page. By the late thirties, machines could still represent the future, hope, industry, and the American dream, just as they had for Henry Adams in 1900; but at the same time they had come to signify a somewhat frightening, inhuman force which no doubt became more and more identified with impending war (as exemplified by such terms as *war-machine* and the *military-industrial complex*). When in 1940 photographs of women interacting with machines appear in fashion magazines, the women in them are not representatives of an elegant, streamlined modernity, but are soldiers and nurses fighting in the war, or women working once again in munitions factories. After 1939, the presence of machines in fashion photography is less a sign of the machine aesthetic than it is a simple documentation of the world in which women lived.

However, unlike the period following the First World War, after the Second World War women (at least as they appeared in fashion magazines) were confined to the house, where the only machines they came into contact with were those designed to help them with housework. Even driving (due to some sudden national fit of female amnesia perhaps?) belonged only to the realm of men. The machinomorphic ideal reverted back for a time to more traditional notions of women's dependence and vulnerability (exemplified by a lyric from *Annie Get Your Gun*, "the girl that I marry will have to be as soft and as pink as a nursery"). The mass-producible assembly-line love goddess became a homebound domestic goddess centered on her family and sweetly oblivious of outside life. The bars of the cage that held her disappeared from fashion photography, but the limitations on her life were perhaps all the more strong for being invisible.

Seen from the perspective of the fifties and sixties, the late twentieth-century phenomenon of the "constructed" female body seems to be a new development. However, if we look closely we can see a link between the female body and machines already appearing in the world of fashion during the twenties and thirties, and in writings from before the turn of the century. Nowadays, women (and men) reconstruct their bodies through surgery, and/or through rigorous programs of "body building"—an option open to more of the population than plastic surgery. The buff woman of the nineties who confidently gets down to business in the gym, does so, ironically, by interacting with a number of machines (multi-gyms, rowing machines, Nordic-trak) in her effort to achieve the current ideal of a body that not only looks good but itself functions like a well-oiled machine.

Notes

1. The fashion industry reflects society's anxieties insofar as it exists in order to create consumer "needs." Naomi Wolf, in *The Beauty Myth*, has perceptively illustrated how the fashion industry continues to exploit women's anxieties. She shows, for example, how ads for facial creams tap into and exploit the fears and pressures experienced by women in the 1990s (114–21). For more on the relationship of women to the magazines that target them as a consumer group, see Janice Winship's *Inside Women's Magazines* and Jennifer Craik, *The Face of Fashion* (50–51). There is also an important body of work, stemming largely from the ground-breaking studies by Laura Mulvey and Teresa DeLauretis, on women as the subject of a male, or male-identified, gaze. Diana Fuss's very interesting contribution to this area of scholarship ("Fashion and the Homospectatorial Look") uses a psychoanalytic approach to analyze the homospectatorial look implicit in fashion photography and advertising, arguing that women are invited not only to

desire images of beautiful women, but to consume them, like vampires, in order to become them.

2. For more on fashion as a cultural signifier see, for example, the work of Juliet Ash, Jennifer Craik, Jane Gaines, Angela McRobbie, and Elizabeth Wilson.

3. This article had its genesis in a seminar on the Machine Aesthetic taught by Susan Fillin-Yeh at Yale University. For more on the Machine Aesthetic, see Fillin-Yeh's *The Technological Muse*, and Joan Marter's review of this exhibition. Also of interest is the "Machine-Age Exposition" catalogue printed in the *Little Review* (New York: No. 11, 1927) which includes articles such as "The Aesthetic of the Machine and Mechanical Introspection in Art" by the Italian Futurist Enrico Prampolini (9–10). I would like to take this opportunity to thank Susan Fillin-Yeh for her invaluable help with this study, and especially for encouraging me to look for the machine aesthetic in fashion photography in the first place. I would also like to thank Craig Atkinson for his excellent work in making slides of the illustrations.

4. In *291*, no. 5/6 (July 1915) [no page number]. Beinecke Library, Yale University, New Haven, Connecticut.

5. In *291*, no. 2 (February 1915) [no page number].

6. In *291*, no. 7/8 (September/October 1915) [no page number].

7. Jennifer Craik points out that the choice of aristocrats and debutantes to model clothes in this period was determined not only by their reflected status on the fashions they modelled, but by the fact that professional models were associated with prostitution (97). However, this attitude changed during the 1920s "as photographers became confident in exploring new techniques borrowed from new artistic movements and moral codes were relaxed" (98).

8. Both in *De Meyer*, ed. Robert Brandau (New York: Alfred A. Knopf, 1976).

9. Sonia Delaunay, an avant-garde artist, believed in applying principles of painting to clothing design, creating garments that were unmistakably modern both in appearance and in function. Jennifer Craik succinctly summarizes the importance of her contribution to design: "Delaunay's approach to clothes was revoluntionary. She combined her interest in the 1920s art movements of cubism, futurism and fauvism with a belief that women's clothes should suit their new lifestyles" (2).

10. Andreas Huyssen looks at the connections between mass production, women, and consumerism, and makes the compelling argument that mass culture itself is gendered as feminine (188–207).

11. Steichen, McAffe Oxfords (1926) in *The Vogue Book of Fashion Photography*, ed. Polly Devlin (New York: Doubleday, 1979), p. 39.

12. Diana Fuss locates a similar loss of identity through fragmentation in the fashion photography of the late '80s and early '90s. She specifically analyzes the prevalence of "decapitation and dismemberment" in fashion shots of women's bodies, and reads this as "the fantasy . . . of a body without a subject" (718).

13. "Bathing Beauties on a Sunday," (1929) from *Style in Motion: Munkasci Photographs '20s, '30s, '40s*, eds. Nancy White and John Esten (New York: Clarkson N. Potter [n.d.], p. 43).

14. Steichen, photograph of Victor Steibel robe, American *Vogue*, January 1, 1935, p. 36.

15. The robot woman was not a new concept in the 1930s. (Arthur Kroker's remark that "women's bodies have always been postmodern" [v–vi] suggests the presence of such images long before the end of the 20th century.) In fact, she appears as early as 1817 as the automaton Olimpia in E. T. A. Hoffman's story "The Sand-Man." The next step for a study of the robot woman would be to locate this image in a wider historical spectrum, which would include for example texts such as *Bladerunner* and genres such as cyberpunk.

16. In *The Vogue Book of Fashion Photography*, ed. Polly Devlin (New York: Doubleday, 1979), p. 47.

III

THE MATERNAL BODY

5

Technologies of Misogyny: The Transparent Maternal Body and Alternate Reproductions in *Frankenstein, Dracula,* and Some Selected Media Discourses

Deborah S. Wilson

In a richly evocative reading, "Assembly-Line Gender and the Postmodern Body," Anne Balsamo argues that under the hostile gaze of postmodern technology, the female body becomes fragmentable, semiotically deconstructable, and when pregnant invisible:

> the maternal body becomes simply an invisible medium to look through. Of course, the womb isn't the only body part to be technologically isolated and symbolically manipulated. But because the womb has historically served as a metonym for the rest of the female body, these media representations of the rest of the technologically fragmented female body offer us an interesting opportunity to witness the interaction between language and materiality; in short, we see how a semiotic deconstruction is chronologically enacted. (Balsamo 7)[1]

Balsamo's essay situates her reading in the decades following World War II, and she deliberately limits her analysis to the technological discourses specific to that era as they center upon the female body: e.g., female bodybuilding subcultures, plastic surgery, current obstetrical technology, and the diet and fitness industries.

If we borrow Balsamo's notion of the invisible maternal body, and couple it with her observation that the "womb has historically served as a metonym for the rest of the female body," we can interrogate cultural history specific to that phenomena. However, unlike Balsamo, I read the maternal body as transparent rather than invisible, for it seems to me that no discursive practice, no matter how hegemonic, can successfully operate without at least the outlines of that maternal body. By one means or another, women's cultural ontology always already predicates upon its metonymic displacement to the womb, and while that displacement may in turn redefine it, the maternal body has never been superannuated.

By preserving those outlines metonymically, various discursive practices can then use the outlines of the maternal body as a transparency through which to screen their particular culturally hegemonic readings, and promote their concomitant political ideologies. Additionally, we observe that other cultural and historical moments offer surveillances and interventions specific to the womb and the maternal body to which it is integral. These surveillances and interventions, whether economic, legal, medical, political, and no matter to what era their technological expression defers, invariably coalesce into a cultural hegemony that would appropriate and reinscribe women's bodies and their reproductive powers. Historically, these reinscriptions and appropriations have chiefly served the interests of patriarchal discourses. Consequently, these discourses frame the outline of this transparent female body specific to the discrete needs of a given cultural and historical moment. As it applies to women, gender oppression here frames itself through a variety of technologies. Through such implementations, these technologies become the technologies of misogyny, for misogyny is what they (re)produce.[2]

Certainly, social surveillances of the maternal role manifest themselves through any number of discursive practices, and their recognition as such is hardly unique to this most recent generation of feminist critics and theorists. Such disparate commentators as the psychoanalyst Karen Horney and the anthropologist Ashley Montagu have taken note of cultural currents that indicate deeply embedded suspicion and/or envy of women's reproductive capacity. Horney, seeking a counterclaim to Freud's theory of female penis envy, opposes to it her own theory of male womb envy (Horney 117; Horney 145). Montagu notes that the men of the Aruta, an Australian Aboriginal tribe, imitate the menses of women, which they regard as magical and powerful. Though the Aruta do not recognize the connection of the menses to pregnancy, through making periodic penile incisions under ritual conditions, they demonstrate envy of the idiosyncrasies of female biology (Montagu 62–64, 328).

Although numerous cultural contexts and artifacts corroborating my thesis abound, I wish to limit my analysis of the technologies of misogyny to a careful sampling of texts: Mary Shelley's *Frankenstein*, Bram Stoker's *Dracula*, the abortion discourse of Planned Parenthood and the Arthur S. DeMoss Foundation, and finally, the Judith Corporation's "Mommy-To-Be-Doll"©, an educational toy. Whether literary or cultural, all these texts mediate between the technologies of misogyny as they cluster about the maternal body and the social forces that would claim, control, or even appropriate that body altogether. Moreover, each of these texts serves as an emissary between the anxieties of technological progress peculiar to their historical moment and their concomitant implications for human subjectivity. All of these texts construct their narratives around the metonym of the womb, not just in respect to the maternal body as a contested cultural site, but as a metonym that accounts for cultural anxieties over competing scientific paradigms, colonial ambitions, and issues of racial supremacy. Finally, we should note here that *Frankenstein* appeared in 1818; *Dracula* in 1897; Planned Parenthood's and the Arthur S. DeMoss Foundation's respectively pro and con abortion campaigns, and the Judith Corporation's "Mommy-To-Be-Doll©," appeared in the 1990s. Clearly, the same phenomena span an historical continuum of nearly two hundred years.[3]

The Masculine Birth of Monstrosity: *Frankenstein*

In an important paper, "Monstrous Absence: The Maternal Body and *Frankenstein*," Kathy Gentile notes that over the last twenty years, two distinct critical schools have disputed just what sort of creation myth we find in *Frankenstein*: "Male critics have taken [*Frankenstein*] as a male myth of the Romantic overreacher or of 'scientific hubris,'" but "feminist critics beginning with Ellen Moers have read [*Frankenstein*] as a birth myth and a psychodrama of Shelley's life as a motherless daughter, a resentful, grieving mother, unfulfilled wife and anxious writer" (Gentile 2).[4] Effectively dismissing both of these readings, Gentile counters that what in this text becomes truly monstrous is an "act of creation perverted by the *obliteration* of the maternal body from the reproductive process," and that "Frankenstein is the modern Prometheus, as the subtitle suggests, because he steals 'fire,' the secret of creation, not from the gods or God, but from woman" (Gentile 3, emphasis mine).

Although her reading accurately asserts that the maternal body disappears from this narrative, Gentile focuses primarily on the text's originary myths; the fate of the maternal body remains subordinate to her larger argument. However, not only do I want to make the status of the maternal body central to my critique of *Frankenstein*, I take issue with her assertion that Frankenstein "completely eradicates the maternal body" (Gentile 4). True, the narrative effectively kills off Caroline, Elizabeth, and Justine so as to interrupt or prevent their possible maternity, yet marginal though they may be, both Margaret Saville and Nature herself (the novel consistently refers to Nature in the feminine) escape and/or resist Victor's agenda. Taking my argument a step further, I will also demonstrate that through *Frankenstein's* extended and impassioned critique of natural philosophy as a perverse paradigm for scientific inquiry, Shelley implicitly argues no matter how sophisticated the medical technology, maternity—even procreation itself—can never really become *solely* male. For even as she foregrounds the issue of a certain male envy of female reproductive powers, Shelley repeatedly calls into question the apparent binaries of male-female, masculine-feminine, and subsequently, the essentialist values such binaries privilege.

Yet readings which privilege binaries dominate much feminist scholarship on *Frankenstein*. For example, Anne K. Mellor's elegant essay, "Possessing Nature: The Female in *Frankenstein*," posits that the Creature's aggressive malice originates not so much in Victor's paternal inadequacies as in the denial of the properly maternal "ethic of care" she locates in the maternal body and role (Gilligan qtd. in Mellor 229). Since Victor has no proper Yin to his Yang, Mellor implies, the logical consequences of Victor's project, should he realize his vision of "fathering" a new race, are monstrous in more ways than one.

> Indeed, for the simple purpose of human survival, Frankenstein has eliminated the necessity to have females at all. One of the deepest horrors of this novel is Frankenstein's implicit goal of creating a society for men only: his creature is male; he refuses to create a female; there is no reason that the race of immortal beings he hoped to propagate should not be exclusively male. (Mellor 220)

Conversely, I would assert that though he tries valiantly to render the maternal body redundant, Victor fails even in his moment of triumph, a triumph he himself immediately pronounces a "catastrophe" (58). Even as he brings the Creature to life through scientific means, he must acknowledge Nature's "maternal" function, and more significantly, he never fully recuperates her gestative powers. For although he turns to science as opposed to woman for procreative purposes, Victor only succeeds in transposing the outlines of the maternal body to a Nature rendered literally, and not just metaphorically, feminine. In other words, even as Victor strives to eradicate the actual need for women and their reproductive powers, he finds he must reinvent them. Victor never quite makes maternity *exclusively* male; the womb may be displaced, the maternal body reinscribed, but it will not remain subsumed.

Even though women seem to disappear altogether from parts of the narrative, they soon reappear. For instance, Shelley frames her narrative along a roughly epistolary model: Victor Frankenstein tells his story to the Arctic explorer and ship's captain, Robert Walton, and Walton in turn relates both his own impressions of Victor Frankenstein and Frankenstein's story in a long letter to his married sister, Margaret Saville. Margaret herself never speaks, either through letters of her own or even through her brother's recollections of his conversations with her. Thus she becomes a synecdoche of the silenced and marginalized middle-class woman, whom Shelley might have calculated as a considerable margin of her audience (Showalter 1977; Poovey 1984). *Frankenstein's* silencing of its women characters is radical: mothers, like Victor's mother, Caroline, either die through acts of literal maternal self-sacrifice or like Justine's mother, repudiate their children. Both Elizabeth and Justine die prematurely, before they can reproduce. Thus the text effectively eradicates only the *literal* maternal body, for Victor briefly forces Nature itself to assume a metaphorically feminine and maternal role.

On one level, *Frankenstein* does become only an allegorical familial melodrama of a bastardized "son," the Creature, demanding acknowledgement from his "father," Victor. Conversely, this narrative offers a critique of the "masculine" scientist's relationship to a "feminine" nature. *Frankenstein* implicitly evaluates the paradigm shift from the older, mystical model of science that the alchemists valorized to the newer, mechanical model of science that the natural philosophers adopted. As an adolescent, Victor becomes as equally conversant with Albertus

Magnus, Paracelsus, and Cornelius Agrippa as he will become with Newton, Davy, and Erasmus Darwin as a university student.

In a study that bears profoundly upon the kind of science Victor will practice, *Reflections on Gender and Science*, Evelyn Fox Keller deconstructs the competing scientific discourses of alchemy and natural philosophy, a competition that played itself out against the larger political conflicts of seventeenth-century England. Keller offers a carefully comparative evaluation of the governing paradigms of hermaphroditism, that is, a perfectly harmonized balance of masculine and feminine qualities and secondary sexual characteristics, which the alchemists adopted, and a patriarchal, heterosexual marital union, which the natural philosophers, taking their lead from Francis Bacon, adopted (Keller 43–65). She notes further that the struggle between the alchemists and the natural philosophers, to determine whose vision would dominate and inform scientific discourse, was very much a social and political struggle, one that had profound impact on the political economy of academic life (Keller 43–65). Over time, succeeding generations of scholars and scientists, whose loyalties and visions lay with natural philosophy, made claim to greater and greater numbers of university chairs, government support, and private patronage. In the end, the natural philosophers dominated academic institutions, and they were therefore in a position to disseminate their readings of material reality to a more general, increasingly literate public. As the son of a prominent Swiss magistrate, Victor Frankenstein figures as a prime example of a newly enfranchised and emergent ethnographic population, the recently prosperous and professionally ambitious sons of the middle class. Tellingly, he matriculates at the University of Ingolstadt, renowned during Shelley's lifetime for its medical school.[5]

Mary Shelley, conversant in the scientific advances of her time, could not have helped but be sensitive to the conflict between those competing scientific paradigms. Not only had she consulted Davy on chemistry and Erasmus Darwin on biology as she worked on *Frankenstein* (Moers 94; Sunstein 127; Spark 156–57), but the struggle for ascendancy between the hermetic and mechanical traditions (the latter eventually gave birth to the Royal Society), had been played out over several generations, its events no doubt still fresh in the living memories of her learned acquaintances, the visitors to her father's parlor. In *Frankenstein*, she constructs a narrative that enacts those conflicts through the mediums of Victor and his Creature. As a young boy, Victor accidentally encounters Cornelius Agrippa, and by reading one of his books (never specified), his interest in science awakens.

Although he later disavows the hermetic model, the study of Agrippa, Paracelsus, and Albertus Magnus so dominates a critical period in his adolescence he deliberately invites mockery from his professors when he cites their work as the source of his scientific training (50–52). Victor repeatedly states that "Natural philosophy is the genius that has regulated my fate" (44), but his ambitions, which lead him to the "the creation of a human being" (53), independent of a woman, or even an isolated womb, resonate strongly of the alchemists' grandiose pursuits. "Life and death appeared to me ideal bounds, which I should first break through and pour a torrent of light into a dark world. A new species would bless me as its creator and source; many happy and excellent natures would owe their being to me. No father could claim the gratitude of his children so completely as I should deserve theirs" (55).

Irony operates at two levels here: the disastrous outcome attendant upon the Creature's "birth," and Victor's having become too much the natural philosopher. "In the hermetic tradition, material nature was suffused with spirit; its understanding accordingly required the joint integrated effort of heart, hand, and mind. By contrast, the mechanical philosophers sought to divorce matter from spirit, and hand and mind from heart" (Keller 44). Victor, Shelley implies, refuses to recognize Nature's autonomy, and in repudiating Agrippa, he repudiates his injunction to "cohabit with the elements." Instead, he wishes, like Francis Bacon before him, to "bind [Nature] to [man's] service and make her [his] slave" (Keller 48).

Under conditions of both war and slavery, women frequently find themselves forced into concubinage; moreover, the rhetoric of even much contemporary scientific discourse constitutes the rhetoric of rape and sexual sadism (Keller 123–24). Just as the mechanical model of science encourages the natural philosopher to force Nature's secrets from her, Victor himself does not hesitate to "rape" Nature. Relentless in his pursuit, he "dabbled among the unhallowed damps of the grave," and "tortured the living animal to animate lifeless clay," as he "pursued nature to her hiding places" (56). By forcibly taking the secrets of life from Nature, Victor forces a metaphorical conception and birth upon her, only to disavow immediately the product of that rape, the Creature, whom he finds hideous (58).

Yet when the Creature finally catches up with him, he refuses to acknowledge his paternal responsibilities toward him. "Abhorred monster! fiend that thou art! The tortures of hell are too mild a vengeance for thy crimes. Wretched devil! you reproach me with your creation; come on, then, that I may extinguish the spark which I so negligently bestowed" (90). The Creature's stalking of the ironically named Victor is both literal and moral. He chases him across Europe and eventually to the Antarctic in an effort to force his "father," Victor, to acknowledge his paternal responsibilities. He consistently addresses Victor as "father" and "creator," terms that ironically echo God's relationship with humanity. But the Creature's pursuit of Victor is also metaphorical, for it becomes redolent of a son avenging his mother's rape, even though he himself knows he owes his existence to her violation. "For," as again Mellor notes, "Nature is not the passive, inert, or 'dead' matter that Frankenstein imagines. Frankenstein assumes that he can violate Nature with impunity. But Nature both resists and revenges herself upon his attempts" (Mellor 226).

Victor's refusal to create a female companion for the Creature, as he demands, seems not so subtly informed by misogyny. "I was now about to form another being, of whose dispositions I was alike ignorant; she might become ten thousand times more malignant than her mate, and delight for its own sake, in murder and wretchedness" (140). Victor claims that his greatest fear is that

> Even if they [the Creature and his proposed mate] were to leave Europe, and inhabit the deserts of the new world, yet one of the first results of those sympathies for which the daemon [the Creature] thirsted would be children, and a race of devils would be propagated upon the earth, who might make the very existence of man a condition precarious and full of terror (140).

Victor never seems to reflect that he could deny her a womb, or ovaries. Of course, it is entirely possible that Shelley herself was ignorant of the function of the ovaries, and assumed that the woman's role in reproduction was solely incubatory. Conversely, it is equally possible that Shelley was slyly commenting on the widespread scientific resistance, characterized by the ovist-animalculist debate raging since the mid-seventeenth century, to acknowledging the function of the ovaries and the probable role of female "seed" in conception.[6]

In *Frankenstein*, Nature represents a maternal body too vast to configure whole; its presence becomes overwhelming and threatening to the scientists like Victor, who seek to subdue her by whatever means they deem necessary. By fragmenting the "body" of Nature, Victor almost succeeds in making women redundant and appropriating for himself female powers of reproduction. Metaphorically, however, Nature reemerges within the outlines of this now abstract maternal body. Figuring herself whole within those boundaries, Nature effectively resists those technologies of a misogynistic science that would render the maternal body transparent and reinscribe it in its own image.

Colonizing the Womb: *Dracula*

Like Shelley with *Frankenstein*, Bram Stoker constructs *Dracula*'s narrative along a modified epistolary model: the story is told through the letters, diaries, memoranda, and journals of virtually all the major characters, but chiefly those of Mina and Jonathan Harker and John Seward. This text densely integrates nearly all the cultural anxieties of late Victorian England, presenting them all at once through an allegory of good triumphing over evil. Most pertinently for my purpose here, *Dracula* draws together the disparate strands of informational technology, imperialist ambitions, sexual dread (particularly when figured as miscegenation), and shifting political economies, locating them—at once metonymically and metaphorically—in the womb. For it is through the bodies of *Dracula*'s female characters that Stoker dramatizes what I shall call the "anxieties of empire."

For example, we can read this text as an ambiguous class conflict: the heroes almost without exception represent an increasingly powerful, professionalized middle class, a class that increasingly sought parity with the aristocracy. Jonathan Harker, a solicitor newly qualified at the narrative's outset, ventures to Transylvania to negotiate a real-estate transaction on behalf of his law firm with the mysterious Count Dracula, who purchases Carfax, an English estate, as well as a London townhouse and other properties in England. The other male heroes, with the exception of Arthur Holmwood, Lord Godalming, all represent resolutely ascendant, middle-class professional men. John Seward like Professor Van Helsing is a physician; Quincey Morris, a self-made man, is a wealthy speculator in land and cattle. That Seward and Morris are old friends of Godalming, and that Harker and Van Helsing quickly become admitted to their circle, suggests the possibility of self-interested alliance between the professional and aristocratic classes, an alliance clearly necessary for preserving commerce and empire. Certainly, these men's friendship and alliance become integral to their hunt for and, ultimately, their destruction of Dracula. Moreover, we ought to note that although both Godalming and Dracula are aristocrats, Dracula is a feudal lord, while Godalming is a parliamentarian one.[7]

On another level, *Dracula*, produced at the apogee of Britain's empire, projects anxious themes of invasion and colonization upon a foreign culture, embodied in Count Dracula himself. As the feudal lord of a mysterious Balkan country, Dracula himself is described in consistently orientalist terms, terms that stress his racial alterity in all but purely negative terms. Not surprisingly, then, Dracula figures in this text as the archetype of a desiccated, corrupt, decadent, and above all, racially other, aristocrat—one who, the text implies, has drained the life's blood of his people and their culture over the centuries. Consequently, Dracula must look for fresh territory to exploit; he focusses his colonial ambitions on England. John Stevenson observes that

> The problem of interracial competition would have probably had an especial resonance in 1897, the year *Dracula* appeared. For several decades, Great Britain had engaged in an unprecedented program of racial expansion: four and one quarter million miles were added to the empire in the last thirty years of the century alone (Seaman 332). British imperialism, of course, was not new, nor was suspicion of foreigners a novelty in a country where, as one eighteenth-century wit put it, "Before they learn there is a God to be worshipped, they learn there are Frenchmen to be detested" (qtd. in Porter 21). Yet the late nineteenth century saw the rise of that great vulgarization of evolution (and powerful racist rationalization), social Darwinism, and heard Disraeli say, "All is race; there is no other truth" (qtd. in Faber 59). *Dracula*'s insistence on the terror and necessity of racial struggle in an imperialist context (the count after all, has invaded England and intends to take it over) must reflect that historical frame. (140)

Too, Britain represented its colonial exploitation of India and Africa as liberatory, freeing the native populations from feudal despotism, ignorance, and superstition, seeking—"altruistically"—to remake the indigenous population in its own image. For its benevolence,

Imperial Britain appropriated the country's natural and human resources as its just due. Similarly, in defeating Dracula, the narrative's heroes defeat both the supernatural forces of darkness and a hostile foreign invader, thereby ridding England, eastern Europe—and indeed the world—of a menacing parasite. Not coincidentally, the heroes, while not all English, are at the very least of immediate northern European ancestry: Van Helsing is Dutch and Morris, from Texas, is clearly of EuroCaucasian ancestry. *Dracula's* text justifies its racialist agenda, to borrow Kwame Anthony Appiah's term, through projection (Appiah 276). Britain's and the United States' allied "manifest destiny" to become the dominant military and economic world powers also becomes essential to human survival. *Dracula* configures that alliance through Morris, with the (North) American's joining his British friends in their battle(s) against the Count.

Finally, as the sexual subtext of *Dracula* has been so thoroughly critiqued, particularly as it enacts misogynistic fear and loathing of female sexuality, we can safely gloss this last issue.[8] Suffice it to say, here, that *Dracula* presents a multi-layered sexual drama, one that enacts the primary contradiction of Victorian sexual hegemony. Women are supposed to be asexual creatures who endured sexual relations with their husbands for the sake of duty, children, and empire. Yet women's sexual modesty must be vigilantly guarded so they will not succumb to their latent sexual appetites and become wholly sexualized.[9] Good women are asexual and to be rewarded with male protection and reverence; bad women are sexual and need to be punished.

We see the contradictions of that Victorian sexual hegemony played out in the scene where the vampire hunters destroy the vampire Lucy. Lucy Westenra has died twice. First in her mortal death from Dracula's attacks; second, because her mortal death at the hands of a vampire in turn makes Lucy a vampire herself, she must be destroyed so that she cannot threaten others with a similar fate. Once the all-but-omniscient Professor Van Helsing convinces her grieving fiancé and friends that Lucy is indeed "undead," Godalming, Morris, Seward, and Van Helsing destroy the vampire Lucy in a scene that simultaneously rationalizes and eroticizes violence against women. As Godalming drives the ritual stake through her heart, Van Helsing, Morris, and Seward read aloud the "Office of the Dead" from the *Book of Common Prayer.*

The Thing [the vampire Lucy] in the coffin writhed; and a hideous, blood-curdling screech came from the opened red

lips. The body shook and quivered and twisted in wild con-
tortions: the sharp white teeth champed together till the lips
were cut and the mouth was smeared with a crimson foam.
But Arthur never faltered. He looked like a figure of Thor as
his untrembling arm rose and fell, driving deeper and deeper
the mercy-bearing stake, whilst the blood from the pierced
heart welled up and spurted through it. His face was set,
and high duty seemed to shine through it. The sight of it
gave us courage so that our voices seemed to ring through
the little vault. . . . And then the writhing and quivering of
the body became less, and the teeth ceased to champ, and
the face to quiver. Finally it lay still, the terrible task was
over. (216)

We should note that only female vampires are ritually destroyed in
Dracula: the stake through the heart, their heads cut off, mouths
stuffed with garlic (217). When Quincey Morris kills Dracula, his
death becomes anticlimactic, for Morris simply stabs him through
the heart with a Bowie knife as Jonathan simultaneously slashes
the Count's throat (377).

As in other, later melodramas aimed at least in part at
rationalizing institutionalized racism, *Dracula* projects the designated racial other as literally rapacious. Male and female alike, the
racial other becomes all but exclusively sexual, calling into question the very binaries Stoker otherwise so assiduously re-affirms.
Dracula presents a double threat for he is doubly the racial other:
Slav and vampire. The Count, like all those potentially marauding,
foreign invaders at the edge of the British Empire, lusts after the
women "belonging" to two of the narrative's heroes: Lucy Westenra,
who was engaged to Godalming, and Mina Murray, who early in
the narrative marries her fiancé, Jonathan Harker. In a particularly campy passage (all but impossible to read with a straight
face), the Count himself explicitly states to the heroes that it is
through the agency of "their" women that he can and does
threaten England itself.

You think to baffle me, you—with your pale faces all in a
row, like sheep in a butcher's. You shall be sorry yet, each
one of you! You think you have left me without a place to
rest; but I have more. My revenge is just begun! I have
spread it over centuries, and time is on my side. Your girls
that you all love are mine already; and through them you

and others shall yet be mine—my creatures, to do my bidding and to be my jackals when I want to feed. Bah! (306)

Blood tropes and retropes endlessly in *Dracula*. Blood represents life ("The Blood is the life!" the mad Renfield chants), sexuality, semen, and racial and gender identity.[10] Above all, the exchange of blood through transfusion represents conjugal intercourse. That becomes clear in Seward's account of Lucy's funeral.

> When it was all over, we [Seward, Morris, and Van Helsing] were standing beside Arthur, who, poor fellow was speaking of his part in the operation where his blood had been transfused to his Lucy's veins; I could see Van Helsing's face grow white and purple by turns. Arthur was saying that he felt since then as if they two had really been married, and that she was his wife in the sight of God. *None of us said a word of the other operations, and none of us ever shall.* (174, emphasis mine)

Repeatedly, wavering, inconstant Lucy hovers between life and death, just as she hovered among her three suitors, asking Mina "Why can't they let a girl marry three men . . .[?]" (59). Godalming, Morris, Seward and even Van Helsing step in several times to donate their blood for the transfusions Van Helsing hopes will save her. Lucy thereby becomes polygamous and promiscuous, as Van Helsing makes clear in his later, private exchange with Seward, during which he explains his hysterical reaction to Godalming's sentiment.

> Said he not that the transfusion of his blood to her veins made her truly his bride?
>
> Yes, and it was a sweet and comforting idea for him.
>
> Quite so. But there was a difficulty, friend John. *If so that, then what about the others? Ho, ho! Then this so sweet maid is a polyandrist*, and me, with my poor wife dead to me, but alive by Church's law, though no wits, all gone—even I, who am faithful husband to this now-no-wife, am bigamist. (176, emphasis mine)

Blood also mediates between the maternal body and the technologies that would control it: first through transfusion, later through the blood-soaked ritual destruction of the vampires. Blood insistently mediates the conflicting claims of Dracula and of his opponents upon the maternal body.

One by one, the heroes destroy Dracula through the women he has "raped": first Lucy, then, as they chase Dracula out of England and back to Transylvania, the three unnamed lamia (who nearly seduce Harker when he stays at Dracula's castle), and, finally, through recuperating Mina Harker herself. Just as Dracula would destroy them—and by extension England—through "raping" their women, they too destroy him by destroying the women of his "race." England itself becomes identified as a maternal body, one whose outline we discern in the island's coast. In Stoker's time, England as maternal body became embodied constitutionally, symbolically and culturally in Queen Victoria, still reigning in 1897. Indeed, at the narrative's outset, Dracula himself personifies England in the feminine third person when he tells an as yet unsuspecting Harker, "I have come to know your great England; and to know her is to love her" (20). In retrospect, his final phrase, "to love her," implies exponentially sexual greed. England feminized becomes by extension the heroine that Harker and the others must rescue, through the mediums of Lucy's and Mina's bodies. Otherwise, through a "fate worse than death" "She" will breed a vampire race.

Dracula, then, becomes an allegory of the struggle for racial ascendancy and gender supremacy, a fabulous epic of stalwart heroes defending their homeland and the women who Dracula and his opponents both regard as vital to their incompatible racial survival. Consequently, Mina, Lucy, and even the lamia become theirs to inscribe and reinscribe according to the exigencies of the cultural or historical moment. As we shall see, because of Mina's fluent and nominally subservient access to all the technologies available to the warring empires of Britain and Dracula, appropriating her body becomes paramount, for through her the victor's cause will advance. Conversely, Lucy, who never lives to marry Godalming, consequently never becomes maternal in human terms, for in her mortal death she presumably dies a virgin. Dracula takes her as a "bride"; her "marriage" to him ends when her transmutation to a fully vampire state is complete; as a full-fledged vampire herself, she becomes his "child." As John Stevenson points out, the economy of vampire procreation is radical, collapsing "the distinction between sexual partners and offspring": wife becomes daughter (143). Unlike human reproduction, however, vampire reproduction requires a new mate for every "birth." Lucy, like the lamia before her, sequentially but unambiguously becomes first wife, then child. If the vampire Lucy had succeeded in seducing Godalming, he would have become first husband, then son.

On the other hand, Mina, Dracula's last female victim, survives in part because she does marry Jonathan before Dracula attempts to make her his next "bride." As Jonathan's wife, she has been claimed for human sexuality. When Dracula attacks her at night in the Harkers' bed, he issues a sexual challenge Jonathan will not later dismiss. Sensing danger after an exchange with Renfield, Seward's patient and Dracula's lackey, Godalming, Morris, and Van Helsing burst through the Harkers' bedroom door. The scene Seward describes parallels forcible fellatio:

> On the bed beside the window lay Jonathan Harker, his face flushed, and breathing heavily as though in a stupor. Kneeling on the near edge of the bed facing outwards was the white-clad figure of his wife. By her side stood a tall, thin man, clad in black. His face was turned from us, but the very instant we saw it we all recognized the Count—in every way, even to the scar on his forehead. With his left hand, he held both Mrs. Harker's hands, keeping them away with her arms at full tension; his right hand gripped her by the back of the neck, forcing her face down on his bosom. Her white night-dress was smeared with blood, and a thin stream trickled down the man's bare breast, which was shown by his torn-open dress. The attitude of the two had a terrible resemblance to a child forcing a kitten's nose into a saucer of milk to compel it to drink. (281–82)

In every way, this scene schematizes Mina's innocent helplessness (though the metaphor of the kitten seems more laughable than chilling): the Count, in black, overpowers her, in white. Yet she cries out soon after, and despite her husband's reassurances, that she is "Unclean, unclean! I must touch him [Jonathan] or kiss him no more. Oh, that it should be that it is I who am now his worst enemy, and whom he may have most cause to fear" (284). Her bloody nightgown suggests defloration, thus marking Dracula's first "possession" of her, a possession secondary and sequential to Harker's own. Mina's body becomes the contested cultural site between her husband and their friends and Dracula.

Whether Mina will remain human and breed human children or whether she will effectively become, as a fully transmuted vampire, his daughter, emerges as the racial stake literally enacted upon her body. By forcing her to drink his blood, Dracula attempts to make Mina his informant: through this act he can force himself telepathically into her consciousness. He will know what she knows and thus can anticipate the strategies his enemies devise against him. However, Mina knows too that her telepathic relation to Dracula can be manipulated to the vampire hunters' advantage, and Van Helsing, resident expert on vampires, affirms its truth to the others. But it is Mina who first suggests that Van Helsing, conversant with Charcot, hypnotize her at night so as to track Dracula's movements and second-guess his plans. Mina implicitly controls and coordinates the hunt against him, just as she controls the text that will become its chronicle: shaping, nurturing, and preserving it. Mina gives birth to the army that pursues Dracula, just as Mina gives birth to the text.[11]

At the outset of *Dracula*, Mina informs the reader that she is fluent in the informational technology of the 1890s. She trains herself as a typist and learns shorthand, so that she can be "useful to Jonathan" (53), and even memorizes train schedules "so that I may help Jonathan in case he is in a hurry" (186). Despite all her nominal insistence that she develops these skills only as a service to her husband, her superficial speeches to the male heroes that she is only "a poor, weak, woman" (330), and her snide diary entries repudiating "the New Woman" (88–89), Mina clearly emerges as Dracula's most formidable opponent. She conceives of the two crucial strategies that ultimately defeat Dracula. She suggests that she type all the characters' writings so as to establish a chronology of Dracula's invasion of England; she constructs and controls the narrative itself. Ever the good bureaucrat, Mina even has the foresight to use manifold so that she can make triplicate copies.[12] Dracula owes his defeat more to bureaucracy and its informational technologies than to magical combat (Auerbach 283). First among his combatants, Mina implicitly grasps that whoever controls informational technology and the material it disseminates rules the empire. Because the narrative and the technologies that produce it become truly instrumental to his defeat, Mina emerges as the narrative's hero as well as its heroine. Yet both she and Stoker remain ambivalent about the androgyny implicit in her shifting role(s). Mina alternates between damsel-in-distress and Boadicea victorious, dropping casually misogynistic remarks about women generally, and the New Woman particularly. Yet despite her unreflexive misogyny, Mina uncritically embraces that silly airhead Lucy as her closest friend and confidante. Ironically, Mina's superior intellect, physical and moral courage, foresight, and talent could support the feminist claims of her time easily and well, even as she plays the Angel of the House. In *Dracula* the ideology of gender is nothing if not ambiguous.

Mina represents a maternal archetype too: she consoles all the men in expressly maternal terms, and she even advocates pity for Dracula himself (308). Mina also embodies a transparent maternity, one on which the discursive practices of racial anxiety and cultural dread, sexual desire and sexual revulsion, colonial rationalizations and middle-class ascendancy, incubate even as they continuously reform themselves, reinscribing her womb in their own interests and images. Nominally, Mina seems reclaimed from the vampire for the purposes of human reproduction. We learn in the epilogue, which Harker writes, that Mina has borne a son whose "bundle of names links all our little band of men together; but we call him Quincey" (378).

Metaphorically, since all these men claim paternity of Mina's son, all but Jonathan indirectly claim her womb. Indeed, Jonathan tells us, Mina secretly believes that their son is Morris reincarnated; his birthday is also the anniversary of Morris's death (378). Her reproductive capabilities, whether textual or physiological, resist the forces that would appropriate them, but the status of her womb remains always in question. Her unacknowledged desire for autonomy remains evident despite her pious protestations of ancillary status as woman. Her ambiguous social and maternal status enlists her efforts in keeping the outlines of the maternal body continually in flux. Mina simultaneously sabotages and supports the social and cultural technologies of misogyny that would reduce women to their wombs, which in turn would valorize their maternal roles even as they also would eviscerate their social effectuality.

Mommy-To-Be©, or Not To Be? Who Answers the Question?

By way of conclusion, I wish to situate my analysis very briefly in contemporary controversies over birth control, abortion, and maternity, particularly as they configure the maternal body in current popular culture. The particular discursive practices I have in mind locate in educational toys, specifically the Judith Corporation's "Mommy-To-Be-Doll"©, and the media discourses of both sides of the abortion debate. I will examine Planned Parenthood's print campaign advocating keeping legal, medically safe, widely accessible abortion, and the television ad campaigns of the Arthur S. DeMoss Foundation, advocating adoption over abortion as a solution to an unwanted pregnancy.

In *Feminism Without Women: Culture and Criticism in a "Post-feminist" Age*, Tania Modleski observes that recent science fiction movies, such as *Alien Nation*, offer allegorical meditations on racial hostility in part because Hollywood usually deems direct representation of that hostility as too "monstrous" (Modleski, 88). Such squeamishness, if you will, applies not only to cinematic representations of the maternal body, particularly in relation to questions of its control, but to other (visual) media discourses as well.

Even contemporary abortion discourse displaces the maternal body, rendering it transparent and ancillary to the cultural debate that should centralize it. On the anti-abortion media front, the conservative Arthur S. DeMoss Foundation offers, through a series of glossy, sophisticated television commercials currently running on cable channels and late night commercial slots, advocation of adoption over abortion as a solution to an unexpected pregnacy. Perhaps not surprisingly, the DeMoss Foundation's commercials rarely show pregnant women, and when a shot of a pregnant woman does appear, the shot literally fragments her body so as to offer an extreme close-up of her vastly pregnant belly. In one such scene, the camera cuts quickly from a long shot of a pregnant woman's whole body to a medium close-up of her huge abdomen, lingering as a small boy puts his ear to her, apparently listening to foetal heartbeats. Other scenes show women literally at the edges of the frames: at family dinners and watching their children play— they never dominate these scenes. In two more recent installments, the maternal body becomes even more insistently remote. In one commercial, we watch a young woman in a choir robe, apparently at a church service. Fair-haired and rapturous, she sings in praise while her voice-over tells us that her mother had tried to abort her. Though obviously she survived the procedure (whether self-induced or clinical, we are never told), she admonishes us that she has had serious medical problems all her life. In the second, we watch a morose young woman walking near a playground, devoid of children at the swings and sandboxes. Shot in black and white, her voice-over tells us that she has never stopped thinking of the foetus she aborted—how old *he* would be now, what *he* would be like, for when this phantom child appears, he is unmistakably male. Throughout *all* of these commercials, a male voice-over intones "There's a growing respect for life in this country . . . All of these children have one thing in common—they were unplanned pregnancies. But their parents [not their mothers] decided against abortion and toughed it out. . . . Life—What a beautiful choice." As of this writing, with the single exception of one commercial that shows a racially diverse group of schoolchildren (whose uniform dress suggests a parochial school), through setting, wardrobe, and locations, these ads focus on an idealized EuroCaucasian middle class. Thus they effectively disallow pressing concerns of economic stability, much less poverty, abusive relationships, or grave medical problems. The implicit anxiety that we see in the DeMoss Foundation's ongoing campaign seems to be over a perceived drop in the EuroCaucasian birthrate. That this television campaign—as of this writing—comparatively under-represents people of color in relation to abortion and birth-rates recalls the racist agenda of the U. S. eugenics movement at the turn of the century. While the eugenicists of an earlier era could and did directly argue their cause in racist terms, the DeMoss Foundation cannot allow itself the luxury of so overtly racist an agenda.

Displacing the maternal body also occurs occasionally on the other side of the abortion debate. For example, Planned Parent-hood, in an ad supporting legalized abortion, similarly dislocates the maternal body. Centrally figured in the ad's upper half is a photographed headstone inscribed "Mother," accompanied by birth and death dates. A long printed text appears below the photo-graph, warning that overturning the United States Supreme Court's 1972 *Roe v. Wade* decision will result in radical increases in the number of women dying from illegal and/or self-induced abortions (see figure 5.1). To be fair, I must note here that the ad in question remains singular and anamolous in Planned Parent-hood's ongoing campaign to protect abortion rights. Not only do the overwhelming majority of their ads center directly on a woman—or women—contemplating her reproductive options, but Planned Parenthood's campaigns also carefully take into account precisely all the issues of economic and social circumstances that the DeMoss Foundation so cavalierly ignores. However, dramatic and highly effective though Planned Parenthood's ad is, it none-theless serves in part to remind us that to be pro-choice does not necessarily mean that we escape the cultural overdeterminations that render the maternal body transparent, making it ancillary to the very discursive practices that should centralize it.

Finally, the Judith Corporation's "Mommy-To-Be-Doll"© em-bodies maternity as glamorous (the doll seems to be modelled on

FIGURE 5.1

Planned Parenthood appeal

Will the Supreme Court's next abortion decision be carved in stone?

Before the 1973 Supreme Court ruling in *Roe v. Wade* made abortion legal, accessible, and safe, countless women were maimed and killed in illegal back-alley abortions.

Different states had different rules about who could obtain an abortion. As a result, women of all ages suffered — teenagers, young working women, mothers who couldn't cope with another unintended pregnancy.

Denied a safe choice, they were forced to sacrifice their health and their lives.

Now, nearly 20 years after this butchery ended, the Bush Administration has asked the Supreme Court to use a Pennsylvania abortion case to overturn *Roe v. Wade,* letting states go so far as to ban abortion outright.

But women are in danger even if *Roe* is left standing.

Recent Supreme Court rulings have already started giving states back the power to interfere with a woman's private choices. And in *Planned Parenthood of Southeastern Pennsylvania v. Casey,* the Court may greatly expand that power.

Pennsylvania's so-called "Abortion Control Act" isn't meant to protect a woman's health

or her privacy. It has been designed to add hardship, expense, and delay:

■ Parental involvement requirements intimidate and endanger teens in troubled families.

■ Waiting periods are a roadblock for rural women who must travel long distances to a clinic, and for working mothers who must arrange child care and time off for two clinic visits instead of one.

■ Husband notification rules target only those women who fear for their safety or their family's integrity if the state forces them into a confrontation.

Pennsylvania's law is no "middle ground." Opponents of a woman's right to choose have deliberately set up these barriers in the path of the most desperate women — the young, the poor, the isolated and abused, women in crisis — to drive them away from the option of a safe, legal, early abortion.

If the Supreme Court permits this kind of frightening interference, *any* state can pass laws designed to deepen the suffering of women already forced to confront the tragedy of an unwanted pregnancy.

The lesson of the past is painfully clear: the more restrictions on safe, legal abortion, the more women are killed and injured.

We must preserve a *national* standard assuring every woman's right to choose a safe, legal abortion without interference — no matter what state she lives in.

Unless this protection is carved in stone, the tragic consequences surely will be.

☐ I'm calling my representatives on Capitol Hill at 1-202-224-3121 and telling them to do everything they can to keep abortion safe and legal.   I'm enclosing my contribution to all your activities and programs, including education and contraception programs that reduce the need for abortion: __$15 __$25 __$35 __$50 __$75 __$100 __$500 or $_____.

NAME

ADDRESS

CITY   STATE   ZIP

Don't wait until women are dying again.

Planned Parenthood
Federation of America

810 Seventh Ave., N.Y., N.Y. 10019-5882

A copy of our latest financial report is available from the New York Department of State, Office of Charities Registration, Albany, New York 12231, or from Planned Parenthood Federation of America, 810 Seventh Avenue, New York, New York 10019. Please write PPFA for a description of our program and activities and/or a list of the organizations to which PPFA has contributed in the last year. © 1992 PPFA, Inc. This ad was paid for with private contributions.

Mattel's Barbie), convenient (a removeable convex panel on the doll's abdomen reveals a smaller foetal doll within), and certainly far more efficient for actual delivery of the baby than either vaginal or cesaerian delivery.

"[P]ro-choice women regard their fertility," Emily Martin notes, in *The Woman in the Body*, "as a handicap to their productive roles; conversely, pro-life women, because productive roles are less able to reward them, regard their [re]productivity as a resource to which other roles must be made secondary" (104–105). Yet the narratives of women on either side of the abortion debate tend also to displace the maternal body, to render it a transparency through which they screen their political ideologies respective to any number of issues, related or not to independent female regulation of reproductive destiny. To the extent that we all do so, we succumb to the cultural mystifications that render our bodies expendable, and the individual women who inhabit them secondary. As we construct discursive practices and technological interventions, informed by metonymic displacements and transparent renderings of the maternal body, we participate in (re)producing misogyny ourselves. What is more, to paraphrase Naomi Wolf, men should pay attention to what is happening to women, because they do not necessarily escape this reproductive fate. Gendered oppression could just as easily frame itself in response to a variety of social and cultural forces impinging on men, reducing them also to their reproductive functions. Those practices and mystifications that separate body from mind, being from consciousness, take control, not simply of reproductive rights, but individual and communal destinies—whether more broadly physiological or otherwise. Indeed, *technologies of misandry* could arise as easily and insidiously, alternately analogous and contradindicated by the technologies of misogyny. In the end, human fate would not be gender-coded if we all were reduced to less than the sum of our reproductive parts: the raw material(s) fuelling the cultural exigencies and political ideologies of reproductive destiny.

Notes

1. I wish to thank Professor Anne Balsamo, of the School of Literature, Communication, and Culture at the Georgia Institute of Technology, for permission to quote from this essay.

2. Perhaps I should clarify here that although my project necessarily owes much to Foucault's work on sexuality and discipline (I have particularly in mind his *The History of Sexuality, An Introduction, Volume I; The Use of Pleasure, The History of Sexuality, Volume II;* and *Discipline and Punish: The Birth of The Prison.*), I refer to him with more than a little reservation. As Lynn Hunt notes:

> Historians of sexuality have been more receptive to Foucault's work than historians of prisons or mental asylums before them. There are at least two reasons for this receptivity: Foucault's work appeared before the field was well-established, and Foucault tied the history of sexuality to a larger philosophical project of reconsidering the meaning of self and history. Thus Foucault gave the history of sexuality a kind of philosophical legitimacy that it had previously lacked. What Foucault himself described as his work on technologies of production, technologies of sign systems, and technologies of power had less resonance among historians, especially those historians outside social history proper, than his last work on the technologies of the self. (79)

While such a project as my own inquiry into what I call the *technologies of misogyny* would not be possible without Foucault's monumental contributions to social theory and intellectual history, as a feminist, I remain thoroughly suspicious of his work on the "techonologies of self" because "the 'individuals' he has in mind are always male" (Hunt 79–80). Indeed, Hunt so thoroughly interrogates Foucault's "unreflective use of the term 'individuals'" in relation to gender and subjectivity that it would be unnecessary for me to do so here. Suffice it to say then that although "his focus on the body as the site for the deployment of discourses (whether the discourses of madness, punishment, or sexuality) opened the way for a consideration of the gendering of subjectivity" (Hunt 80), like Hunt, I am nonetheless surprised at his "relatively warm reception among feminist historians [social theorists and literary critics]" (Hunt 79). Furthermore, the important question of Foucault's unreflective sexism aside, it seems to me that rubrics such as "philosophy" or "history," when taken as totalizing discursive practices, are antithetical to feminist inquiries and methodologies, especially as they relate to rigorous inquiry into gendered subjectivity. Instead, I turn to feminist interventions into the Foucauldian model of social, cultural, and biomedical surveillances of the female body.

This is not to claim, of course, that gender oppression does not apply to men, or that patriarchal surveillance and control do not focus upon the male body, male sexuality, or the male role in human reproduction. I dismiss out of hand callow, oppositional arguments that oppose all-women-as-victims to all-men-as oppressors. However, I do not think that we should therefore collapse the necessarily different surveillances of the male and female body—*especially* as they relate to human reproduction—together under a loosely constructed rubric of "gender studies." Such gestures typically subsume marginalized subjectivities, whether gendered, racial, ethnic, or sexually oriented (or some combination of any or all of these differences), into the presumed subjectivity of the dominant discourse. In short, we would only succeed in replicating an oppressive discursive practice, just as we would only preserve the blind spots replete in Foucault's analyses of the technologies of self rather than refine them further.

    3. Over the years, I have frequently taught *Frankenstein* and *Dracula* in my Women in Literature classes. Not only do they quite effectively illustrate these issues, but in these texts originate extraordinarily powerful and widely familiar myths relative to gendered identity and roles, reproduction—even sexuality itself. My students respond with great enthusiasm to reading Stoker's and Shelley's books; their enthusiasm grows no doubt out of a favorable predisposition to reading the texts, for the majority presume that contemporary understanding of the Frankenstein and Dracula legends originates from them. However, that in the novel Frankenstein's Creature is intelligent, articulate, and capable of very sophisticated, even erudite philosophical discussion always comes as a shock. Their understanding, like most people's, of the Creature actually originates in the 1931 Universal production of *Frankenstein.*
    Whether or not they have actually seen Universal's original film (and, as many of them have not, I make a point of showing it in class), their understanding of the general plot, as well as the characters of Frankenstein and his Creature, derives from this film, for all subsequent film productions refer to it in some way, just as all actors who subsequently play these roles refer to Colin Clive's mad doctor and Boris Karloff's monster. While Boris Karloff successfully humanizes the Creature, thereby encouraging viewers to see him as at least somewhat sympathetic, if not tragic, he still remains very much a dumb brute animal. In a crucial scene, cut at Universal's insistence over the objections of both Karloff and director James Whale, the Creature comes across a little girl, who, completely unafraid of him, engages him in play. They toss flowers into a lake and watch them float; the Creature then playfully tosses the little girl into the lake as well. To his horror— expressed by his gutteral cries, anguished face, and hand-wringing—she sinks like a stone. Initially, the studio cut only those frames that showed the Creature's distress, making his action seem deliberately malicious. Later, the entire scene was cut, only to be restored when the film was re-released in the 1970s.
    Conversely, film versions of *Dracula* foreground male sexuality through the character of Dracula himself in ways that far more closely parallel the novel's take on female sexuality. The evil old Count Dracula's menace is far more directly sexually attractive in virtually every film

version—with the notable exception of F. W. Murnau's 1922 *Nosferatu*. In *Nosferatu*, Max Schreck's makeup and performance unequivocally represent the Vampire as horrible and disgusting. Inserts show streams of rats leaving his ship after it docks in Bremen, carefully equating his menace to vermin and plague. In this respect, *Nosferatu* follows far more closely both Stoker's text and the folk traditions that provided his source material. As with Karloff's Creature and Clive's scientist, no actor to play the Dracula role can escape referring to Bela Lugosi's interpretation, preserved in Universal's 1931 production.

In 1823, after Mary Shelley declared her authorship of *Frankenstein*, possibly as many as five stage versions were mounted; new productions continued to appear well through the mid-twentieth century (Glut 28–57 *passim*). With the advent of the cinema, both novels provided the basis for the earliest horror films. The Edison Film Company made the first-known film version of *Frankenstein* in 1910 (with Charles Ogle playing the Creature), and there followed two more very early film versions: *Life Without Soul*, in 1915, for the New York–based Ocean Film Corporation (starring Percy Darrell Standing as the creature, though devoid of the grotesque makeup that we've come to expect), and an Italian production, *Monster of Frankenstein*, in 1920.

With the enormous success of *Frankenstein* in 1931, Universal produced six more sequels: *Bride of Frankenstein*, 1935; *Son of Frankenstein*, 1935; *Ghost of Frankenstein*, 1941; *Frankenstein Meets the Wolf Man*, 1943; *House of Dracula*, 1945; and *Abbott and Costello Meet Frankenstein*, 1948. On the other hand, Universal only made a few direct sequels to 1931's *Dracula*: for example, *Dracula's Daughter* (with Gloria Holden in the title role) in 1936.

From the late 1950s to the late 1970s, Britain's Hammer Studios, remade both *Frankenstein* and *Dracula*. Hammer's *Frankenstein Created Woman* appeared in 1965, followed, for instance, by *Frankenstein Must Be Destroyed*, 1969; and *Frankenstein and the Monster from Hell*, 1974. Between 1959 and 1978, Hammer produced a total of eight sequels to its own first version of *Dracula* in 1956: *Dracula, Prince of Darkness*, 1966; *Dracula Has Risen from the Grave*, 1968; *Dracula, A.D. 1972*, and *Dracula and the Seven Golden Vampires*, 1978, to note only four series' titles.

Additional foreign and independent versions of both stories abound, most notably Andy Warhol's 3-D versions, *Andy Warhol's Frankenstein* (1974) and *Andy Warhol's Dracula* (also 1974), and the cult-favorite *Rocky Horror Picture Show*, (1975) a musical-comedy parody. Tim Curry as "Transylvanian transvestite" Dr. Frank N. Furter fashions his creature as a young blonde muscle number. The most recent version would be Kenneth Branagh's 1994 film (with Robert de Niro playing the Creature to Branagh's Victor Frankenstein). Branagh's $42 million budget produced an effort as grandiose as Victor's ambitions. Ironically, as many critics have observed, *Mary Shelley's Frankenstein*, despite the opulent production values and exaggerated performances that make it the film version closest to the Romantic tradition, demonstrates that the original story no longer frightens us.

As we might gather from Universal's last sequel to *Frankenstein*, that story had long ago become so familiar that perhaps self-parody was inevitable, twenty-six years before Mel Brooks' released his 1974 send-up, *Young Frankenstein* (with Gene Wilder and Peter Boyle playing the scientist and his Creature, respectively). In fact, the Frankenstein story has become so comfortably familiar that a children's cereal, "Franken-berry," first marketed in the 1970s, remains widely available at super-markets, along with its aristocratic companion, "Count Chocula." The story provided the basis for a television situation comedy, the 1964–65 CBS show "The Munsters" (Fred Gwynne's Herman Munster renders the Creature as a typically (for sit-coms) dim-witted *paterfamilias*; Al Lewis is a grandfatherly Count Dracula); comic shorts, such as Tim Burton's "Frankenwienie" (1984) about a little boy, Vincent, who tries to re-animate his dog after it gets run over by a car; Halloween costumes and decorations depicting the Creature as warm and cuddly; and even a commercial for Pepsi-Cola products, shown as of 1995 for the last several years around Halloween. The Creature seizes an entire Pepsi-Cola truck to bring to a Halloween party, hosted by Count Dracula. The Count then goes into a snit when he sees the Creature brought chips too, but not dip.

The first theatrical version of *Dracula*, however, was not staged until 1924, no doubt because the copyright laws designed to protect an author's financial interests had appeared in English or American law codes, in time for Stoker to benefit from them. Because copyright laws had not been enacted until quite late in the nineteenth-century—decades after Mary Shelley's original publication date of 1818—neither she nor her heirs could legally demand permission and royalties from theatrical producers. Paying royalties would necessarily represent a financial bur-den significant enough to deter all but the most determined and/or well-financed producers, and the copyright laws benefitted Stoker's estate where they could not have Mary Shelley's. For example, when F. W. Murnau failed to get permission to use Stoker's *Dracula* for his film, *Nosferatu*, he simply went ahead and made it anyway. Stoker's widow sued successfully, but was unable to collect as the company went bankrupt. Although the courts ordered all prints of the film destroyed, at least one survived to take its place as one of the greatest films—horror or otherwise—ever made (Farson 168).

Hamilton Deane, an old friend of Stoker's who was himself an actor, wrote the first stage version of *Dracula*, which ran in London on and off from 1925 to 1941 (Farson 165–67). The Broadway production proved equally successful, launching the career of the then-obscure Bela Lugosi. An enormously successful revival of *Dracula* appeared again on Broadway in the 1977–78 season, and ran for a total 674 performances.

Frank Langella, like Bela Lugosi before him, played the role on stage before reprising it in the 1979 film version.

Most recently, Francis Ford Coppola's *Bram Stoker's Dracula* appeared in theaters in 1992 with Gary Oldham in the title role. The Coppola release's lackluster performance at the box office may have been in part due to numerous parodies of the Dracula character, a staple of American television variety-show comic sketches, from "The Red Skelton Show" in the 1950s to "In Living Color" in the 1990s. Roman Polanski's ill-fated feature-film parody, *The Fearless Vampire Hunters*, appeared in 1967, but 1979's *Love At First Bite* proved far more successful, partly because it manages to be both funny and poignant, with George Hamilton's witty if uneven performance never really descending into caricature.

4. I wish to thank Professor Kathy Gentile, of the Department of English at the University of Missouri—St. Louis, for permission to quote from her essay.

5. Ingolstadt, an ancient Bavarian city, functions still as one of Germany's more major industrial and shipping centers. The University, important to the German Humanist and Counter-Reformation move-ments, had been founded in 1472. In 1802, the University relocated to Landshut, and then relocated again in 1826, this time to Munich, where it remains today, though it retains its original name. Shelley's narrative, set in the 1790s by Walton's journal, accurately sends Victor to Ingol-stadt for his university career.

6. The ovist-animalculist debate, relative to human and other mammalian reproduction, raged in the European scientific community from 1651, when Harvey, refining ancient notions of spontaneous gener-ation, proposed that all human and other mammalian life originated in degeneration, until 1875, when Hertwig demonstrated the inextricably cooperative roles of the ova and sperm and their originary roles in gestation, both human and mammalian.

Leeuwenhoek, credited with the invention of the microscope and the discovery of microorganisms, first conjectured human sperm were in fact *homonucleui*, literally "little men" that the male implanted in the female's womb—gestation he thought to be purely a matter of enlarge-ment. As an animalculist, Leeuwenhoek equated movement with life, basing his assumptions on the obviously self-propelling capabilities of the microorganisms he first saw moving in the drops of water he examined microscopically. He concluded that the ova, apparently immo-bile cells, were dead tissue and thus incapable of generative functions. Conversely, he argued that sperm, demonstrably mobile and therefore living cells, were the sole generative cells. To de Graf, his contemporary who speculated that the female's follicle, or the ovary itself, was in fact the egg that germinated and gestated mammalian life, Leeuwenhoek pointed out that the follicle was clearly too large to move through the fallopian tube and into the uterus. Leeuwnhoek's theory became widely accepted and we still have extant his drawings—depicting the homonecleus cramped inside the sperm cell as "little creatures in the sperm"—and reproductions of these drawings are fairly widely available (Martin 419).

In 1826, K. E. von Baer postulated again an ovist argument, widely and obstreperously disputed in the nineteenth-century medical and scientific communities—and one generally repudiated, until Hertwig's successful demonstrations of 1875.

Von Baer's theories and the controversy over them could therefore have very possibly been known to Shelley well before her 1831 revision of *Frankenstein*. Certainly, Shelley was more than likely aware of the entrenched ovist-animalculist controversy, reemergent and reconfiguring continuously through the eighteenth and nineteenth centuries, given her early and lifelong interest in scientific progress.

Recently, Emily Martin has cited new evidence in medical research that suggests the female's ova, like the male's sperm, are also self-propelling cells and that they have rough, sticky surfaces with which to capture sperm. Such evidence invites serious revision of contemporary scientific and popular sources, which currently insist that the ova are passive, free-floating cells, while sperm are aggressively active. This new evidence suggesting oval mobility, should it prove true, as Martin notes, is not without problematic implications for the social construction of femininity:

> the egg has become [in scientific papers documenting new evidence about the nature of the ova] an aggressive kind of vagina dentata, a predator. Spider images are used. She's like a horrible fearsome creature in the middle of a sticky web just lying there in a lair waiting for these poor hapless sperm to float by. And when one happens to bump against her, Bang! she gets him (Martin 422).

7. Many critical readers of *Dracula* note that Lucy Westenra's surname suggests "the light of the West," and I agree. I would further point out that certain other characters' surnames similarly allude to their mythopoetic functions. For example, Jonathan Harker, whose journal notations begin and end the novel, is the first to sound the alarm about Dracula's threat to England, the Western Hemisphere, indeed, the whole of humanity itself: "Harker" suggests "hark" or "harken." Similarly, Arthur Holmwood, who assumes the aristocratic title "Godalming" after his father's death, will of course sit in the House of Lords, and thus should literally and figuratively assume *noblesse oblige*. He is unfailingly generous to the narrative's other heroes and heroines in every possible way: with his friendship, his connections, his wealth, his energy. "Godalming" suggests "God's alms" and thus firmly if subtly reiterates

the divine justice guiding the vampire hunters' cause, as well as the rewards that will befall them when they successfully complete their mission.

Contrast Godalming's actions with Dracula's, particularly in that scene where Jonathan Harker stumbles on the dusty, anachronistic coinage Dracula hoards as he seeks to escape Dracula's castle (47), or later, when money literally showers from Dracula's clothes, after the vampire hunters confront him in his London townhouse (306).

8. See, for example, Nina Auerbach, "Magi and Maidens: The Romance of The Victorian Freud," in *Writing and Sexual Difference*, ed. by Elizabeth Abel (Chicago: U of Chicago P, 1981), 281-300; Thomas B. Byers, "Good Men and Monsters: The Defenses of *Dracula*," in *Literature and Psychology*, xxxi (1981), 24–31; and John Stevenson, "The Vampire in the Mirror: The Sexuality of *Dracula*," *PMLA*, 103 (1988), 139–49.

9. See Steven Marcus, *The Other Victorians* (New York: Basic Books, 1966), *passim*, for his classic analysis of the cultural contradictions informing Victorian sexual life.

10. In a gesture redolent of class prejudice, and homophobic in its implications, Van Helsing refuses to ask the Westenras' servant women to serve as blood donors for Lucy. This despite the tremendous amounts of blood she has needed, and that he, Seward, Godalming, and finally, Morris (but notably *not* Harker), have donated dangerously (for them) large reserves of their own blood (148).

The scandal caused by Oscar Wilde's trials, two years earlier, would have been reverberating when Stoker set to work on this novel. Stoker had also married Florence Balcombe, who had rejected Wilde's marriage proposal, before later accepting Stoker's. As both men lived in London, and had active careers in theater, they not only socialized together, but no doubt became mutually well acquainted.

If we bear in mind the generally heightened awareness of sexual "deviance" during this period, and along with the demonstrably widespread use of the word "blood" as not simply as a metaphor, but also a synonym, for race, class, and family, and the exchange of blood as metonym of sexual intercourse, the connection becomes both clarified and prominent.

11. I owe the latter insight to my co-editor, Christine Laennec, whose editorial advice on the drafts of this essay proved invaluable.

12. Immediately before his attack on her, Dracula finds a single copy of the whole manuscript, and throws it, along with Seward's wax cylinder diaries, on the fire. As with Harker's shorthand diary that frustrates him earlier, Dracula cannot understand the significance of the typewriter and its capability of producing typescript in triplicate.

For a lucid and witty analysis of the relations between vampirism and informational technology as the infrastructures of competing empires, see Jennifer Wicke, "Vampiric Typewriting: *Dracula* and Its Media." *ELH* 59 (1992), 467–93.

6

SEXUAL SILENCING:
ANESTHETIZING WOMEN'S VOICES IN CHILDBIRTH, 1910–1960

Cynthia Huff

In Sylvia Plath's *The Bell Jar* Esther Greenwood contrasts a 1953 birth with her vision of her own birth experience. As she and Buddy Willard watch through the hole in the delivery room door, Esther is struck first by the medieval torture table and the separation of the mother's body from her face and then by the "unhuman whooing noise" caused, as Buddy tells her, by twilight sleep.

> I thought it sounded just like the sort of drug a man would invent. Here was a woman in terrible pain, obviously feeling every bit of it or she wouldn't groan like that, and she would go straight home and start another baby, because the drug would make her forget how bad the pain had been, when all the time, in some secret part of her, that long, blind, doorless and windowless corridor of pain was waiting to open up and shut her in again.

When someone tells Mrs. Tomolillo her baby is a boy, she doesn't respond at all, and Esther observes:

> For some reason the most important thing to me was actually seeing the baby come out of you yourself and making sure it was yours. I thought if you had to have all that pain anyway you might just as well stay awake. I had always imagined myself hitching up on to my elbows on the delivery table after it was all over—dead white, of course, with no makeup and from the awful ordeal, but smiling and radiant, with my hair

down to my waist, and reaching out for my first squirmy
child and saying its name, whatever it was. (Plath 53–54)

These contrasting ways of birthing—one with the doctors and
by extension the medical establishment as the principal actors
while the mother is anesthetized from herself, her child, and the
experience of birth; and the other with the mother as the sentient,
controlling agent who interacts with her newborn while the atten-
dants are erased from the picture—indicate the complex ramifications of sexual silencing through the obliteration of women's
voices in childbirth in this century. Yet the powerful contrast in
this passage between a controlling male medical establishment
and a prostrate birthing woman only partially tells the story of the
continuing conflict and accommodation as well as the ideological
underpinnings of parturition. In this paper I will argue that childbirth is an ideology with a psychosocial and economic history
which affects our metaphorical construction and personal experience of birth, the maternal body, and generally, the discourses on
and about women's bodies. I will also discuss how conceptions of
the optimum birthing experience change over time, how these are
influenced by factors of race and class, medical and social beliefs,
and the individual and cultural interactions between the birthing
mother and her caregivers.

On the most obvious level, how we construe birth depends on
whose voices we hear; whether we speak of birthing a baby or a text
as paramount; whether we give credence to birth at all, except as a
worn-out metaphor so separated from its root as the physical act of
bringing new life into the world that it is silenced by our dismissal.
To hear women's voices in childbirth would seem to give us much
that we have been lacking, to give us what Adrienne Rich tells us
we need: "the one group whose opinions and documentation we
long to have—the mothers—are, as usual, almost entirely unheard-
from" (130). Nor is Rich the only one who notes the lack of mothers'
voices. In *Pain, Pleasure, and American Childbirth: From the Twilight
Sleep to the Read Method, 1914–1960*, Margarete Sandelowski
notes that among physicians, nurses, and childbearing women, the
group who is least articulate is the last (139). In this essay I
foreground two differing birthing experiences of one woman, Bessie
Siebert, to indicate how autobiographical accounts of birth can be
situated. Other critics, such as Dale Bauer and Mary Poovey, deal
respectively with the implications of class and race in fiction,
namely Edith Wharton's novel, *Twilight Sleep*, and the medical

establishment's ideological construction of gender in Victorian England. More recently, in *Reproducing the Womb: Images of Childbirth in Science, Feminist Theory, and Literature*, Alice E. Adams combines literary texts with her experience as a birthing woman to argue that in their birth narratives women "(re)negotiate the terms of their subjectivity" by speaking as individuals not just as community subjects. My analysis is indebted to the important, thought-provoking work these scholars have done, but it differs from theirs by choosing to focus on personal accounts of childbirth rather than fictional or medical ones.

My focus on autobiography provides another textual dimension to contemporary and historical debates about who reads birth and the import of various readings; and by examining the cultural bedrock of personal narrative, I show the common ground between the narrative terrain of fiction and autobiography and point out how women's birth accounts are embedded in the stories of childbirth our culture transmits. Theorists of autobiography repeatedly emphasize that autobiography "defies generic stabilization," as Sidonie Smith and Julia Watson observe, precisely because our readings of autobiography are so dependent on the cultural constructions of a historical moment (xviii). Autobiography plays a central role in the construction of our ideologies of childbirth and the maternal body, mirroring and affirming the stories culture tells, a site at which readers confirm their cultural beliefs, a site at which writers reflect, revise, and internalize ideology. "The reader sees not so much herself in the autobiography," writes Leigh Gilmore in *Autobiographics*, "as the representation of her position in relation to other familiar positions within cultural scripts" (23). As these theorists assert, fiction and autobiography are best read, to borrow Gilmore's phrase, as cultural scripts.

I suggest, as well, how the scripting of birth narratives depends not only on an individual, Bessie Siebert, whose personal experience of her maternal body changes over time, but also on the intricacies of the cultural space in which she gives birth. In *Writing a Woman's Life*, Carolyn Heilbrun contends that it is not a woman's life that writes her story, but rather it is received narratives that dictate how a woman will pen her life. The issue for Heilbrun, as for many other critics of narrative, is not whether we can locate truth in one form and falsehood in another, but whether we can understand how history, fiction, and non-fiction prose all transmit the era's prevailing ideologies and how various narrative forms affect how we read, write, and dream. A similar point is made by Leigh

Gilmore, who argues that a "triangulation" exists in autobiography as well as fiction, between writer, reader, and ideology (23).

Heilbrun envisions women breaking away from the closure that has determined their lives and their autobiographies. Following her cry to metamorphose narrative and experience, I think that if we are to reimagine the discourses written on and about women's bodies, we need to begin by looking at what is arguably the most culturally-laden and least problematized area: the maternal body. The need for this approach is particularly acute in autobiography studies. As Shirley Neuman writes in *Autobiography and Questions of Gender*, "for all the emphasis in feminist theory of autobiography on the gender difference of women's autobiographies, the maternal remains practically unaddressed as a gender issue" (Neuman 6). Bessie Siebert's two accounts of her birth experiences help redress this lack and lead us, too, to consider how our received narratives of birth might be re-envisioned to open up new possibilities for our cultural and individual experiences of women's bodily discourses.

Although women's voices are normally absent in many published sources about childbirth, accounts by women of their birth experiences exist in magazines, diaries, and birthing manuals. The number of women who will respond to queries about their birth experiences, whether the medium is an interview or a call for autobiographical accounts, is perhaps even more poignant and culturally indicative, because their overwhelming response to any medium that offers women a voice indicates that women will be heard if people will listen.[1] The issue of where women are allowed any voice is complex and significant. Embedding childbirth narratives in texts such as hospital manuals that are designed not to validate women's birth journeys, but primarily to insure patient cooperation with medical routine and hence suppress mothers' experiences if they conflict with doctors' orders, indicates a form of spatial silencing, or anesthesia. Women's birth narratives are not given primary place in this medium of hospital manuals. Rather, birthing women are only allowed to speak here if their birth narratives support the medical view of birth.

Textual silencing by manipulating space correlates with owning the birthing place. The history of birthing practices in America shows that ownership and control of space is important to women's conception of birth and to whether or not women's voices and experiences will be blotted out. As the historians Judith Walzer Leavitt and Richard W. and Dorothy C. Wertz point out, the move from home to hospital in the twentieth century is highly significant. With the death rate from puerperal fever for women of childbearing age second only to that from tuberculosis throughout the later part of the nineteenth century, middle- and upper-class women, in particular, began to turn to hospitals in the early decades of this century as an environment which could protect them from the ravages of septicemia. The safety from disease and death that the medical profession promised women if doctors could practice asepsis in the controlled space of the hospital appealed to child-bearing women. Hospitals had formerly been places where indi-gent mothers and those lacking the support system necessary for a home confinement had gone to have their babies, but as more economically secure women also found themselves without the help necessary for a home birth, they too began increasingly to consider hospitals as the chosen location for birth.

By the second decade of this century upper-class women, many of them feminists, were actively campaigning for the obli-teration of pain through twilight sleep, a combination of scopola-mine and morphine, which physicians argued could best be admin-istered in a hospital. Society women wrote articles in popular magazines and participated in department store rallies where they exhibited their twilight sleep babies as proof that the anesthetic produced a more perfect child. Their choice of alleged safety over any consciousness of actively giving birth helped determine that most twentieth-century American women would deliver their children anesthetized from any conception of themselves, rather than the physician and the medical establishment, as the con-trolling agent. And the commodification of children dovetailed with wealthier Americans' preoccupation with eugenics to move the site of birth away from the home.

Some middle-, upper-, and even working-class women in the second decade of this century insisted that the ideal way to give birth was through the anesthetized condition of twilight sleep, and this insistence complicates the issues of choice and control in the birthing process, highlights distinctions of class and place, and underscores the dynamics of group interaction in determining individual and historical birthing possibilities. Ironically from our contemporary vantage point, middle- and upper-class women in the second decade of this century argued that the availability of twilight sleep was an issue of who would control the birthing process—the American physicians who in the teens were largely opposed to twilight sleep because they considered it unsafe, or the women who advocated it and forced its acceptance by the medical community because it kept women from experiencing pain and consequently gave them control over their own bodies. Judith Walzer Leavitt interprets the outcome of the conflict over twilight sleep births as a victory for women's right to control their bodies, yet notes that the historical implications meant a loss of control for women (see Leavitt, "Birthing and Anesthesia"). Esther Greenwood's interpretation of the twilight sleep experience for Mrs. Tomolillo can be read from the perspective of the Natural Childbirth practices of the late forties and fifties when educated women and some physicians advocated that safety and satisfaction in birth meant a sentient mother (Sandelowski 85–105).

Yet the twilight sleep debate and its aftermath had additional implications for our construction of the birthing maternal body and how we read it. Dale Bauer points out the class and ideological basis of the debate when she discusses its eugenic implications; and fictional accounts of pregnancy, birth, and childbearing likewise show how the birthing body can be situated in terms of race, class, and prevailing ideologies as well as gender (see Bauer). Once the movement for racial purity gained momentum in the second half of the nineteenth century, conceptions of parturition showed this ideological imprint. Prior to the setting for *The Bell Jar* in the early 1950s, novels such as *The Awakening*, *Weeds*, and *The Bluest Eye* contained fictionalized sociohistorical accounts of motherhood that illuminate cultural concepts of women's bodily and social roles and indicate narrative transmission of maternal body ideologies.[2]

Set at the end of the nineteenth century, *The Awakening* deals with the reactions to motherhood and birth of the bourgeois Edna Pontellier, whose process of awakening culminates after she witnesses the confinement of Adele Ratignolle, who, unlike Edna, is the perfect mother-woman. Responding to Mr. Pontellier's concern about Edna's changing behavior, Dr. Mandelet describes women as "delicate organisms." Mandelet's reactions to Edna's dread during Madame Ratignolle's labor underscores the racist, classist, and eugenic bases of his judgement that it was cruel for Adele to insist that Edna be present during her labor. He declares: "youth is given up to illusions. It seems to be a provision of Nature; a decoy to secure mothers for the race" (171). As a *fin de siècle* lady, Edna would have been expected to be delicate, unlike working-class women and women of color, and to produce children to secure the hegemony of the white race. Protecting Edna from the knowledge of the pain of birth has its corollaries a few decades later when twilight sleep advocates argue that this method of birthing would cause more women to procreate because they, too, would not know pain.

Accounts of motherhood in *Weeds* set during the 1910s and *The Bluest Eye* set in the 1930s and 1940s indicate no such sheltering of women from parturition. *Weeds* depicts the Kentucky tenant-farming life of Judith Pippinger Blackford, whose three children are delivered at home, not in a twilight sleep hospital; and although Judith is no more a mother-woman than Edna Pontellier, no one speaks of her duty to provide children for the race. Pauline Breedlove in *The Bluest Eye* chooses a hospital birth for Pecola, perhaps because of her desires to identify with wealthy, white society, but her experience is unlike white women's. Because she is African American, the doctors assume Pauline feels no pain giving birth, tell each other that these women deliver right away just like horses, and never speak to her, but only look at her stomach and between her legs. The objectification and silencing of Pauline's birth experience by the white medical establishment derives from their racist assumption that women of color are only animals and, as Pauline realizes, their lack of observation and empathy for mares whose eyes show pain during foaling. Protesting her silencing, Pauline moans hard "to let them people know having a baby was more than a bowel movement. I hurt just like them white women" (99).

In the twentieth century, home as a birth place came increasingly to symbolize both the childbirth trauma suffered by Victorian women and the poverty and foreignness of immigrant or rural Americans who delivered with a midwife. In their campaigns to stamp out the practice of midwifery, doctors published photographs of poor and minority women with captions emphasizing their lack of skill and playing on racial and class biases.[3] Thus, the space where birth took place carried with it the ramifications of historical consciousness and race, class, and gender. If the location of the birth was at home, the voice of the mother would not be heeded because of her lack of status; if the birth occurred in a hospital under the anesthesia of twilight sleep, the mother could picture herself as directing the birth because she chose its method, yet ironically the supposed oblivion from pain necessitated her silencing herself by giving her body over to the physician.

Upper- and middle-class American women lost control of the traditionally gendered space of the birthing room when they chose hospital over home. In the centuries preceding this one, and still in most parts of the world, childbirth is a ritual from which men are excluded. Pictures of eighteenth- and nineteenth-century lying-in rooms show the birthing mother foregrounded while her midwife and female friends and relatives gather around to provide succor. Similarly, written accounts of childbirth from these periods indicate the mother's spatial control, for she typically recounts who attended the birth and where it occurred (see Huff *passim*). Even when male midwives began to be present at births in the Victorian period, their role was still largely determined by the birthing woman and her family. In "Architecture in the Family Way: Lying-In and the Design of Middle-Class Motherhood," Annmarie Adams argues that for Victorian women their place of confinement functioned as an extension of their body and that both spaces were to be cared for scrupulously. Articles instructed women about the intricacies of home inspection to insure that laborers had properly prepared the site of confinement. Before the twentieth century, middle- and upper-class women were in charge of the space where they gave birth as well as of those in attendance: a doctor or midwife and a support system of female friends and relatives.

The same cannot be said for poor women who historically entered charity hospitals when their baby was due. Emily Martin points out in *The Woman in the Body* that the metaphorical description of the uterus as a machine began in seventeenth- and eighteenth-century French hospitals; and the correlation between physicians' mechanistic view of childbearing women's bodies and the layout of hospitals to insure the smooth running of separately demarcated tasks meant that poor, parturient women did not control either the space of their bodies or the site of childbirth (Martin 54). Poor women's bodies provided the raw material for scientific experimentation; and the powerlessness of these women in the face of mechanistic models underscores the anesthetizing that women's voices could undergo once the move from home to hospital was affected, if women lacked an economic control.

The mechanization of women's bodies and birth has its textual as well as its historical manifestations. If Esther Greenwood in the autobiographical novel *The Bell Jar* contrasts her hoped-for birth experience with her observation of Mrs. Tomolillo's, two childbirth narratives by Bessie Siebert (formerly Hathaway) show the distinctions between a birth where the mother exercises control over what happens to her body and a physically far easier parturition where the doctor and the medical establishment regulate her body and place of birth. Her differing accounts are illuminating not only for readings of gender but also for the historical and personal complexities of class, choice, geographic location of birth, and the dynamics between birthing woman and caregiver. Examining these different and interrelated factors in one woman's two birth accounts helps us understand how birth stories, whether classified as autobiographical fiction or women's non-traditional narrative, borrow from and contribute to our conception of the maternal body. As Alice Adams argues, there is no "real" birth separated from the story of our birth or our birth experiences. Still, Adams claims, "the closest we can come to reconstructing our origins is to ask our mothers to tell us their stories" (Alice Adams 8)

Bessie Siebert's first pregnancy and birth occurred when she was only fifteen in the frontier town of Campo, Colorado, early in this century. Her age, class status, and geographic location influence how Bessie gives birth; and her autobiographical account points to an experience far different from that of wealthy, twilight sleep mothers delivering on the East Coast, who, unlike Bessie, could choose whether or not to be anesthetized. Bessie describes herself as largely ignorant of her body's functions during pregnancy and birth; and her girlish preoccupation with her popcorn ball, spoiled by a fall on the day she goes into labor, shows she is more child than woman. She is oblivious to her body's signals that she is in labor after her waters break, as the "notch stick" indicates that she isn't due for another month. But when her mother arrives from the fields to the chaos caused by her screaming daughters, potatoes boiling over, and a tearful Bessie crying because her skirt is wet, Bessie is immediately brought to reality by her mother's command: "Stop that, Poochie, you're going to need your strength for better things—let's get busy. Child, you're going to have a baby."

Initially Bessie assumes that the baby will come along with the country doctor and depends on her mother for nurturing support, but after several hours of first pulling on her mother's hands and then on the reins tied to the bedpost to relieve the pain from the overwhelming contractions, she looks in the mirror to see her mother and the doctor consulting in the kitchen. When the doctor pulls a scalpel from his black bag, Bessie concludes he's intending to perform a caesarean and vows she'll have none of it. But after her mother tells her that the doctor intends to perform a craniotomy to save her life, Bessie declares: "Something came over me, girl that I was. I was only a little past fifteen, but at that moment I grew up. Releasing Mother's hand, I pushed her away. 'Get that doctor back in here, I'm going to have a baby. If not, we'll go together!' As she opened her mouth to argue, all I said was, 'Never.'"

Six hours later Bessie Hathaway delivers her son Jim breech and her feelings of triumphant strength are obvious: "We'd made it! He was 7 pounds and 11 ounces, and 21 inches long. He didn't cry, but he was alive! He was too weak to cry. He had been on a long journey too." Bessie's recovery was long and slow, but her belief in her endurance, her will to decide what was best for herself and her infant is apparent. Bessie's metaphor for the birth is a shared journey, hard but ultimately rewarding. She sees Jim's birth, too, as an event which results in personal growth, for it is the turning point from girlhood to womanhood. It is especially significant that Bessie achieved this transition through her own powers, aided by her mother and the doctor, but nevertheless remaining the one in charge of her own and her child's destiny. She is not anesthetized from her body nor from herself as she grapples with the "birth forces" to complete her journey. In Bessie Siebert's account of giving birth at fifteen there is never any question of who the principal actor is nor who controls the space of her body or the place of birth. The doctor and Bessie's mother may think the only way for Bessie to complete the arduous task of birth is to take the baby in pieces, but theirs is not the voice that triumphs. Over half a century later, Bessie's determination rings loud and clear. Her autobiographical birth account is filled with specific details of place, participants, and actions and framed by paragraphs that indicate her acceptance into a woman's world where motherhood and marriage are the keys to admittance. As Bessie Siebert's "My Jim" shows, giving birth at home puts her in control, for here she is the agent who brings herself and her Jim into the world together. Given the economic and class factors informing Bessie Siebert's birth experience, it is difficult to believe that she would have had equal agency in a hospital setting. Although twilight sleep mothers generally had the economic clout to exercise some control over the hospital space and its manipulation by their caregivers, Bessie had no such class privilege.

Bessie's inability to control hospital space is apparent when she bears her third child, Howard. The resolve and control the fifteen-year-old Bessie exhibited at home is sapped from her. Immediately frightened by the cold sterility of an alien place and ignorant of the routine to which she would be subjected, Bessie looks for the reassuring face of her doctor. Instead, she is forced to participate in "a ritual that I was sure would shame me to death."

Told to bathe herself and forced to dress in a skimpy hospital gown which exposes her body, Bessie is further humiliated by the required enema and the shaving of her pubic hair. Left alone in a small, cold room with only the pains of childbirth for company, Bessie is eventually wheeled into the delivery room. Transferred from one metal table to another, she wonders why there are so many rooms when one had always been enough to deliver her two previous children:

> My legs were raised, spread apart and placed in high iron stirrups. Completely exposed, very conscious of my shaven body, ashamed and in misery, I was strapped down and assured "it won't be long now." Of that fact I was positive. I couldn't wait much longer.
>
> The door opened and a stranger entered. Gloved and frocked, the face I saw was not Dr. Johnson. Amidst swirling pain and helpless rage, I screamed for Dr. Johnson. The very thoughts of a complete stranger ministering to me was sickening. Fighting my pain, the restraints, raving and lurching, I finally felt a sharp stab in my arm and eventually I knew no more. Never having had a shot before, I didn't know what they had done to me.

Bessie eventually awakes to find Sargent, the nurse who tended her dying mother and who Bessie had expected to be with her during her confinement, shaking her shoulder. After Sargent extracts a promise from Bessie to be good, the nurse agrees to bring Bessie's baby boy to her. Fearful that her impotent rage at the medical establishment has created a monster, Bessie is relieved to look at "the pink cheeked perfection of my son." When she is completely conscious, Bessie vows never again to give birth in a hospital.

The contrast between Bessie Siebert's birth experiences is telling. At fifteen, delivering in her home, Bessie works with her body to birth her son, but in the alien environment of the hospital Bessie's body is controlled by others. The medical routine, which historically evolved as a tacit agreement between primarily upper-class women and their physicians as a way to create and maintain a sterile field and hence allegedly combat puerperal fever, functions to anesthetize Bessie from the work of her body. What has been established during the twentieth century in America as the "safe" way to give birth acts to invest power in the routine and those who control it. Each part of this parturient ritual—washing the body, giving the enema, shaving the pubic hair, isolating the mother from others, moving her from place to place, surrounding her with strangers, exposing her body, tying down her hands and feet, and finally blotting out her memory—takes away the woman's power to control her maternal body. As the birthing woman is subjected to less and less control, she becomes increasingly alienated and powerless. Reduced to a uterus, which can only function if the physician-mechanic operates it, at the moment of birth the mother becomes an anesthetized body.

This method of twentieth-century American birthing, where the mother has no choice over how she will give birth, awake or anesthesized, is the perfect symbol of labor, so separated from its producer that the process of creating the work is blotted out. At the moment of Howard's birth Bessie Siebert is anesthetized from her labor by a shot that renders her unconscious. The sexual workings of her body are silenced because Bessie and her maternal body are influenced by the Victorian ideology which decrees that childbearing women are to suffer and be still, a phrase often used by nineteenth-century clergymen as they argued that women were fulfilling their God-given function as daughters of Eve to withstand in silence the pangs of childbirth. Bessie and her maternal body are also silenced by a class history that has given economically advantaged women a greater say in their own birthing experiences and an influence over how other women will deliver. Bessie violates these ideological and historical influences when she screams and rages and fights the binds that hold her down. The response of the medical establishment, the institutional body upholding both the conception of women as out of control—unless quiet—and the superior economic power of the advantaged, is to render Bessie mute. The compliance of laboring women must be affected in other ways as well. Bessie is made to feel guilt for her sin of wanting control of her labor. Nurse Sargent agrees to bring Bessie her baby only if Bessie promises to be good, to be complicitous in her own alienation from her labor and her body. Nurse Sargent's actions fit the description of the perfect obstetric nurse in *Pain, Pleasure, and American Childbirth*, for she was to manage patients as an extension of the obstetrician, a role which Margarete Sandelowski notes was often an uneasy one for nurses.

The interrelationships among historically based socioeconomic factors, racial and medical ideologies, and the ways women give birth are complex and reflect differing subject positions. Examining these interrelationships shows that a woman's agency during childbirth derives from the interconnectedness of her individual birth experience with her race, class, and historical situation. To consider any woman's birth story without also seeing how it is embedded in a narrative that is itself part of the cultural legacy of the maternal body, is to miss the multiple layers that make up our complex experience of birth. Situating Bessie Siebert's accounts of her different birth experiences within the contexts of fictional and historical stories of parturition illuminates the ways in which class and ideology can silence the mother's voice, the effects of the birthing place and the caregivers' roles in determining agency, and the cultural information we exclude if we fail to hear the mother's voice.

Adrienne Rich points out in *Of Woman Born* that "to change the experience of childbirth means to change women's relationship to fear and powerless, to our bodies, to our children; it has far-reaching psychic and political implications" (Rich 182). Rich is arguing here that until we revision the maternal body so that in giving birth all women have agency, we can not change human society. The contrasting autobiographical accounts of Bessie Siebert bear out Rich's analysis. Bessie Siebert's perhaps accidental naming of her first account, "My Jim," and of her second one merely "Howard" may indicate, in a seemingly small but significant way, the implications Rich finds in the way women bear their children. Bessie labored with her body to bring forth *my* Jim as the product of her own labor and determination. But when Howard was born Bessie was alienated from the workings of her body; Howard seems to exist alone, outside of her efforts. The history of childbirth, whether embedded in the ideological assumptions of a cultural body or the personal accounts of a woman's experience, always has a voice. Whose voice triumphs and whose is muted depends upon how we conceptualize labor, whether we see it as a woman giving birth or as a body anesthetized and controlled by an institution.

Notes

1. For autobiographical accounts of childbirth experiences in America in the 1950s, see "Journal Mothers Report on Cruelty in Maternity Wards," *Ladies Home Journal* (May 1958): 44–45, 152+, and "Journal Mothers Testify to Cruelty in Maternity Wards," *Ladies Home*

Journal (December 1958): 58–59, 135+, both edited by Gladys Denny Schultz.

2. By Kate Chopin, Edith Summers Kelley, and Toni Morrison, respectively. For other critical analyses of childbirth in British and American literature, see Hollenberg; Cosslett, "Childbirth from the woman's point of view," "Childbirth on the National Health," and *Women Writing Childbirth*; and Frantz. More general theories of childbirth narratives include Yaeger's recent article, and earlier pieces by Upton and Carpenter.

3. Wertz and Wertz note:

Magazines also treated immigrant midwives as curious anachronisms, repeating horror stories replete with racial and ethnic slurs about "rat pie among black midwives" or deformed babies allegedly delivered by Italian or Russian Jewish midwives. Photographs of such older women, attired in the shapeless black clothes frequently worn by European widows, contrasted sharply with the pictures and advertisements showing fashionable women. One article captioned the picture of an elderly black midwife: "A former slave, 98 years old, still actively engages in the work of midwifery! A direct transplantation into a progressive American city of African voodooism" (216–17).

IV

THE BODY-MIND CONNECTION

7

LOCKE, DISEMBODIED IDEAS, AND RHETORIC THAT MATTERS

Catherine Hobbs

The feminine is not a category; diverse and disruptive, it subverts (while also shoring up) efforts to categorize. Reverberating within and against cultural codes, it opens "woman-in-the-feminine" to self-difference.

—Shari Benstock, *Textualizing the Feminine*, (xvi)

But the dramatic notion of language as a risky practice, allowing the speaking animal to sense the rhythm of the body as well as the upheavals of history, seems tied to a notion of signifying process that contemporary theories do not confront.

—Julia Kristeva, "The Ethics of Linguistics" (34)

The classical configuration of matter as a site of generation or origination becomes especially significant when the account of what an object is and means requires recourse to its originating principle. . . . This link between matter, origin, and significance suggests the indissolubility of classical Greek notions of materiality and signification. That which matters about an object is its matter.

—Judith Butler, *Bodies That Matter* (31)

More than a decade of scholarship has now explored the intricacies of sexuality and textuality. Various and divergent attempts have been made to "write the body;" to understand the relationship of the female body to writing and to a corpus of texts produced primarily by males; to understand the relationships of various "feminines" to textuality; and most recently to comprehend the processes of producing or materializing a sexed body in conjunction with the processes of "writing."

Poststructuralists have formally explored the feminine and woman's body as trope, the "textual feminine" figuring embodiment itself, rupture in the symbolic order, the irrational, disturbance, ultimately death of the body. Explorations of embodiment and textual practice have described women's writing as mute, as a sign of the body. Theorists of the textual feminine have at times sought to challenge dominant discourses by introducing the "feminine" as a positive deviation or disturbing element in an unwelcome stasis. Feminine discourses have been characterized as those that emanate from the body and that have been ignored or repressed in texts. Dominant modernist discourses have valued sight, so these discourses privilege the nonvisual—including bodily elements such as rhythm and sound, in addition to other textual features such as punctuation and marginalia. This preoccupation with the textual feminine has culminated in critiques perhaps expressed best by Judith Butler's reported challenge, "But what about the materiality of the body, *Judy?*" (*Bodies* ix).

A Bakhtinian notion of text as practice and process widely accepted today emphasizes its emanation from a materially embodied speaking subject. Butler's *Bodies That Matter* inquires into this issue of the materiality of the body and the processes of its production in relation to language practices. She holds that "the materiality of sex is constructed through a ritualized repetition of norms," bound up with citations, or signification. This view brings history into play as the subject, always in process and situated at the crossroads of various discourses, and invokes previous language or repeats citations that sediment over time into recognized practices.

Poststructuralist theorists in particular have worked to reactivate, deconstruct and defamiliarize sedimented citations of the "textual feminine" and woman's body as trope in western philosophy. This is not an idealist project, for as Butler (and others) argue, our practices of signification are not clearly separable from our bodies. Yet neither are language practices laid over already existing, unmarked physical bodies, serving to construct them. Instead, language practices are material practices that embody us—bodying us forth as sexed beings. Materialization becomes a "process of sedimentation of repeated citations" (15) that in practice produces bodies, and subjects.

It is just this relationship between signification and the body that is at issue at this site of inquiry into Locke's *Essay Concerning*

Human Understanding, perhaps the key text informing Enlighten-ment debates over language. This reading, focusing on represen-tations of embodiment and the feminine, remains an analysis postmodern scholars have in many ways gone "beyond." One way they have gone beyond is by imbricating gender with ethnicity and other "identifications" to show the complexities of embodiment. Yet a historical inquiry into the network of traces of the "textual ordering of sexual difference" (Benstock xv) can function to fore-ground textualities that have sedimented into normative practices producing us in various ways as bodies and as subjects.

In addition to "woman as trope," I discuss here the trope of catachresis, or the abuse of language, both implicit and explicitly discussed in the text of Locke's *Essay*. I follow these tropings in Locke's text from embodiment to disembodiment, from the senses to ideas of sense and understanding, from woman to man. The body and discipline, desire and prohibition, rhetoric and phil-osophy go hand in hand in Locke's text. Here, the repeated citation produces its effects so that: "sexuality and its representations. . . continue to be the ground for determinations of law and order, so that the unsayable, inexpressible pleasure, also becomes unspeak-able, unlawful, disorderly, obscene" (Lyon 6). Woman and the body are figuratively distanced from Locke's *Essay*, but their traces remain to ravel the edges of the text he has scrupulously knotted together. The feminine generally represents disruption of desired order, although at some textual moments, woman is linked with truth and order in Locke's text.

As Bakhtin theorizes, language is heterogeneous, containing both centrifugal and centripetal forces, homogenizing and strati-fying forces, serious royal and comic jester forces (425, 272–73). It is fully embodied in sound—melody, harmony, rhythm, repetition; in vision—images, color, light, dark; and in other elements both bodily produced and expressive, and productive of desire, plea-sure, and pain. Because of this heterogeneous quality of language, it would be impossible for Locke's *Essay* to be homogeneous, con-sistently banishing the textual feminine, presenting a purely "mas-culine" theory and text. (It may be just these multiplicities and inconsistencies in the texts and citations we repeat that provide us with the spaces for subjectivity and agency.) With this caveat, however, I turn to Lockean themes that signify the feminine in ways that since have been repeated and reinforced.

Significantly, the *Essay* begins with the body—woman's body, in particular, citing a verse from the book of Ecclesiastes: "As thou knowest not what is the way of the spirit, nor how the bones do grow in the womb of her that is with child: even so, thou knowest not the works of God, who maketh all things" (XI. 5). Linked with this is a quote from Cicero, in Latin, on the contingency of knowledge. Thus Locke's treatise opens by foregrounding epistemology, origins, production, and reproduction. Butler opens her discussion of materiality by tracing a set of etymologies of classical terms linking materiality with *mater* or *matrix*, associated with the womb and reproduction. In addition to these terms, in Greek "*hyle* is the wood or timber out of which various cultural constructions are made, but also a principle of origin, development, and teleology which is at once causal and explanatory" (31). Thus, as in this chapter's final epigraph (Butler, above), materiality is closely bound up with origins and signification, something Locke seems to imply in various places in his *Essay*. Locke's own epigraphs point out that the origin of knowledge—much as the origin of our bodies—is an ungraspable, mysterious process. He links but also opposes spirit and flesh, the flesh figured as a woman with child.

However, Locke quickly moves away from the physical body to the mind. The classical and Christian body/soul duality as well as the Cartesian split between body and mind comes to parallel the age-old conflict between rhetoric (embodied) and philosophy (intelligence/esprit). Throughout the exploratory discourse of his treatise, Locke moves similarly from the body to the understanding, one of the faculties of the mind, as he pursues the way of ideas. A primary move from body to intellect is represented by his familiar two-step path to knowledge, from perception to reflection, from the senses to *ideas* of sense and reflection. The second move is his corresponding progression from simple to mixed modes in his theory of ideas, and the third is his swerve from woman to man in his explanation of how particulars should lead to generality and abstraction. This progression from woman to man results in what Walker has termed the "fade of the female." Through it all, the body is paradoxically represented as closer to truth, and yet it is feared, mistrusted, ultimately silenced. Locke's scrupulous exploration does ultimately lead him to recognize that language is central to thought. However, fearful of the connections between language and the body, he then directs much of his energies to the control of language.

Locke's move away from embodiment rests on his linguistic theory that words are signs for ideas, not for things, and thus all humans can ever know are their own ideas of things, not the "real essences" of the things themselves. Because knowledge begins with the senses, the senses are sometimes portrayed as closer to true ideas (although by the *Essay's* end, it becomes clear that human judgment rules over the senses as determinant of truth). This seems to some a primary rupture in the history of language theory, yet Locke never strays too far from a representational theory of language, a theory of language as naming, in this case, primarily the naming of immaterial ideas.

Locke's "ideas," created by external or internal perceptions (perception and reflection), are first classified as simple or complex. Further the "modes" of his complex ideas are themselves divided into simple and complex. This split echoes ancient Greek atomic theory that everything in the universe is reducible to simple notions, or "simple natures," which serve as the building blocks of everything else in the world. For Locke, simple ideas cannot be learned from language through a process of definition but must be obtained directly from things, which produce their various effects on our bodies' nervous systems. Complex ideas are combinations of simple ideas, so that much of the abuse or confusion of language can be unraveled by a return to the simple ideas closest to things. While this foundation in sensation seems to privilege the body, Locke nonetheless restricts understanding to the mind to eliminate the body's hegemony. Since all we can ever know are ideas, knowledge itself for Locke consists in the "perception of the connexion of and agreement, or disagreement and repugnancy of any of our ideas" (525, IV.1.2). This lessens the pure determinism of the world acting on our bodies, and yet all knowledge becomes either cognitive, as in mathematical thought, or spiritual, as in revelation. The body and its passions loom threateningly and centrally yet are left behind. It might be protested that Locke's dependence upon pleasure and pain for the mainsprings of human action reveals an inevitable reliance upon the body. Yet even in the debate over pleasure and pain, pleasures of the mind versus those of the body, both are ultimately ceded to the mind. Although they may arise from the body or the mind, as in perception or reflection, Locke makes clear that ultimately all pleasure and pain are properly to be attributed to the mind (258, II.21.41).

Locke's rhetoric of ideas structures itself in a progression from simple to mixed modes, paralleling the rise from perception to reflection. Simple modes, such as number, space, motion, or light, can't be defined, but must be directly experienced from nature. Mixed modes, a type of complex idea, are abstract terms that form our ideas of such concepts as triangle, beauty, gratitude, or moral terms. Locke says these are nothing but bundles of simple ideas tied together by words used as a "Knot" (417–19; III.3.17–19). He tries to keep these mixed modes "pure" in his atomistic scheme by presupposing the existence of separate simple modes first experienced in the world and subsequently tied together by a Name or a Knot. As Bennington points out "it is clear that the length of time the bundle of ideas could be held together by the mind without the securing knot of language is unthinkably small" (114). For Locke, a word is usually a token in the service of a natural entity, but in the case of mixed modes, words produce the entities they signify with no equivalents in nature. This, as Paul de Man points out, is the classic definition of catachresis, a textual disruption that threatens to reveal the weakness of the whole structure. Thus mixed modes must be kept tightly bound to the notion of "archetypes," a mysterious disembodiment similar to Platonic forms Locke heavily leans on without attempting to define.

In the *Essay*, the banishment of the body is manifested primarily by Locke's effort to control language, specifically, to exclude a devalorized feminine Rhetoric from Philosophy as well as excluding the figural from literal philosophical language. This effort also works to exclude the social from human understanding, another way of purifying Rhetoric from Philosophy, but it is an exclusion that ultimately fails. However, it produces a rational-empirical theory of language with long-term implications for rhetorics from aesthetics to science. The move works as a wedge along the fault lines of the classical philosophy/rhetoric debate, helping to construct our contemporary polarity of scientific and poetic languages.

Locke posits a "bad" feminine rhetoric of passion and the body in opposition to a "good" masculine rhetoric of ideas. Since classical times, rhetoric had been figured as feminine, but the figure was more often held up for adulation—as is the indomitable allegorical warrior figure of Rhetorica in Martianus Capella's work. In an oft-repeated citation, Locke's *Essay* figures rhetoric as feminine. Here however, rhetoric is not a goddess, but a seductress, a "perfect cheat" hampering the search for truth. This analogy of the deceitful female to a figural rhetoric does not stand alone in the *Essay*, but is part of a textual system of fearful or disparaging images of women's/rhetoric's deceptions in regard to language.

Notably, Nietzsche begins his course in ancient rhetoric by citing Locke's "aversion" to rhetoric as the most notable example of the disrepute into which the classical art of rhetoric had fallen in the nineteenth century (200, n.1). Nietzsche quotes this familiar passage by Locke as his proof: "But yet, if we would speak of Things as they are, we must allow, that all the Art of Rhetorick besides Order and Clearness, all the artificial and figurative application of Words Eloquence hath invented, are for nothing else but to insinuate wrong Ideas, move the Passions, and thereby mislead the Judgement; and so indeed are perfect cheat." (508; III.10.34).

This denunciation of a figural, passionate rhetoric by Locke occurs at the end of the chapter titled "Of the Abuse of Words," where he names seven abuses in preparation for offering remedies for them. These abuses include first, using words with no clear ideas; second, using words inconsistently; and third, using jargon or an "affected obscurity." The fourth and fifth are related to each other: taking words for things instead of ideas, and making words stand for the real essences of things. The sixth is using words whose meaning is unclear to others, and seventh is using figurative speech, which is "perfect cheat" in a discourse intended to instruct, where objective judgment might be influenced by the passions.

The passage ends on this "witty" note:

> 'Tis evident how much Men love to deceive and be deceived, since Rhetorick, that powerful instrument of Error and Deceit, has its established professors, is publickly taught, and has always been had in great Reputation: And I doubt not but it will be thought great boldness, if not brutality in me, to have said thus much against it. Eloquence, like the fair Sex, has too prevailing Beauties in it, to suffer it self ever to be spoken against. And 'tis in vain to find fault with those Arts of Deceiving, wherein Men find pleasure to be Deceived. (508; III.10.34)

Taking on the role of self-deprecating gallant seeming to fear appearing ridiculous or "brutalizing," Locke dismisses figural rhetoric as deception, much as Plato and others dismissed the sophists and their rhetoric of the body, replacing a figural rhetoric by a self-evident, commonsensical process of arriving at and communicating truth. Despite his playfulness in the passage, we can note the masculine gendering of philosophy in contrast to the feminine figure of rhetoric. In his interdiction of rhetoric and figurality, he attempts to construct a closed, masculine space for philosophy apart from the deceit of embodied, feminine rhetoric.

The duality of this scheme—the dangerous sensual rhetoric versus the pure rhetoric of truth—echoes the growing seventeenth-century split between courtly and an oppositional parliamentary language described by Fumaroli. In courtly societies, a hierarchical structure where speech was strictly controlled, the courtier does not speak openly, but persuades powerful figures indirectly through a sensual, insinuative rhetoric. In France, where Locke spent some time, this was in contrast to a plainer-style rhetoric of the aristocrats in parliament vying for power with the monarchy. Although French salon life was more open than courtly society, the more elaborate, aesthetic language of the salons remained polite and courtly, deferential and "feminine." Locke's feminine coding of seductive rhetoric carries some of the same valences, paralleling criticisms of the "artificial" language of the salons. Although he claims to allow for the bodily seductions of rhetoric in the civic realm, his masculine-figured philosophy of ideas nonetheless expands to encompass all of language, leaving no space for "rhetoric" at all. Yet repressed and denied its own legitimate space, the body and rhetoric return to pervade all of language.

Locke's moment of allowing a separate sphere for rhetoric, his eloquent admission of the existence of discourses where we seek "rather Pleasure and Delight than Information and Instruction," is paradoxically the moment when "philosophy" begins to crowd out the space for rhetoric:

And therefore however laudable or allowable Oratory may render them in Harangues and popular Addresses, they are certainly, in all Discourses that pretend to inform or instruct, wholly to be avoided; and where Truth and Knowledge are concerned, cannot but be thought a great fault, either of the Language or Person that makes use of them . . . (508; III.10.34)

Here, rhetoric and pleasure are linked in popular persuasion, but denied space where any inquiry into Truth is concerned. Feminine rhetoric here seems restricted to something like stand-up comedy in a disreputable, even obscene, club. The body and passion, beauty, error, and pleasurable deceit are linked to the feminine and to rhetoric. Truth is opposed to pleasure, instructional to popular, and the mind to the body. Traditionally, rhetoric concerned itself not only with reason or logos, but with pathos and ethos, bringing in social, emotional, and physical events of language. Locke's text performs this theory: it is precisely this "traditional," passionate eloquence that he uses so well to violate the very conditions he has stipulated. As Locke's own use of eloquence shows us, rhetoric will not stay in its place. Bennington points out that the borders of rhetoric and philosophy must be policed because rhetoric in Locke is not a simple abuse of language that can be corrected, but a planned deceit (105), whose very ground is in principle illegitimate. Rhetoric is the femininely "perfect cheat," and there is no remedy. Locke casts a veil over the body of rhetoric and moves on, while this "feminine" rhetoric moves on to undermine the ground he stands upon.

In Susan Bordo's analyses of Descartes, a transcendence of the body and birth of inwardness and privacy are linked with later efforts to reject the values associated with the old female universe of the Middle Ages and Renaissance. Bordo's narrative interprets the shift to a new discursive pattern of science as a "rebirthing," a "re-imaging" of knowledge and the world as masculine. The masculine is a world of detachment, clarity, and objectivity opposed to the feminine world of connection between knower and known, ambiguity, and empathy. What Bordo calls a "flight from the feminine" she explains in psychological terms as a reaction-formation brought about by the anxiety of separating from the material universe, resulting in a defining or a policing of the boundaries of the masculine. Efforts to fix and police language and meaning in the new discourses of science can be seen as part of the "masculinization of thought" she describes as a legacy of Cartesian theory.

Locke's quest for control and mastery logically associates language with women, desire, and the body and enacts prohibitions against their free circulation. This forms part of a network of textual citations of terms and images criticizing women's practices or subsuming woman in man. Images of women in the text are relatively rare, but when they appear they are almost always negative, and ultimately women disappear. As William Walker points out, woman occurs at the origins for Locke (including his title page reference to a child in the womb), but she then "fades" out. This "fade of the female" is associated with the disappearance of the concrete and particular (mother, nurse) in the formation of abstract thought, allied with the male (father). For example the mother and nurse known by a child as particulars are ultimately displaced in Locke's scheme of language development by the child's progressing to the general concept Man (Walker 254, Locke 411; III.3.7–8). As Walker comments:

That is to say that the ideas of qualities that constitute gender which are ostensibly omitted in the formulation of the general term for and idea of humanity obviously return as possible designations for the general term. If female gender is cut deepest in the process, male gender is restored and healed as a possible designation of the new general term. (256)

In this fashion, Locke's *Essay* is constructed on universal principles that are, in the final analysis, abstract and male. Woman and the body remain bracketed, relegated to the origins, origins which are once more inseparable from language and signification. When woman does appear in the *Essay*, her image echoes that of the "seductress" Rhetoric. Locke repeatedly insinuates these images, old familiar citations, alluding to women as promiscuous, women as deceitful, women as adultresses, or women as uneducated and untrustworthy in regard to child-rearing, constructing a curiously negative, yet embodied ideal of womanhood.

As echoed in his education treatises, Locke here seems most concerned that fallible women are responsible for the upbringing (and language training) of children; as such, they can be held responsible for monsters in the male mind. As Walker notes of Locke's woman: "It is . . . not surprising that she also resides at the origins of the disease, the madness, that is the foundation of the greatest errors in the world: the association of ideas" (251). Having also discussed negative images of women in Locke, Walker goes on to deconstruct them with the *Essay*'s more rare, but positive figurations of woman, primarily as a symbol of Truth. Images of Truth figured as a female are of Truth receiving a male caller "intimately" into her private rooms (3) and of Truth as a lover (285; II.21.72). These textual citations essentially cast Truth as a (chaste) woman being courted by a man. Walker argues that Locke's text and his presentation of mind are neither consistent, nor simple, nor unified and points out textual instances of the feminine and woman representing other than madness, disruption, and death. And yet woman's embodiment of Truth remains here ambiguously disembodied.

If Locke can be charged with dematerializing the word and the world through his emphasis on reason and intellect, one counterargument might be that some of Locke's contemporaries and successors believed him to be a materialist. Christian theology along with some "pagan" classical texts held that men are made up of a clearly demarcated material body and an immaterial soul.

The orthodox believed the immaterial soul was the site of thought, that "no organization of matter and motion could ever produce thought, and that God could not without essentially changing the nature of matter, make matter think" (Yolton, xi). Thus, Locke dismayed many when he wrote in his *Essay* that we might conceive that "GOD can, if he please, superadd to Matter a Faculty of Thinking. . ." (4.3.6). This throwaway remark was part of a longer discussion of the limitations of human knowledge about our ideas of "*Matter* and *Thinking*." In this passage, Locke says that contemplating our own ideas about such issues will not lead to the truth of the matter, unless there is some revelation from God. However, Locke himself speculates that "the first eternal thinking Being" should be able to create thinking matter even if he himself is not matter (IV.3.6, 541). Because of these remarks Locke was read by some such as Samuel Clarke in the eighteenth century as actually promoting the view that matter can think. However, throughout the *Essay* Locke inclines more to a sort of Platonism, of a Christian variety, referring to "archetypes" of our ideas as if they needed no definition or explanation. The point is that again, Locke's text is not homogeneous, and that citations to it are as various as have been the nearly three hundred years of readers. However, while different moments and values in the text may favor materialism, Locke tenaciously and faithfully holds onto the spiritual in his explorations of epistemology. Despising or controlling the body and its desires is consistent with both Platonic and Christian values.

In that vein, it is not surprising that the "feminine" is linked with the body and suppressed, even though the textual network of images of women in the *Essay* neither purely praises nor blames them. But it generally foregrounds Locke's figuration of Rhetoric as deceitful seductress and devalues or "fades" women and the flesh. Following a trajectory set by Bacon and Descartes, Locke outlines a "masculine" discourse of philosophy stressing a plain, clear, and correct style, an empirical "seeing is knowing" epistemology, and a primarily individualist rationality.

But if language is first social, even today retaining its familiar origins with mother and child, if it is material, binding mind and body with its rhythms and tones, it is always thoroughly rhetorical. Such a view of language as embodied brings into play multiple voices—citations from within and without—in the process enfolding the body and rationality, passion and morality, politics and power at every turn. Locke's own use of heightened rhetoric, exceeding purely logical calculations, as well as inconsistencies such as his reliance on undefinable terms such as "ideas" and "archetypes" are obvious but necessary points of stress in the logic of his texts. These texts helped form part of discursive practices that figuratively and literally helped materialize women's bodies in particular ways in western culture. Today women of various ethnicities and sexualities require different tropings, new discursive classes, citations, and practices yet to be worked out. We cannot simply return to Bordo's Renaissance universe of the nurturing mother in this postmodern age. Moreover Butler and others have warned of the dangers of elevating gender or decontextualizing it from other factors such as sexual orientation or race in trying to understand our subjectivities and potential for agency. Meanwhile we still live within the norms and practices created by discursive citations and structures such as Locke's, norms and practices that create inequities in social relationships of all sorts. What rearticulations of citational practices might accord with truer partnerships and friendships between and among men and women in the present and future? In exploring new alternatives, we might do well to accept, celebrate, and rearticulate Locke's "deceitful feminine" body, the site of desire, the site of rhetoric, and the site of history. Whether this body be the cybernetic organism described by Donna Haraway or a future body as yet unknown and unknowable, women's own writings in their various voices and rhetorics will help to produce it and its social nexus. This is why a broader study of rhetoric and rhetorics truly matters.

8

"I'VE GOT YOU UNDER MY SKIN":
CYBER(SEXED) BODIES IN CYBERPUNK FICTIONS[1]

Cathy Peppers

In 1985, Donna Haraway proposed the image of the cyborg as an icon for our post-humanist bodies and subjectivities. In "A Cyborg Manifesto,"[2] Haraway argues that "from [one] perspective, a cyborg [identity] might be about lived social and bodily realities in which people are not afraid of their joint kinship with animals and machines, not afraid of permanently partial identities and contradictory standpoints" (154). In a time when any notion of a singularly identifiable "natural body" has been radically undermined, and the "discursive body" of our theorizing has been fundamentally inscribed by a rhetoric of technology, Haraway's claim that "we are cyborgs" (150) sounds less like a "manifesto" than a description. A wide range of feminist and postmodern cultural analyses have focused on exposing the ways that technologies—scientific, medical, industrial, discursive—have determined what counts as our bodies. From feminist analyses of the ways reproductive technologies construct definitions of the reproductive body,[3] to analyses of the ways legal, medical and literary discourses create raced bodies,[4] to Foucaultian-inspired analyses of the ways postmodern bodies are always already constituted by discursive technologies,[5] much current cultural theory indicates we live in a time in which the traditional boundaries which have separated "organic" from "technological" have grown increasingly porous.

Within this context, Haraway's call to embrace a cyborg identity, which exists precisely where such boundaries are crossed, is about refusing "an anti-science metaphysics, a demonology of technology" (181), which she sees not only in traditional humanism, but also in a feminism that celebrates a nostalgic return to the "natural" female body. As Haraway shows throughout her work, in the "Manifesto" and the other articles in *Simians, Cyborgs, and Women* as well as in *Primate Visions*, while feminists might want to argue for one story of the body over another for strategic reasons, images of the "natural" body are the products of the culturally powerful discourses of biology. And biology is a "logos," a discursive technology which (at least) mediates how we know our bodies, and such "technologies . . . [are] instruments for enforcing meanings" of the biological individual (Manifesto 164).

In "The Biopolitics of Postmodern Bodies," Haraway describes how current immune systems theory has questioned what constitutes the "individual body." Evelyn Fox Keller, in *Secrets of Life, Secrets of Death*, notes that new theories in molecular biology have had a similar effect, and even Luce Irigaray, a feminist theorist most often cited for espousing an essentialist difference of the "natural" female body, has published an interview with Helene Rouch, a French biologist, in which new knowledge about the relation between the fetus and the pregnant woman's body figures a promising new "placental economy" based on neither fusion nor aggressive parasitism between the "self" and the "other." Such bio-technological stories of the body indeed offer us the opportunity to ask, as Haraway does, "why should our bodies end at the skin?" (Manifesto 178) Feminists, who have long been aware that the female body exists on the boundary between sex and gender, nature and culture, and who have theorized the pregnant body as a key boundary-crossing ontology, have much to gain from entering into contests over how technologies, in Haraway's broad definition, enforce meanings of the self. For these reasons (among others), a cyborg identity does indeed sound appealing. But while the image of the cyborg who escapes all the old dualisms, such as organic/technological, nature/culture, body/mind, sounds like a productive place from which to struggle over definitions of identity, and while it would certainly also help feminists avoid the exclusionary essentialism that so often attends on claims of an "innocent" category of "woman," I'm not sure I'm ready to agree with Haraway's claim that the cyborg also escapes the familiar man/woman dualism. As she puts it: "The cyborg is a creature in a post-gender world; it has no truck with bisexuality, pre-Oedipal symbiosis, unalientated labor, or other seductions to organic wholeness through the appropriation of all the parts into a higher unity" (150). Such a postfeminist cyborg sounds like a deconstructionist's dream come true, but the reality that a cyborg might equally be represented by a fighter pilot plugged into his intelligent headgear as by the "ideal" replicants in *Blade Runner*, by Robocop as well as by Laurie Anderson in performance, should give us pause. If cyborgs can equally be represented by the technofascist bodies of a Terminator or a Robocop, as by the "women of color" affinity identities Haraway describes, can the cyborg really be "post-gender"?

While Haraway's utopian image of a subject who takes pleasure in boundary confusions sounds charming, it also sounds suspiciously like the deconstructionist's eagerness to embrace a "dissolved" subject in order to avoid the disruption of feminists' concerns with gendered subjectivity. If deconstructionist postmodernism is all about shattering what Susan Bordo calls the illusion of the "modernist, Cartesian view from nowhere," replacing this with the "postmodern imagery of a body whose own unity has been shattered by multiplicity," then it appears we are left with "a new imagination of disembodiment: a dream of being everywhere," which is also a "resistance to the recognition that one is always somewhere, and limited" (143–45). Bordo's point is a forceful reminder of Haraway's own warning that we should "take responsibility for [the] construction" of representations of the cyborg (Manifesto 150). While it is true that she claims the cyborg to be "post-gender," the Manifesto also notes that, though "the cyborg is a kind of disassembled and reassembled postmodern self," for feminists who would insist on a continuing struggle over the technologizing of the (cyborg) body, "this is a self feminists must code" (163). The Manifesto, then, though it dreams of a postgender cyborg, can also be taken as a call to read the gender encoded in the "organic" half of the cybernetic organism, as well as the way gender is encoded in the structural relation between technology and the body. And science fiction is obviously one ideal site for finding representations of cyborgs; as Haraway says, science fiction writers, in "exploring what it means to be embodied in high-tech worlds . . . are our theorists for cyborgs" (173).

Mainstream academic critics, recognizing that science fiction is, as Mary Ann Doane notes, "a genre specific to the era of rapid technological development," have increasingly turned to analyses of the ways this genre "envisages new, revised bod[ies] as a direct outcome of the advance" of technologies (163). Recent studies by feminist critics have focused on the ways women writers have used science fiction (and "speculative fiction," in the widest sense, including utopian and fantasy fictions) to explore the ways technologies destabilize sexual identity and gendered social structures.[6]

But within the critical rush to take science fiction seriously, it is cyberpunk that has generated the most hyperbolic critical attention. It has been hailed in academic circles as the "apotheosis of postmodernism" (Csicsery-Ronay 182), as "the literary manifestation of postmodernism" or at least as the genre which "literalizes . . . what occurs in postmodern fiction as metaphor" (McHale 150), as perhaps even indicating the very "future of narrative" (Slusser and Shippey). And yet these analyses of our most likely body of texts to "theorize cyborgs" remain largely indifferent to considerations of gender, forgetting (ignoring) Doane's reminder that "when technology intersects with the body . . . the question of sexual difference is inevitably involved" (163).[7] For this reason, cyberpunk offers an ideal site for tracing the conflict between postmodernist and feminist theory that Susan Bordo describes, as this conflict is crystallized in constructions of cyborg subjectivity.

To interrogate how gender is constructed in these texts, I will focus on only three writers—William Gibson, James Tiptree (Alice Sheldon), Pat Cadigan—to set up an intertextual dialogue between men's and women's texts within this genre.[8] I will show that, while each of these fictions represent cyborg bodies whose blurring of boundaries are more pleasurable and radical than in traditional science fiction, in each case there is a limit to that pleasure, and the most problematic boundaries concern gendered subject/object relations. For this reason I will be using Klaus Theweleit's work on male subjectivity, which might be read as the definitive theoretical account of (techno)fascism, and Jessica Benjamin's theory of "intersubjectivity," which I think might be our closest theoretical account of a utopian subjectivity founded on the pleasure of boundary confusions.[9] The cyborg bodies in these texts are inscribed by technology differently (hence my term "cyber(sexed) bodies"), and this difference hinges in part on whether the text represents a subject who enters another body or space via technology, or a subject who is entered.

(En)gendering the Genre

In cyberpunk texts, where technologies and the "technologies of gender" (de Lauretis) are marked literally on the bodies of the characters, I am concerned by Veronica Hollinger's claim (which has been echoed by most other writers on the subject) that cyberpunk's "anti-humanism," the genre's "breakdown" of "the oppositions between the natural and the artificial, the human and the machine" (30), offers such a "radica[l] decenter[ing of] the human body" (33). Her description of the radical deconstruction of the subject in cyberpunk (texts mostly written by white men) leads her to argue (briefly) "that most feminist science fiction," which includes no writers of cyberpunk (her one female cyberpunk writer, Pat Cadigan, is lumped in with the rest of the boys), "given the exigencies of their own . . . political agendas . . . rather supports than undermines the tenets of liberal humanism" (33). Unfortunately, because the scope of Hollinger's "Cybernetic Deconstructions: Cyberpunk and Postmodernism" did not permit her to pursue this suggested contrast between feminist and postmodern science fictions, the subsequent critical discussion of cyberpunk has tended to carry on with the (by now familiar) danger often seen in "deconstructionist" readings: the assumption that feminist science fiction is "political," while men's is not.

To read from this position does not include the questioning of how masculine/feminine or subject/object oppositions are "deconstructed" (or reinscribed). However, it is precisely my intention to examine the way gender is encoded in the cyborgs that are constructed in cyberpunk texts, and to examine the "intertextual dialogue" that might be found between men's and women's texts in this same genre, before I readily embrace the cyborg as the utopian ideal Haraway describes. At the risk (with the pleasure) of sounding like a feminist killjoy, struggling under the weight of "political exigencies" and "humanism," I am not ready to leave the field of contested notions of the cyborg subject to Gibson's cyberpunks.

Cyberpunk, as the name implies, presents readers with hacker/street punk heroes who subvert monolithic corporate technocracy, and the tools of their subversion are the pirated programs, viruses, and genetic manipulations the technocracy has spawned. Cyberpunks do not stand outside technology, they interface with it and subvert from within. Bruce Sterling, the movement's most vocal spokesperson, cites the following generic characteristics of cyberpunk:

> For the cyberpunks . . . technology is visceral . . . utterly intimate . . . not outside us but. . . under our skin. . . . Certain themes spring up repeatedly in cyberpunk. The theme of bodily invasion: prosthetic limbs, implanted circuitry, cosmetic surgery, genetic alteration. . . . Mind invasion: brain-computer interfaces, artificial intelligence, neurochemistry. (*Mirrorshades* xi)

Hailed as *the* postmodern revolution in science fiction, cyberpunk's obsession with the breakdown of boundaries between human and machine, its "radical deconstruction" of the humanist body, is described as being solely responsible for bringing the genre out of its "doldrums;" as Bruce Sterling notes, "in the late Seventies, [Science Fiction] was confused, self-involved, and stale" (*Burning Chrome* ix).

While cyberpunk does stand in stark contrast to most traditional science fiction, which tended to be concerned with keeping the human at the center of things in the face of invading technologies, what repeatedly gets elided in accounts of the literary inheritance of cyberpunk is the fact of the first full-scale "invasion" of women writers into the traditionally male world of science fiction. The critical work on postmodern science fiction has its own origin stories, written by the likes of Bruce Sterling and Larry McCaffery. In these stories, Gibson is cited as the male progenitor of cyberpunk; if the origin story looks for earlier ancestors, as does, say, Kadrey and McCaffery's *Storming the Reality Studio* (17–29), which also includes the influences of musicians and mainstream writers, writers like Alfred Bester, Thomas Pynchon, and William Burroughs are cited as sort of sympathetic uncles, but the lineage is primarily male. The Kadrey/McCaffery story makes an obligatory nod to Mary Shelley's *Frankenstein* as source for science fiction in general, and mentions Tiptree as the only other woman science fiction writer (though she is not included in the actual anthology). While Joanna Russ's *The Female Man* often gets an honorable mention as a precursor to postmodern science fiction, feminist science fiction is generally characterized in the manner Hollinger's article indicates, or as merely nostalgically utopian and in need of cyberpunk's tough edge (see Joan Gordon in *Storming*). This amnesia about women science fiction writers between Mary Shelley and Pat Cadigan is indeed curious, considering that women writers first gained high visibility in the genre in, you guessed it, the "stale," "self-involved" late 60s and 70s.

If traditional "hard" science fiction was dead there for a while, it seems it was women writers who killed it. Ursula Le Guin describes this "invasion:" "When women invaded science fiction they brought a lot of luggage with them . . . things the devotees of wiring-diagrams and weaponry had little knowledge of, things like men, women, and children" (52).

Women's science fiction, often called "soft," often not considered to be "true" science fiction at all, tended to be concerned with questions of biological determinism, genetic manipulations, and in general, the issues of how technological inscriptions on the body affect gender roles (and definitions of "human"). As random examples, we can consider Anne McCaffrey's *The Ship Who Sang* (1969), the story of a parapelegic woman whose neurocircuits are meshed into the body of a spaceship. Ursula LeGuin's *The Left Hand of Darkness* (1969), and many of Tiptree's stories published in the 1960s and 1970s, show a concern with the effects of biological and other technologies of gender; and Joanna Russ's *The Female Man* (1975), in particular, stands as a novel most resolutely committed to exploring divided subjectivity.[10]

My point in reinscribing the missing mother into the commonly invoked Oedipal drama of the cyberpunk sons rebelling against their traditional fathers is not just to "give the women their due" (although it is also that);[11] my point is to place cyberpunk fiction historically in reaction to the emergence of feminist concerns regarding the technologized body and the resultant boundary confusions that occurred both in science fiction and in the culture at large. Cyberpunk fiction could be seen in the context of a host of radical disruptions of the security of white male privilege in the 1970s.[12] If it is a fiction obsessed with dissolving boundaries, it is also possible to see the genre's emergence as the privileged site for postmodern subjectivity as a reenactment of Susan Bordo's description of deconstructionist postmodernism's embrace of a "disembodied view from everywhere" as a way to remain indifferent to concerns about gender, and to the women writers who brought that concern to science fiction. The male cyberpunk writers, such as William Gibson, have also essentially stepped into a generic space first opened by women writers, and have, as we shall see, engendered that space. It is perhaps for this reason that, as technology gets more "intimate" with the body, more "under our skins," it also gets "feminized."

Cyberspace: (A Semiotic Scrubbing of) the Final Frontier

In Gibson's fictions, we would not expect to find "panic male bodies" fleeing from the fluid mass of the feminine, nor hysterically insisting on fortifying the "tower of the bodily boundaries" in the face of threatened dissolution which Klaus Theweleit describes as marking the fascist subjectivity of the soldier males in *Male Fantasies*. On the contrary, Gibson himself critiques the fascist desire to create a post-apocalyptic "totality machine" of the future, and the Nietzschean super-bodies who would populate that future, in one of his earliest stories, "The Gernsback Continuum." The protagonist has a nightmare vision of the "perfect" future as it is envisioned by those who would rid the world of "impurities." He sees the "heroes" of this future as they stand facing the "ideal" city:

> They frightened me. . . .
>
> They were Heirs to the Dream. . . . They were white, blond, and they probably had blue eyes. . . . They were smug, happy, and utterly content with themselves and their world. And in the Dream, it was their world. . . .
>
> It had all the sinister fruitiness of Hitler Youth propaganda. (32–33)

As Sterling notes in his "Preface" to *Burning Chrome*, this story critiques the traditional "technolatry" and "rock-ribbed Competent Men of hard science fiction" (xi). Gibson is here also critiquing not only naive scientific utopianism, but also the "ideal" humanist body as a product of a fascist "dream logic" (Gernsback 32). But there are really no cyborgs in this story; it is especially in his novels, and a story called "Burning Chrome," that we can find the cyborgs Gibson creates instead of the (techno)fascist bodies, with their nostalgic visions of coherence, he critiques here.

In Gibson's quintessential cyberpunk trilogy of novels, *Neuromancer* (1984), *Count Zero* (1986), and *Mona Lisa Overdrive* (1988), we are introduced to a world where the constructions of cyber-subjects are manifold: Molly, an assassin, sports implanted lenses for eyes and razor knives under her fingernails; street gang members genetically engineer their facial features, hair styles, body shapes, and wear hologram designed clothing as a sort of body-literal wearing of the colours; various characters have sockets in their skulls into which they can plug programs for direct mental access to all manner of coded data. One particular version of the cyborg condition which occurs frequently in Gibson's fictions concerns the linking of two characters via brain-interface rigs, called simstim. This vision of "cyborg sex" stands as a literal representation of what Kroker and Kroker would call "hyperreal sex: sex without secretions . . . the ultimate out-of-body experience [which] avoids the terror of the ruined surfaces of the body" (15). We see this high-tech parable of pornography repeated over and over again in Gibson's work, but he seems incapable of imagining the hyperreal experience of simstim from the point of view of the woman entered.

And it is always a woman's body which is entered via this technology, indicating that the boundary that remains most problematic in Gibson's work is the one between male subject and female object. In Jessica Benjamin's "A Desire of One's Own," she critiques the traditional Western model of individuation through differentiation from the mother, claiming it both reinforces male objectification of women, and constructs a model for female desire that is passive. She argues instead that "individuality is properly, ideally, a balance of separation and connectedness, of the capacity for agency and relatedness" (82), and offers as a new ideal psychic mode the notion of "intersubjectivity," which avoids the two poles of domination of the object of desire and submission to it. An intersubjective relation would undo the boundary between subject/object and allow "the desire to lose oneself in the other and really be known for oneself [to] coalesce" (93). Donna Haraway's ideal cyborg would, it seems to me, experience intersubjective desire; Gibson's cyberpunks, despite repeated attempts to merge with the "other," ultimately do not.

Case, the cowboy-hacker hero of *Neuromancer*, is a "virgin"; that is, he has no implanted circuitry, viruses, or other technology. He has only contempt for embodiment: Case "lived for the bodiless exultation of cyberspace. . . [he felt] a certain relaxed contempt for the flesh. The body was meat" (6). In this, he is like all of Gibson's male protagonists; just as men are never entered via simstim, neither are their bodily interiors penetrated in any way. Male interiors are not in question in Gibson's fictions, only their relationship with the interiors of female characters and cyberspace are. And having access to a female character's bodily interior, even via electronic mediation, is too intimate. Thus, when Case's job requires that he be plugged into his co-conspirator Molly via a simstim link, the sensation is described this way:

> For a few frightened seconds he fought helplessly to control her body. Then he willed himself into passivity. . . .
>
> Her body language was disorienting. . . .
>
> She slid a hand into her jacket, a fingertip circling a nipple under warm silk. The sensation made him catch his breath. She laughed. . . . He had no way to reply.
>
> He began to find the passivity of the situation irritating. (56)

The potential for intersubjectivity here is not pleasureable to Case, despite the gratuitous nipple caress. Disrupting the masculine privilege of agency is not part of Gibson's deconstructive impulse; this is somehow perverse.

But amidst all of Gibson's myriad techno-bodies, the privileged cyber-construct remains the relationship between the cowboy and cyberspace, and this relationship undergoes something of a sea-change.

Cyberspace is defined as "a consensual hallucination . . . a graphic representation of data abstracted from the banks of every computer in the human system" (*Neuromancer* 51), and cowboys access this space via electronic brain interface rigs that allow them to project their disembodied consciousnesses. Cyberspace is a representation of the collective unconscious which exists as a virtual reality on the other side of computer screens, similar to the way Theweleit describes the unconscious of the soldier male: "The unconscious emerges here no longer as a productive force, but as a product of the body, a substance which, once released, becomes ungovernable . . . laying waste the boundaries of the body" (II 7). While Theweleit's soldier males seek to destroy this exteriorized (and feminized) unconscious at all costs, in order to keep the self from dissolving, Gibson's cowboys exhibit a more complex relationship to it. As Luce Irigaray notes, "the unconscious is historically censored femaleness" (Theweleit I 432), and cyberspace in Gibson's work is constructed as a feminine space. But over the course of Gibson's fictions, cowboys show a chronological shift from desiring to conquer this space to desiring to merge with it.

In "Burning Chrome," a story set in the same fictional world as the *Neuromancer* trilogy, we read Gibson's first version of this relationship. In this story, a cowboy decides to "burn"/pirate the database of a brothel owned by a woman named Chrome. Here is a typical description of cowboy activity from the story:

> Bodiless, we swerve into Chrome's castle of ice. And we're fast, fast. It feels like we're surfing the crest of the invading program.
>
> Somewhere we have bodies, very far away.
>
> We've crashed her gates disguised as an audit and three subpoenas, but her defenses are specially geared to cope with that kind of official intrusion. Her most sophisticated ice is structured to fend off warrants, writs, subpoenas. When we

breached the first gate, the bulk of her data vanished. . . . (173)

Eventually, their virus program is able to "penetrate" Chrome's defenses, and the narrator responds with a "Ride 'em, cowboy." Like cowboys who rode out to tame the "virgin territory" of the west, the cyberspace cowboy in early representations is reminiscent of Theweleit's description of the fascist hero's relationship to the landscape:

> The fascists . . . gain experience through piracy; they raid and annihilate all things alien. . . . Where once a peaceful landscape gently mirrored the feelings of the wandering onlooker, the landscape now only exists in symbiosis with the body of the man racing across its surface . . . the landscape itself crouches in tense anticipation of the moment when it will devour him. (II 366)

In "Burning Chrome," then, cyberspace is constructed as the exteriorized unconscious, coded as feminine, and the cowboy leaves his body behind as he enters the space, intent on destroying what he finds there before it finds him.

While, on one level, this "interface of the human and the machine radically decenters the human body, the sacred icon of the essential self" (Hollinger 33), it is a male body which is "decentered," not the position of the masculine subject relative to the feminine object. And, considering that the historical space for cyberpunk writers like Gibson was initially opened by women science fiction writers intent on exploring the interzones between human/machine, male/female, Gibson's construction of the cowboy's relationship to cyberspace stands as a telling metaphor for the way the space of the feminine is objectified and engendered by masculine subjectivity.

In *Neuromancer*, Case maintains a certain limited longing to merge with the still feminized cyberspace. While cyberspace here is not coded as so overtly feminine as in "Burning Chrome," it still represents what Theweleit calls a female "territory of desire." Case's quest is now not to destroy what he finds there, but to change it fundamentally; the space he longs to enter remains "raw material . . . awaiting socialization" (Theweleit I294). Near the end of the novel, Case's relationship to cyberspace is coded in mother/ son imagery; his body is described as "afloat in a loose fetal crouch" (256), with the "umbilical cord" of his deck connected to the central computer. His goal, however, is less to give birth to himself than to precipitate the birth of a new form of cyberspace. His job is to literally provide the word ("socialization") that will enable two artificial intelligences existing separately in cyberspace to know each other and gain sentience—this moment will be known as "The Change" in future novels.

Case's sacred role here is similar to Theweleit's description of the fascist male subject's assertion of control over the procreative function: "Men create the future . . . totalities evoked in the concept of 'form'. . . . Though childbirth has become masculine, it still requires a body" (II 88), in this case, the maternal body of cyberspace (also called the "matrix"). Case accomplishes procreation in the penultimate scene of *Neuromancer* by literally locating (naming) the space encoded as feminine; rather than entering into an intersubjective relationship with the feminine/maternal space, he "creates the future" and withdraws, and, in fact, the epilogue to the novel indicates he gives up his cowboy activities altogether. Case, it seems, prefers living in the "meat" of his own "virgin" body, and retaining that body's masculine privilege, to mucking about in even a de-maternalized space.

Once cyberspace has been fundamentally changed by Case, it is no longer coded as "feminine;" Case has effected a semiotic cleanup of this maternal "womb" in much the same way as Apollo recodes the female womb in Aeschylus' *Eumenides* as an empty space that houses man's seed without having any blood relationship to it. By the time Bobby Newmark enters the scene in *Count Zero* and *Mona Lisa Overdrive*, it seems safe for him to desire to merge completely with cyberspace because it is no longer so resolutely "other." But, before this is possible, cyberspace must be rid of a few more ghosts of "otherness." When Case brought about "The Change," and cyberspace became sentient, it fragmented, and "the fragments sought form, each one, as is the nature of such things. In all the signs [humans] have stored against the night . . . the paradigms of voudou proved most appropriate" (MLO 257). In *Count Zero* and *Mona Lisa Overdrive*, the "ghosts in the machine" are no longer feminine, but black, the loa of voudou.

If feminists are concerned with deconstructionist postmodernism's indifference to gender, making it "magically disappear" through claims of a "radical deconstruction" of the subject, we should be equally concerned with Gibson's co-option and erasure of racial difference by having his white boy hero, Bobby, and white girl heroine, Angie, become the chosen favorites of the voudou loa. Here is another danger of a "view from everywhere" which refuses to recognize that "one is always somewhere, and limited": in the deconstructionist move to disembodiment, it ceases to matter (deconstruction is indifferent to) who occupies the structural position of the "other," which erases the very racial specificity one might expect to be explored by Gibson's choice of voudou as the new "paradigm" for cyberspace. Despite the presence of all the black characters in *Count Zero*, it is Angie who is chosen most often to be ridden by Legba. But then, Angie also represents the "truest" cyborg in all the novels: her father has implanted circuitry directly into her brain, so she has direct, unmediated access to cyberspace without needing an interface deck. She is no "virgin," nor does she have any control over her access. As cyberspace is an exteriorized and feminized unconscious, Angie has privileged biological access to it, which represents the same old Freudian story of women being "closer" to the unconscious, and, indeed, "ridden" by it, as Angie is "ridden" by the loa.

By the time we arrive at *Mona Lisa Overdrive*, all the black characters are gone, and Bobby is completely merged with cyberspace. His body is only present as empty "meat" strapped to a stretcher, while his consciousness exists completely within the virtual world. The force of the plot is to bring Angie into cyberspace with him so they may complete a "marriage" arranged by the voudou gods. Bobby is in complete control of cyberspace now, and when the marriage is completed, cyberspace realigns itself into a new "totality principle;" with all the fragmented intelligences unified, Earth's cyberspace can now make contact with another "other" on Centauri, and Bobby and Angie not only leave their bodies, but also Earth, completely behind.

Ultimately, then, I find that the cyborgs Gibson constructs, while they do disrupt the boundary between man and machine, are not what I would consider "radically deconstructed subjects." While his constructions of bodies traced literally by technology are seductive, and there are moments when boundaries between subjects blur pleasurably, we are, in the end, presented with the same old fantasy of transcendence beyond the body, the feminine, and racial "otherness," with the masculine rather firmly reinscribed at the center of this newly constructed, and quickly colonized, space. Gibson's cyborg subjects know only domination over or submission to the other, and they rather prefer the former. Where moments of potential intersubjectivity appear, the narrative sweeps them ruthlessly away. Gibson's cyborgs are more willing to flirt with boundary confusions than, say, Robocop, but they are still trapped in a technofascist economy of the same.

"Fruitful Couplings" within an Erotics of Domination?

I find it positive that Istvan Csicsery-Ronay, who has called cyberpunk "the apotheosis of the postmodern," is also willing to consider it as the "apotheosis of bad faith" as well, primarily because he sees the genre as suspending questions about "whether some political controls over technology are desirable" (Cyberpunk 193). In "Futuristic Flu, or, the Revenge of the Future," he describes the "ideology" of cyberpunk as defining "the human project as a technological autoevolution" (29), which "undermin[es] the morale and freedom necessary to create an open . . . future, free of technological determinism and constructed through conscious choices" (33). The "inevitability" of the future, as presented by writers like Gibson, brackets any ability to contest the forms the future might take, willing to settle instead with the "thrills" available to technobodies. Csicsery-Ronay also notes that cyberpunk leaves largely untouched the difference between male and female, which he assumes might "someday" be remedied by a "feminist futurism." While I admire his brief recognition of the need to struggle over a reproduction of the same old gendered dualism, I find it curious that he doesn't go on to read work by writers such as (at least) Pat Cadigan (who is a contemporary of Gibson, whom he does read).

As I have suggested, if cyborgs are to be the "hopeful monsters" for feminists, as Haraway envisions, their "fruitful couplings" might be modeled on Jessica Benjamin's notion of intersubjectivity. But I don't think that the women writers of cyberpunk offer the utopian "antidote" that Csicsery-Ronay hopes for. (And why does his wish to be rescued from "bad faith" by women remind me so much of the hope that women's entry into corporate culture will somehow heal that culture with a healthy dose of domestic virtues and spiritual meaning?)

Neither Pat Cadigan's nor James Tiptree's stories offer representations of cyborgs completely liberated from the tyranny of cultural coding; nor do they attempt to reinscribe their female subjects with a rhetoric of the "natural" body. Rather, it is important to consider these two cyberpunk texts by women writers because they are overtly concerned with the effects of technology's inscription on gendered bodies, a consideration which, as we have seen, is left un-problematized in Gibson's fictions. Unlike, say, Anne McCaffrey's *The Ship Who Sang*, which rests on an essentialized split between a unified female subject "brain" complementing a male subject "brawn," both Tiptree's and Cadigan's fictions construct "a gendered and heteronomous subject (subject in two senses of the term: both subjected to social constraint and yet subject in the active sense of maker as well as user of culture, intent on self-definition and self-determination)" (de Lauretis, Fem Stds 10). As I noted in describing Gibson's work, despite the blurring of boundaries we find there, we do not find representations of technological invasions of the body from the perspective of the entered subject, the subject forcefully "subjected to social constraint."

Which is not to say that "The Girl Who Was Plugged In" (1973) or "Rock On" (1984) tell tales of female victimization. They do, however, offer evidence for Arthur and Marilouise Krokers's claim that "women's bodies have always been postmodern because they have always been the targets of a power which, inscribing the text of the flesh, seeks to make of feminine identity something interpellated by ideology, constituted by language. . . . Women's bodies are an inscribed text, this time in skin, not philosophy" (24). These two stories, then, may be read as responses to Gibson's resorting to a fantasy of transcending the body altogether; as any anorexic knows, simple denial of the body is not the answer.

Tiptree's "The Girl Who Was Plugged In," written in 1973, before the term "cyberpunk" was coined, is further proof that "women's bodies have always been postmodern." In fact, this story, which is in a sense a tale of "Cinderella transistorized," (Girl 289) though without the happy ending, offers a reminder that women have been aware that their bodies have been marked by technology (does your foot fit the slipper?) and ideology (if you stay out too late, poof!) since before the advent of deconstructionist postmodernism. And, of course, even fairytales may be seen to operate as "technologies" for enforcing meanings.

The protagonist of "The Girl Who Was Plugged In," Philadelphia Burke, is literally split into two subjects by means of technological manipulation. P. Burke is "the ugly of the world" (286): in a world of pollution, poor street girls like P. Burke cannot afford decontaminated water, "body lifts," "nose filters," plastic surgery; her body is described as resolutely grotesque: "When she smiles, her jaw—it's half purple—almost bites her left eye out . . . [she has] a jumbled torso . . . mismatched legs" (286). After she tries to commit suicide, her "fairy godmother" appears—in this case, corporate advertising executives who are looking for a social nonentity who will not be missed. They train her to operate, via a complex neuroelectric interface system, a vat-grown beautiful body—"the darlingest girl child you've EVER seen" (290)—who they name Delphi. Delphi's job is to sell products.

While the story as a whole is a clear critique of advertising as a technology that contributes to women's divided subjectivity— with P. Burke and Delphi representing an "authentic" self and a self which is produced by the patriarchal ideal, respectively—this fundamental division is not left un-problematized. Tiptree's narra- tive insists on the ugliness of P. Burke, and on her happiness at remaining physically in a cabinet hundreds of miles underneath Carbondale, Pennsylvania, while her consciousness travels with Delphi as she scoots off to all manner of exotic locales. We might say that this is just an example of the false consciousness which is a product of a woman internalizing a self-image created by the patriarchy, and to some extent, it is.

But even when P. Burke notices that Delphi's body has "blankspots" of missing sensation, "certain definite places where her beastly P. Burke body feels things that Delphi's dainty flesh does not," we are told that P. Burke simply "forgets it" (297). Even the loss of sexual feeling in Delphi's body does not mark P. Burke's original body as "privileged;" her original body has already been marked by culture. "For her, sex is a four-letter word spelled P-A-I- N;' as the narrator says, "You don't want the details," but having grown up on the street, it is implied that P. Burke has been (always already?) raped (297). Tiptree insists that living through Delphi is an improvement; certainly, she has more control over her Delphi body.

The division between P. Burke and Delphi is further eroded when we see signs of Delphi "coming alive" on her own (she murmurs when P. Burke is unplugged), and when P. Burke's attitudes disrupt Delphi's docility. P. Burke/Delphi might well have gone on happily in this divided/unified state, but she/they meet "the prince"—Paul, the errant revolutionary son of the corporate boss—who falls in love with Delphi, and insists on seeing her as a victimized martyr who must be saved. The problem is, he can only conceive of Delphi as the "real" woman, who he sees as a pawn in his power play with his father. The other problem is that P. Burke/ Delphi is willing to love him masochistically, to the point of denying her divided reality completely.

In the end, P. Burke/Delphi dies when Paul tries to "rescue" her from his father's clutches. Tiptree's story critiques Paul's desire to reduce P. Burke/Delphi to just Delphi as the object of his love. But I don't think the story supports a "humanist" conception of the female subject, either. When Paul rejects P. Burke, we are asked, "Wouldn't you, if a gaunt she-golem flab-naked and sprouting wires and blood came at you clawing with metal studded paws"? (318), and the grotesqueness of this description does not allow us to sympathize with some "essential" self. P. Burke, too, is guilty of denying the reality of her divided self, and even after she dies, Delphi stays "alive" a bit longer, implying that the "real" P. Burke/Delphi is just that, and not reducible to either a purely "essential" or purely "constructed" subjectivity. While Tiptree's cyborg comes to a tragic end, her tragedy is a result of her refusal to realize that she is a subject who occupies a space both inside and outside cultural inscription. P. Burke/Delphi is not offered the option of transcending the body, as Gibson's cyberpunks are. If Paul had been able to recognize the truth of P. Burke as an agent of desire, only then might this story have had a "happy ending."

Pat Cadigan's story "Rock On," the only story by a woman writer included in the influential cyberpunk anthology *Mirrorshades*, does not exactly offer a "happy ending" either, but its resolutely ironic, flip tone defies any attempt on the reader's part to feel pity for the protagonist, Gina. "Rock On's" scrutinizing of the parallel between technological invasions of the body and rape, standing in stark contrast to the comparatively gleeful explorations of the power conferred on technologized bodies in Gibson's stories. Not that Cadigan has constructed her cyborg as simply a high-tech incarnation of a rape victim; her story problematizes the notion of the entered body in a complex way. Gina is a "synner," the literal embodiment of a human synthesizer. Her artistic role is to provide band members with "rock'n'roll visions straight from the brain" (39); she is the musical source, the embodiment of musical memory, which band members "plug in to" via brain socket interface. In a sense, this cybernetic construction is parallel to the relationships in Gibson's fictions between both the cowboy and cyberspace, and Case's simstim link with Molly. Only this time, we get the story from the point of view of the entered subject.

In the story, Gina has run away from her former rock "boss," Man-O-War, the guitar player who holds her contract. Though Man-O-War legally "controls" Gina, it is clear that he is "the clown" (40) who merely receives the musical substance Gina feeds him, "giving him the meat and the bone that made him Man-O-War" (39). In this "other side" of the story of cyborg subjectivity, the power dynamics of gender are clearly marked, only, with subjectivity granted to the embodiment of the equivalence of Gibson's "cyberspace," Cadigan has turned the "cowboy" into a "clown," and focuses instead on the fundamental power of Gina's role as synner:

> you had to get everyone in the group dreaming the same way. You needed a synthesis, and for that you got a synthesizer . . . somebody—to channel your group through, to bump up their tube-fed little souls, to rock them and roll them the way they couldn't do themselves. And anyone could be a rock'n'roll hero then. Anyone! (39–40)

Although Gina "loves it," takes pride in her ability as a synner and has a clear sense of the importance of her role, Gina has run away from Man-O-War, and when she is kidnapped by an insignificant band called Misbegotten, she resists being forced to be their synner.

Misbegotten physically forces her to play the synner for their band: "Five against one and I couldn't push them away. Only, can you call it rape when you know you're going to like it" (38)? Here is the question that is begged by cyberpunk's concern with the bodily invasion of intimate technologies, but it can only be asked from the perspective of the entered subject. At first, Gina's phrasing of the question itself sounds like a refusal to acknowledge rape for what it is, and unpleasantly echoes that old sexist shibboleth that all women secretly "desire" rape. But as the passage continues, Gina's attitude shifts from resignation to a sense of pride/pleasure in her "synning" ability:

> Well, if I couldn't get away, then I'd give them the ride of their lives.
>
> The big boy faded in first, big and wild and too much badass to him. I reached out, held him tight, showing him. The beat from the night in the rain, I gave it to him, fed it to his heart and made him live it. Then came the lady, putting down the bass theme. She jittered, but mostly in the right places. (38)

In the end, Gina is able to "[give] them better than they deserved, and they knew that too . . . . They were never better" (38–39).

While we might still consider this a rape, the narrative's tone does not encourage us to see Gina as a victim, and Gina herself seems to be in control.

I think that, beyond the rape, what is being represented here is a construction of Jessica Benjamin's notion of an intersubjective relation which includes the idea that "the interior of the body and the space between bodies form an elusive pattern, a plane whose edge is ever-shifting" (94) which can allow for both "recognition in and by the exciting other, and the holding that allows the self to experience desire as truly inner" (96). In this scene from "Rock On," Gina does take pleasure from the band members' positions both inside and outside her self, and she is both recognized by the others, and able to hold them "inside." No one is objectified here; the breakdown of bodily boundaries between Gina and the band members is a blurring of subjects. But if her role as a synner affords her this intersubjective pleasure, then why does she want to run away from Man-O-War, and from synning altogether?

Her primary reason for running away from synning has to do with being used as an object; in a time when any old "clown" can be a "rock'n'roll hero" if s/he has the right synner, the mutual give and take between player and synner seems to be skewed in the direction of synners doing most of the giving. And Gina leaves Man-O-War the minute he says "I'll never let you go" (40); his claim of ownership reduces her to the status of object, and she is refusing to play into his domination. As Jessica Benjamin warns:

the idea of inner space or spatial representation of desire can be associated with subjectivity only when the interior is not merely an object to be discovered or a receptacle in which to put things . . . [this space] should be understood as a receptacle only insofar as it refers to the receptivity of the subject. (95)

If Gina cannot enact her receptivity as an agent, as a true subject of desire, she doesn't "want to be a synner, not for . . . anyone" (42).

In a world organized around the phallic economy of the desire for domination, Gina, as a synner, is objectified, and her body is entered without her consent/control. Rather than live as an objectified receptacle of music memory, Gina says instead, "I want to go to a cheesy bar and boogie my brains till they leak out the sockets" (42). Gina is clearly not ready, or even able, to leave her body behind in favor of transcending into a purely mental space. Sadly, despite constructing the possibility of intersubjectivity, Cadigan can present us with no utopian ideal of the cyborg body. As Man-O-War reminds Gina before he takes her "home," "'But all the bars are gone and all the bands. Last call was years ago; it's all up here now. All up here.' He tapped his temple" (42).

Conclusion

In these constructions of postmodern cyborgs, I've found that, despite some "fruitful couplings" and pleasurable blurring of boundaries between humans and technologies, none presents a subjectivity that lives up to Haraway's ideal. Gibson's male cyberpunks are still "seduced to wholeness" in their move toward a "disembodied view from everywhere," and Tiptree's and Cadigan's female cyberpunks are unable to maintain both "partiality" and "intimacy" in a world that operates under the "erotics of domination." These cyborgs might be post-a-lot-of-things, but they are not "post-gender."

I find myself in the fundamentally negative position Julia Kristeva recommends for feminist practice, "at odds with what already exists so that we may say 'that's not it' and 'that's still not it'" (137). Perhaps this is a useful position to take as a feminist who is unwilling to allow the question of sexual difference to "magically disappear" within the "dissolution" of the deconstructionist postmodern subject. As Teresa de Lauretis reasons, "if antihumanism so badly needs to claim feminism in its ranks, it is because of that epistemological priority which feminism has located in the . . . body" (de Lauretis 11). As we have seen, what is at stake for women in the deconstruction of the subject is more than a philosophical play with boundaries; what is at stake are the very terms under which we will know our bodies. The women writers of cyberpunk fiction show why we should not be in a hurry to leave those bodies behind.

On the other hand, Pat Cadigan's novel *Synners* (the novelistic extension of "Rock On") shows why feminist cultural critics should also not abandon the reading of subjectivities created by technologized bodies altogether. In lieu of a reading of the novel, I would like to close with Gina's final remarks to another character who has chosen a neo-Luddite rejection-of-all-technology reaction to the dilemmas I've been mapping here:

"The door only swings one way. Once it's out of the box, it's always too big to get back in. Can't bury that technology. All we can do is get on top of it and stay the fuck on top."

He shook his head. "Appropriate technology. That's how I live."

"Yah?. . . Think on this one. All *appropriate technology* hurt somebody. A whole lot of somebodies. Nuclear fission, fusion, the fucking Ford assembly line, the fucking airplane. *Fire* for Christ's sake. Every technology has its original sin. . . . Makes us original synners. And we still got to live with what we made." (435)

Notes

1. This article is a revised version of a paper delivered in the session on "Bodily Discursions" at the November 1991 Midwest MLA Conference in Chicago. My thanks to Deborah S. Wilson, Christine Laennec, and the reviewers at SUNY Press for their helpful suggestions toward revision.

A historical note is in order: much has happened since I first began this article in 1991, not the least of which has been a virtual explosion of critical work on science fiction + postmodernism + feminism, and on cyberpunk in particular. In 1991, Veronica Hollinger's article was the only other published article on cyberpunk I had access to (a few other early articles were later reprinted in *Storming the Reality Studio*), and I, along with many other critics, owe much to her first sophisticated establishment of a theoretical context within which to study these texts. Since 1991, much other work has emerged—some of it announcing that "cyberpunk is dead," much of it continuing to explore the convergence of methods and concerns between postmodernism and cyberpunk, little of it noting how gender is being left out of consideration—and in this article I have endeavored to come to terms with as much of it as time and space constraints allowed. Revision in such a context resembles nothing so much as "playing ball on running water."

2. Originally published as "A Manifesto for Cyborgs: Science, Technology, and Socialist Feminism in the 1980's" in *Socialist Review*, Vol. 15, No. 80, 1985, pp. 65–107. The essay has since been reprinted in a number of places. I will here be quoting from "A Cyborg Manifesto: Science, Technology, and Socialist Feminism in the Late Twentieth Century," in *Simians, Cyborgs, and Women*.

3. For example: Corea, et al, Eds. *Man-Made Women: How New Reproductive Technologies Affect Women*, 1987; Emily Martin, *The Woman*

in the Body: A Cultural Analysis of Reproduction, 1987; Irene Diamond, "Babies, Heroic Experts, and a Poisoned Earth" in *Reweaving the World*, Diamond and Orenstein, eds., 1990; Marina Benjamin, Ed. *A Question of Identity: Women, Literature, and Science*, 1993.

4. For example: Henry Louis Gates, Ed. "Race," *Writing, and Difference*, 1986; Hortense Spillers, "Mama's Baby, Papa's Maybe: An American Grammar Book" in *Diacritics*, Vol. 17, no. 2, 1987, pp. 65–81; Sandra Harding, Ed. *The "Racial" Economy of Science*, 1993.

5. For example: Kroker and Kroker, Eds. *Body Invaders*: "For we live under the sign of Foucault's prophecy that the bourgeois body is a descent into the empty site of a dissasociated ego, a 'volume in disintegration,' traced by language, lacerated by ideology, and invaded by the relational circuitry of the field of postmodern power" (20).

6. Some of these recent studies include: Lucie Armitt, *Where No Man Has Gone Before*, 1991; Marleen S. Barr, *Lost in Space*, 1993; Donawerth and Kolmerten, Eds., *Utopian and Science Fiction by Women*, 1994; Sarah Lefanu, *Feminism and Science Fiction*, 1989; and Robin Roberts, *A New Species*, 1993.

7. Since 1991, I have seen only two sustained discussions of the "problem" of gender in cyberpunk appear in print: Nicola Nixon's 1992 article "Cyberpunk: Preparing the Ground for Revolution or Keeping the Boys Satisfied?" notes cyberpunk's "complicity with '80s conservatism" (231), including an anxious repression of feminist gains and goals; and Jenny Wolmark's 1994 *Aliens and Others*, in Chapter 5, decides that "cyberpunk is marked . . . by unresolved anxiety about gender relations" and "cannot escape from a predominantly patriarchal view of social relations" (126).

8. I have chosen Gibson because he is considered to be the "quintessential" cyberpunk writer; Cadigan because she is the only woman included in the *Mirrorshades* anthology, and one of only three women included in the *Storming the Reality Studio* anthology; Tiptree because she may be the only woman writer before the mid-1980s "creation" of the cyberpunk genre whose work nonetheless fits the generic characteristics of cyberpunk. Obviously, there are many other science fiction works containing constructions of cyborgs, both before and since the advent of cyberpunk, but I am limiting my examination here to cyberpunk texts because of its current privileging in academic circles. As Haraway herself suggests, I intend to perform my readings from "within the belly of the beast."

9. Though Haraway warns against "pre-Oedipal symbiosis" as a grounding for cyborg subjectivity, and in fact is quite critical of psychoanalytic theory in the Manifesto, feminist versions of psychoanalytic

theory remain the most powerful stories for subjectivity we have, and I'm not sure Haraway herself offers any alternative site for subjectivity. Benjamin's theory of intersubjectivity is the least dependent on images of utopian pre-Oedipal fusion between mother and child; it is also a theory of subjectivity which suggests some interesting parallels to Irigaray's biologically based "placental economy."

10. For more examples of women's science fiction of this period, see Le Guin's "The World of Science Fiction" and Bonnie Zimmerman's "Feminist Fiction and the Postmodern Challenge," as well as the works listed in note 6 above.

11. Samuel Delany, in an interview with Takayuki Tatsumi, has also suggested that feminist science fiction can be seen as cyberpunk's "absent" (and repressed?) "mother." It is unfortunate that, while *Storming the Reality Studio* did a great service to critics in reprinting many hard-to-find early writings on cyberpunk, Delany's interview is conspicuously absent (repressed?) from this "casebook."

12. See Nicola Nixon's article for more on this topic.

9

WILL THE REEL WOMAN IN *BODY DOUBLE* PLEASE STAND UP?

Roberta Schreyer

A week after the film *Body Double* opened in New York in 1984, Nina Darnton's review of it headlined the controversy many viewers have long associated with De Palma's work: "Is Brian De Palma Crossing the Line between Art and Pornography?" Given both the film's explicit sexuality and its violence, most feminists would have to nod assent to her question. To demonstrate De Palma's fascination with violence, and frequently with violence directed against an unsuspecting female, Darnton proceeds to chart the history of De Palma's choice of weapons, from the icepick in *Murder a la Mode*, to a razor in *Dressed to Kill*, to a chainsaw in *Scarface*, and finally to an oversized electric drill in this controversial release. In *Body Double* the murderer stalks a beautiful woman, who has just performed an unusually explicit erotic dance, and impales her with an electric drill. The finishing touch is seen from below, as the drill bit whirls through the ceiling dripping blood. This scene, contends Darnton, crosses the line from art to pornographic titillation (Darnton 2).

Body Double is a fascinating and disturbing film for some of the same reasons Darnton's critique suggests, but I want to complicate her thesis by examining how "gender technologies" or the shaping of gender roles by ideology and language occurs within the Hollywood genres that *Body Double* incorporates into its screenplay. In the order of the film's diegesis these include the horror or vampire movie and the romantic melodrama engendered by boy-meets-girl and boy needs to rescue girl. Interspersed throughout *Body Double* are the presence of hardcore porn, porn stars, the presence of Hollywood with its fabulous homes, the fabled Rodeo

Drive, and fantasy as the catalysts for the process of production and the reproduction of meaning and desire in the viewer. Despite the violence that very nearly drove this viewer out of the theater and that lingers like the deferred action of a traumatic event in all my subsequent viewings of the film, I want to argue that *Body Double* exceeds the equation misogynistic hatred = female viola- tion/annihilation. The intentions behind the film and its represen- tation are more complex, contradictory, overdetermined, and, if possible, even more disturbing than the misogynist equation. There is a space for female desire and identification within the dis- course De Palma has set in motion: although the female space is not as large or obsessively constructed as it is for male subjectivity and identification, it is a possibility for the female spectator within the patriarchal hegemonic orchestration of virtually every scene in *Body Double.*

In both *Sisters* and *Dressed to Kill* De Palma organizes his psychological thrillers around characters in whose split conscious- ness there is a repressed double or other self that emerges in the course of the film as the agent of a homicidal fury frequently directed against women. The Jekyll-Hyde thematic is a familiar one to the psychological thriller, but De Palma shows a special fondness for it. Its implicit presence can be felt in Jake's career as a vampire in the movie-within-a-movie that opens and closes the main feature of Jake as voyeur and failed knight-errant. In *Body Double* De Palma's vision becomes more complex as the repressed assumes wider dimensions that include not only the voyeuristic hero who suffers from a claustrophobic fear of enclosed and womblike spaces, but extends to the culture at large replete with Hollywood hype, horror movies, television talk shows, and pornog- raphy whose content is always about victimization/objectification of the female. The topos of hero-as-voyeuristic-detective that De Palma inherited from Hitchcock's *Rear Window* and *Vertigo* assumes parodic dimensions as our hero, Jake Scully, becomes an actor in "independent, low budget" horror flicks and later a sophomoric actor in the "cum shot" of the pornographic epic *Body Talk.* (I will have more to say about the plethora of resonating "bodies" as my argument unfolds.) What unifies Jake's activities both on screen and off is obsession and sexual fascination with woman as "other"; yet as the grisly murder at the movie's dis- placed center proves, obsession with the feminine conceals mech- anisms of control, regulation, and finally misogynistic fury aimed at exterminating that mysterious female otherness. As the reflexive quality of *Body Double* implies (especially in its obligatory closing homage to Hitchcock's *Psycho*, but this time with Jake-the-vampire instead of Norman Bates in the bathroom), villains aren't the only ones who stalk unsuspecting females, so, at least in fantasy, does the average man—the man likely to go to a movie like *Body Double* in the first place. Freud first defined scopophilia or love-of-looking as an autoerotic instinct in his "Instincts and Their Vicissitudes" essay in 1915. Scopophilia is institutionalized by the cinema's dominant regime, its commerical ideology and consumerist traffic in women who are alternately fetishized objects of desire or part-objects: i.e., breasts, face, or whatever fragment of the anatomy may be in demand. *Body Double* insists upon the anatomization/fetishization repeatedly: in Holly's response to Jake's compliment, in Gloria's/Holly's exhibitionism, and in the final shot of blood streaking down a woman's breast. Anatomization is clearest in Gloria's penetrated corpse holding the entire framework of the film together. Given the scopophilia of a male audience and male cinematic apparatus, where is the woman spectator in all this?

A partial answer finds the continuity between the genres of romantic melodrama, horror, and pornography as they are portrayed in this film, and reveals their workings as institutionalized rituals within patriarchy for domesticating the female body and its subversive *jouissance*. The insistent equation of woman with spectacle and man with vision elides and obscures the real narrative of the male subject shocked into a visual confrontation with what Lacanian psychoanalysis terms man's own "lack." Instead, the cinematic apparatus functions as the fetish does to simultaneously reveal and conceal lack, not in the object of vision, but in the ideologically constructed fictions of male coherence and plenitude enshrined in cinema's most popular genres—horror and pornography. The unusual degree of reflexivity in *Body Double* makes cinema and its ideological operations the interior of the diegesis in a way that foregrounds the lack upon which cinema as an institution is founded.

Jake Scully: Vampire, Voyeur, Hero

After its opening shot of the generic southern California palm trees, the camera quickly establishes Jake's lack: his claustrophobia in the vampire's grave/daytime bed immobilizes him in terror before the camera so that he is unable to prey upon his food/sexual partners. We never learn directly why Jake is susceptible to hysterical panic, but in a later scene with his acting coach we learn that as a child he hid from his older brothers behind a refrigerator where he became stuck. Unable to cry out for fear that his brothers would laugh at him, Jake has reached his thirties still victim to a panic that will render him powerless at crucial moments of the narrative, as it does when he pursues the mysterious Indian into the womblike tunnel in pursuit of Gloria Revelle's stolen purse. Again his hysteria will strike when he is trying to save Holly Body from being buried alive; his mastery of his fear in a moment of combat with the murderous villain will, of course, cathartically free him of what may be an infantile or Oedipal fixation. It seems that De Palma uses this flaw to signify his hero's anti-heroic status and his commonality with the viewing public and to reflect the moral ambiguity and confusion inherent in the voyeur-heroes of *Rear Window* and *Vertigo* from whom he is descended. Freud, however, made interesting connections between phobias as a class of "anxiety-hysterias" and phobia's hysterical symptoms as a manifestation of the fantasy scenarios that the subject creates during autoerotic activity, scenarios later repressed for fear of discovery and castration. The link between dread of castration and the taboo on autoerotic activity as part of the logic of the unconscious inscribed in *Body Double* need to be kept in mind if we are to make any sense at all of the punishment inflicted on the "transgressive" Gloria Revelle who ostensibly "revels" in satisfying her own sexuality. The origins of claustrophobia as a form of hysteria tied to autoeroticism is consistent with Jake's panic whenever he is in a private space, (often one that he lies in horizontally,) and when the acting teacher's response to his phobia is "you're a baby." What I want to stress are the notions of lack and defensive adaptation to the threat of castration—looking—inscribed in the hero's characterization. Film theorists Teresa de Lauretis and Laura Mulvey have seen lack in terms of castration in the male subject which necessitates a female as mirror and spectacle rather than as a subject in her own right. In this argument woman is both the ground for the representation and nowhere present with her own specificity outside the male gaze that idealizes or degrades her. In later discussion of Gloria Revelle, Holly Body, and the body double mechanism, I will argue that such a feminist argument is and is not true to De Palma's film, arguing instead for a specular instance of subversion of the dominant code in the improvisational freedom De Palma granted Melanie Griffith (Holly) in allowing her to invent a character outside normative preconceptions of who a porn star is and what she is apt to do and say. If Jake's mysterious phobia has links with his sexuality, an interesting parallel links him to the woman he watches masturbate quite openly. Freud argued that scopophilia was an "active" manifestation of the autoerotic, the predecessor in fact to the more "passive" scopophilia of exhibitionism (Freud 130). If we recall that Jake is an actor as well as a voyeur then the ambiguity, contradictions, and heterogeneity in his positioning before the gaze and the object of desire becomes more obvious. The illusory unity of his gaze, able only to mis-apprehend representations or flee from them in phobic avoidance, is the narrative vehicle for De Palma's assembly of all the mirrors cinema provides for the subject's *méconnaissance*.

The mirror phase, according to Jacques Lacan, is a stage in the constitution of the human individual between the ages of six and eighteen months. Though still in a state of powerlessness and motor incoordination, the infant jubilantly anticipates on an imagi-nary plane the apprehension and mastery of its bodily unity. This imaginary unification is actually a misrecognition or *méconnais-sance* brought about by means of identification with the image of the counterpart as total *Gestalt*; it is exemplified concretely by the experience in which the child perceives its own reflection in the mirror.

One of the most crucial mirrors for his and the audience's identification or disavowal is the female body. A more overt con-nection, however, links Jake with castration and feminine *jouis-sance*. Returning home after his claustrophobia attack, Jake discovers that the ecstatic noises he hears coming from the rear of the house belong to his wife positioned astride her lover. Recalling the memory to his new friend, Sam Bouchard, he confides that she was "glowing," an adjective Sam greets derisively as he admits that his wife never glowed for him. I hear a subtext of male wonder, resentment, and dread in this exchange that is part of the uncon-scious logic threading its way throughout the film. Moments earlier we had learned that Jake's acting credits included *Vampire's Kiss* and *The Taming of the Shrew*. Both texts are transformations of the feminine by a male agent, although Shakespeare's text at least has the possibility of a woman's ironic relation to the transformative effects of male discourse and the male gaze. Domestication of the female subject is at least covertly embedded in De Palma's concern with male agency and recuperating its potency. The enigma of female pleasure haunts *Body Double* in the image of the adulterous wife, the masturbating woman Jake peers at through a telescope, in Holly Body's fastidiousness about what she will and will not do on-screen for the camera, and in the final repetitive scene of the movie where yet another "body double" appears do the nude scene with Jake and instructs him in how to caress her breasts. While *Body Double* takes male desire seriously, the quest to establish knowledge about the identity of the masturbating female, and to reestablish Jake's authority, potency, and masculinity, the case it establishes for the female participant in this drama of substitution and desire is very different.

Pornography is the vehicle for Jake's reintegration as a competent male hero; for the freedom its fantasies offer him allows him to begin to move beyond his claustrophobic inhibitions. In this context De Palma is concerned with pornography and its liberating effects for the male consumer and is intent on refuting feminist arguments against pornography as an institution for the subjugation of women. The case he builds in *Body Double* for empowerment of the viewer of pornography is an interesting one with suggestive implications for women who also find pornography erotically enhancing rather than degrading to women.

Hollywood: Gloria and Holly Body

Jake is offered a place to live in exchange for housesitting a spectacular "house" atop the Hollywood hills, a house complete with rotating circular bed and telescope, which rival any *Playboy* reader's dream. Sam leaves for a theatrical tour after instructing Jake in the real view the house offers: a beautiful neighbor who regularly dances in front of a mirror in diamonds and high heels as she ritualistically excites herself and masturbates. On first viewing this scene in a theater I was amazed by the audacity of the shot and initially relieved to see that the cinematic apparatus recognized the autonomy of female sexuality apart from the usual romantic formulas, even as I knew that the cinematic code of woman-as-spectacle was being rigidly enforced. (In a short time I was to learn how naive my response was.) Jake, too, becomes a ritualistic consumer of this rite, and a few days later follows the woman, Gloria, to Rodeo Drive in what he believes is an effort to protect her from an Indian he believes wants to harm her. En route to a beach front motel to meet her lover after her husband has physically abused her, Gloria stops at a lingerie store to buy new underwear. Watching her activity through a store window, Jake is assumed to be a voyeur by the saleswoman and security personnel. Convinced now that a grotesque Indian is following Gloria Revelle, Jake pauses to retrieve her old panties from a trash can and stuff them into his pocket. In a later police interrogation where the concealed panties cast doubt upon Jake's motives in observing and following Gloria, Jake is unable to explain the nature of his desire, leaving the police to conclude that Jake's fetishism, voyeurism, and mistimed interventions in Gloria's life undoubtedly make him responsible for at least some of the violence directed against her.

But is this all a scenario of unconsummated passion with Jake on the beach following Gloria who is being pursued by a sinister Indian? Finally after a long interval with no spoken dialogue, a reflection of De Palma's belief in imaging rather than language as the vehicle for narrativity, Jake confronts Gloria on the beach to tell her she is being followed. A chase after the Indian ensues, which leads Jake to the menacing tunnel he cannot endure because of claustrophobia, and Gloria leads him from the tunnel. A long kiss with 360-degree camera pan derived from *Vertigo* follows, and Gloria hastily leaves. That night Jake watches through the telescope only to see the Indian in Gloria's bedroom robbing her safe. Gloria enters in a bathrobe and the Indian proceeds to strangle her. Jake runs to the house in an effort to save her while the grisly murder with an electric drill takes place. De Palma insisted in directing the murder on a terrified but essentially passive Gloria who is impaled by the drill, in a scene shot through the angle of the killer's leg, enormous drill-as-phallus between them, standing above the prone woman. All the cinematic conventions and patriarchal codes conspire to punish the offending woman who seeks her own sexual satisfaction as *penis normalis dosim repetatur* is brutally enacted in this scene. The viciousness of the scene seems proportionate to the degree of eroticism displayed in the earlier scenes. Watching the film later, I saw how carefully the audience is prevented from caring about Gloria as anything other than another object of desire. She speaks seldom and only once for any length on the phone; we know nothing about her apart from her wealth, her unseen lover, and her brutal husband. What we know best about Gloria is her erotic dance that incites desire in Jake and, presumably, in the audience. Her non-personhood becomes even more marked when we and Jake discover that the dance was not Gloria's, but a body double—Holly Body.

It is hard to overlook De Palma's symbolic equation between Hollywood, the cinema's traditional home, and the pornographic empire presided over by the porn queen who is the real object of Jake's desire rather than the falsely eroticized, but now very dead, Gloria. The synecdochic equation between the woman's body and both legitimate and pornographic cinema cannot be missed as *Body Double* foregrounds movie sets, casting calls that may attract respectable actors and actresses, and the look that both camera and audience direct toward images in a complex system of identification, inscription, and desire. The echolalia between Hollywood and Holly Body could scarcely be clearer.

In Jake's quest for the one true image that will authenticate his imagined relation to Gloria and to his career he discovers only the endless circularity of body doubles: substitutions or repetitions with which he began his quest. In postmodern fashion, De Palma suggests that the real object of quest in an authentic relation to an object, an other, or even to the self is a *mise en abime* of displacement and illusion. What De Palma does seem certain of is the connection between popular cinema and pornography. The film theorist Yann Lardeau has argued that cinema is the pornographic medium par excellence. In the pornographic film, the camera close-ups exhibit the woman's sex as the object of desire and

> the definitive place of jouissance only in order to ward off castration, "to keep the subject from his own lack": "too heavily marked as a term—always susceptible of castration—the phallus unrepresentable. . . . The porno film is constructed on the disavowal of castration, and its operation of truth is a fetishistic operation. (Lardeau, qtd. in de Lauretis, 26)

Mainstream or patriarchal cinema repeats the same operations of fragmenting and fabricating the female subject in its camera maneuvering and light and color effects as the cinematic apparatus reproduces in its representations alienated social relations and sadomasochistic sexuality. It was widely reported that De Palma almost hired a real porn actress, Annette Lavers, to play the role of Holly, and Lavers did instruct Melanie Griffith in the mechanics of a masturbatory routine she used in her own movies. De Palma's penchant for a kind of documentary authenticity in making pornography so prominent a feature in his own work reflected what he identifies as the audience demand for a glimpse inside a tabooed underworld and allowed him to comment, however obliquely, on the workings of his own industry (Dworkin, 39). With the introduction of Holly and the milieu in which she works, De Palma demonstrates that the line between voyeurism in the consumption of pornography and voyeurism in the consumption of erotica may well be hopelessly blurred.

Up to and including the murder, the film recounts the cultural archeplot of power. There is power, however ineffectual, on the side of the hero, and there is powerlessness incarnated in the victim-object. What Holly adds is skepticism, refusal to meet any and every demand even if she is in the "skin trade" and a deafening storm of words to undo the unnatural silence surrounding the film's presentation of Gloria. She is a parodic porn queen, skilled in the one-liner and put-down. With her entry the film's tone of savage violation becomes a compound of black humor and farce. She remains woman-as-spectacle but articulate woman is no longer as object-like, as passive. Remembering my first viewing of the film, I think it would be too much to see this atypical characterization of a porn queen as an internal subversion of the dominant Oedipal narrative concerned with Jake. But Melanie Griffith does manage to recuperate a space for female identification, even if the identification is not with her occupation or the rescue fantasy acted out by Jake on her behalf but with her resistance to male manipulation. Awakening after the males' battle at the gravesite, she is blissfully uncomprehending of the situation but in enough control of her fate to refuse Jake's touch, arguing instead that "I've seen you on late night TV. You're a necrophiliac."

Surrounding his suspense thriller with transgressive cinematic creations—vampire films and pornography—De Palma represents to the audience its simultaneous fascination with excess and with disavowal of lack, with sexual ambiguity and excess in androgynous vampires and the phantasmagoric gymnastics of pornography. While the violent murder seems misogynistic, and I have argued it is a result of male fear and envy of female sexuality, it is also a staple in both the cinematic and literary canons. Although Edgar Allan Poe argued in "The Philosophy of Composition" that the death of a beautiful woman was "the most poetical topic in the world," I find it confusing to argue, as Darnton does, that violence is "pornographic." Little consensus exists as to the definition of the pornographic or the effects it has on the viewer. One woman's pornographic subjugation to male power is another woman's erotic enthrallment before the demands of anarchic sexual instincts. I would characterize my own response, as I have done earlier, as one of horrified shock, not least because of the close conjunction of explicit autoeroticism with savage extermination. I do know that titillation was a compound in my reaction, and that I still find it difficult to sum up my reaction to *Body Double* in a phrase; at the very least it was characterized by double identification with the male subject active in trying to establish some epistemology that would allow for active "seeing" rather than solely sexually motivated gazing and by identification with the female object of his gaze. A female spectator may even enact a narcissistic or desiring relation with the image of a woman uninhibitedly masturbating, only to find her own eroticism repressed and punished in Gloria's fate. Certainly this was a factor in my reaction to the film. Whether or not she can recuperate that earlier freedom in Holly's defiant rhetoric or cinematic status remains problematic. The most likely avenue for the female viewer's identification is Oedipalization similar to Jake's own, a fluid identification with the vicissitudes of the male protagonist's quest, given the insistent emphasis De Palma gives Jake's detective pursuits.

The movie remains difficult to classify and poses interesting questions about viewer response, the space for a female spectatorship, and pornography's relations to the archeplots of power and the taboo. The dominant cinematic apparatus often compels female spectators to take a position where both identification and dissociation with the representations sanctioned by patriarchal heterosexist ideology is operative. John Berger's formulation of the female dilemma still rings true as I find myself seeking an elsewhere of vision before the conundrum of woman-as-spectacle, wishing for a body double who will spare me from psychic assault. Berger writes, "Men look at women. Women watch themselves being looked at. This determines not only most relations between men and women but also the relation of women to themselves. The surveyor of woman in herself is male: the surveyed female. Thus she turns herself into an object—and most particularly, an object of vision: a sight." (Berger, 41) Further, as Carol Clover argues, horror and the pornographic are the two "body" genres devoted to audience arousal and stimulation of archaic feelings of the uncanny and the sexual. As she makes clear, the real target of these genres in depicting the body in threat and the body in sex is actually our witnessing body. Hitchcock left an explicit statement of the equation victim = audience in the margins of his shooting script for the shower scene in *Psycho*, a scene, as I have noted, that De Palma incorporates with interesting changes into *Body Double*. Hitchcock wrote, "The slashing. An impression of a knife slashing, as if tearing at the very screen, ripping the film" (Spoto

431). In Jake's shower scene as vampire preying upon seduced female, the body double is called in for a camera close-up of her breasts while Holly tells the original actress that now she'll get lots of dates as a result of this movie. The credits unfold as we watch a trickle of blood run down the exposed breast, presumably from a bitten neck, but the camera's insistent focus on the breast suggest that for all the film's insistent attention to bodies, the real locus of the Oedipal narrative is with the breast and with Jake's cry of "Oh, mother" as he rushes to Gloria's aid. Linda Williams writes that "like dreams and hallucinations, cinema facilitates a temporary regression on the part of the viewing subject to a psychically earlier, pre-Oedipal mode of merger in which the separation between the body and world is not well defined and in which 'representations' whether of the unconscious or of the film 'are taken as perceptions'" (Williams, 44).

As a process, identification for the viewer of a film like *Body Double* is not gender exclusive. Roger B. Rollins explains that "common experience suggests that it is possible for a male to identify with a Madame Bovary, a Scarlett O'Hara, or even a Linda Lovelace as it is for a female to identify with a Raskolnikov, a Rhett Butler, or a Harry Rheems. Identification is so free floating that children can identify with adults (*Dirty Harry*), adults with children (*The Wizard of Oz*'s Dorothy), anyone with animals ("Benji") or even machines (Herbie, the Disney Volkswagen)" (Rollins 8).

Thus it is possible for the female viewer to glimpse anxiously pleasurable strategies of empowerment within Jake Scully's resolutely voyeuristic gaze in *Body Double* because of his alignment with the subversive posturings of Holly Body in De Palma's amalgamation of genres —romantic melodrama and hard-core pornography. As Linda Williams's eloquent anticensorship study frames the conundrum of viewership, "Hard core is not the enemy. Neither are fantasies which by definition are based on unruly desires rather than politically correct needs. The one speaks to us plainly about bodies and organs; the other describes the often circuitous roles these bodies and organs can play in satisfying our desires. Pornography speculates about both" (Williams 277).

V

DISEASE IN THE BODY POLITIC

10

WOMEN AND AIDS: BODILY REPRESENTATIONS, POLITICAL REPERCUSSIONS[1]

Susanmarie Harrington

In 1987, Simon Watney's article "The Spectacle of AIDS" detailed the way homosexual men had become a touchstone for British fears about HIV and AIDS. Hysterical press coverage of AIDS had created a "public masque in which we witness the corporal punishment of the 'homosexual body,' identified as the enigmatic and indecent source of an incomprehensible, voluntary resistance to the unquestionable governance of marriage, parenthood, and property" (83). In the United States, as in England, public discourse about AIDS grew out of and in turn has amplified fears about homosexuality; rather than conveying information about how to prevent HIV transmission, the discourse offers moralizing discussions about behavior. Thus the "facts" about AIDS appearing in media discussions simply reflect and reproduce hatred and stereotypes, while speaking "confidently on behalf of the 'general public,' viewed as a homogenous entity organized into discrete family units over and above all the fissures and conflicts of both the social and the psychic" (Watney 73). In the face of this pressure to maintain the fiction of the "general public," he warned that we are "witnessing the precipitation of a moralized bio-politics of potentially awesome power," which seeks to destroy distinctions between private and public, and place the "family" as the central point of reference for social structures. This political discourse can have disastrous consequences, for it prevents rational attention to epidemiological knowledge that can be used to prevent HIV transmission, and encourages a callous response to the hundreds of thousands whose lives have been affected by HIV.

Watney's analysis of the AIDS discourse in Britain in the mid-1980s rings as true years later as it did at the time of first writing. His description of "an essentially modernizing universalizing discourse of 'family values,' 'standards of decency' and so on" could have been written in response to Patrick Buchanan's vitriolic address at the 1992 Republican National Convention. It is true that there have been some prominent signs of attitude shifts about AIDS, shifts which reflect an increasing sense that AIDS is a public health problem that needs to be responded to with compassion and education appropriate to different age and social groups, such as teens, women, gay men. The Ryan White Act, although it has never been fully funded, provides federal funds for AIDS education and prevention, and Bob Hattoy, Elizabeth Glaser, and Mary Fisher, all people living with AIDS, addressed both the Republican and Democratic 1992 National Conventions and called for prompt and compassionate government response to the epidemic. Nonetheless, the HIV/AIDS pandemic remains a site of political and social conflict, and the bodies of people with AIDS have become a prime symbol in the conflict.

In the United States, widespread attention to a particular body with AIDS first grew in response to Kimberly Bergalis, the Florida woman who became infected with HIV after a visit to her dentist. Because her infection has never been explained, she crystallized fears that AIDS could creep into the lives of "ordinary" Americans, the "general public" so threatened by AIDS. Pictures of Kimberly Bergalis showed the nation the debilitating progression of the disease, and news reports described her symptoms in great detail, an unusual feature of AIDS reporting. Bergalis was not the first person with AIDS to have made national news—Rock Hudson's final illness received international press attention, and Ryan White, the Indiana boy who had been kept out of school in Kokomo, had also received widespread attention. But Hudson's homosexuality, perceived by many to be at odds with the Hollywood roles he had played, received more press attention than the particulars of his illness, and White's case was covered because of the political and educational policy issues it raised. Some coverage may have mentioned, generally, the medical aspects of AIDS, but the illness itself was not the object of discussion. AIDS memoirs, such as Paul Monette's *Borrowed Time*, often detail the physical progress of AIDS in great detail, but the popular press has not attended to the manifestations of opportunistic infections in the same way. Although *People* published a long article in which Ryan White's last days were chronicled with some attention to his failing health, the coverage of Bergalis stands out for the detail with which reporters covered her symptoms. *People* reporter Meg Grant's retrospective on Bergalis, for instance, focused as much on Bergalis's symptoms as on her fight for protective legislation.

This foregrounding of Bergalis's decaying body became a symbol of "fear and rage," Abigail Trafford noted in the *Washington Post*, and set the stage for the AIDS body to act as a lightning rod for public fear. Although competing symbols emerged in later dis-course—pictures and speeches of Elizabeth Glaser, for instance, depicted an apparently healthy woman seeking to disrupt the rhetoric of blame that blossomed around Bergalis—the body of Kimberly Bergalis and the discourse her infection spawned remain potent symbols in the national AIDS discourse.

Bergalis had, I will argue, a profound and lasting impact on the way the U.S. debate about AIDS was constructed in terms of guilt and blame. In order to understand this impact, it is neces-sary to examine the ways in which language functions in the debate about AIDS. To explore the ways in which the rhetoric of blame percolates though AIDS discourse on many levels, I will examine the presentation of AIDS information by Bergalis herself, by news reports about her, and by those testifying and speaking in Congress; I will also examine the ways in which AIDS is presented in the popular press for women, since the political rhetoric of AIDS is echoed in subtle—and dangerous—forms in publications for women.[2] Taken together, these different sites of conflict about AIDS are a laboratory wherein popular passions, prejudices, and epidemiological factors can be examined. As time passes, Bergalis is less and less frequently mentioned in public discussions of AIDS, but it is crucial that we understand the ways in which her case influenced later public debate. When I first became interested in this subject, Robert Dornan, one of the key figures in the Bergalis discourse, was a representative from California who was hardly nationally known, and Jesse Helms, another advocate for Bergalis, was a powerful senator seemingly destined to serve out his career in the minority party. As I prepare this essay for publication, Dornan is announcing his candidacy for the presidency of the United States, and Helms and other conservatives hold the majority in the United States Congress. Although Kimberly Bergalis is no longer in the center of AIDS debate, her legacy shapes the terms of debate. The rhetoric of blame and guilt seen in the debate about the wisdom of mandatory HIV-testing of health care workers may now be found in the debate on welfare reform, for example; we must understand the logic of this rhetoric in order to understand and shape current political debates about AIDS and other matters.

As these debates unfold, we understand AIDS in large part through the language used to describe it; the way we characterize AIDS affects cultural and political responses to it; furthermore, language perpetuates attitudes about AIDS. As Paula Treichler notes, "the very nature of AIDS is constructed through language" (31). The "AIDS body," too, is constructed through language, and the debate about AIDS often depends on the assumption that if the gay body (and gay sex) could somehow be contained, HIV transmission would end. Angela Wall's examination of the Surgeon General's mailing on AIDS reveals precisely this logic and demonstrates its consequences: epidemiological information is obscured or not presented at all. Yet this constraining rhetoric of blame is only one of many discourses that explain and construct AIDS differently: AIDS is, depending on who is speaking, a lifestyle issue, the natural consequence of immoral behavior, a gay disease, a drug users' disease, a viral disease, a public health challenge, a plague. The implications of all these discourses create "a nexus where multiple meanings, stories, and discourses intersect and overlap, reinforce, and subvert one another" (Treichler 42). Treichler explores the ways these meanings "write" the gay male body, and Wall explores the ways these meanings "write" gay sex; these meanings also "write" the bodies of people with AIDS in ways that stress the tension between the beauty of innocent youth and the evils still associated with AIDS in the popular imagination.

This focus on language is not to say, of course, that AIDS is not a very real phenomenon affecting millions of people worldwide. The medical problems associated with HIV are all too real. But AIDS itself is a syndrome, a category created by doctors and scientists, and the many meanings of AIDS are created through language use and policy implementation. AIDS is both "an epidemic of a transmissible lethal disease and an epidemic of meanings of signification. Both epidemics are equally crucial for us to understand, for, try as we may to treat AIDS as 'an infectious disease' and nothing more, meanings continue to multiply wildly at an extraordinary rate" (Treichler 32). As these meanings multiply, it becomes increasingly difficult to untangle the social from the political from the medical.

This tangle of meanings is nowhere more evident than in the discourse surrounding Kimberly Bergalis. Bergalis is the most prominent example of a curious phenomenon that has emerged in the United States. Even as discourse about homosexual men remains prominent in debates about AIDS, the rhetorical landscape has changed somewhat, in ways that bear careful examining. The white, middle-class woman with AIDS has become another touchstone for fears about AIDS. In many respects the body of a woman with AIDS has become the discursive site Watney foretold: this figure represents, paradoxically, the spectre of HIV spreading unchecked through the "general" population, and the simultaneous promise of protection from HIV, the promise that safe barriers can be found to protect the uninfected. The Bergalis case illustrates how the white female body functions in the construction of attitudes about AIDS in the United States. Regrettably, Kimberly Bergalis came to symbolize a view of AIDS that serves to reinforce the notion that AIDS is a disease of Them and not Us, one which can only affect Us through some unpredictable tragedy that we must erect costly barriers to prevent.

Linda Singer's *Erotic Warfare* provides a helpful framework for the analysis of women's symbolic role in AIDS discourse. Singer traces the historically specific operation of what she calls "epidemic logic," noting:

> as metaphors of sickness and health come to dominate the representation of the social, we are confronted by an ever increasing number of cancers, viruses infecting the body politic through mechanisms of contagion and communicability. In order to represent a phenomenon as socially undesirable, be it divorce, drug use, single motherhood, teenage pregnancy, one need only call it epidemic (27).

This practice is more than a rhetorical flourish, for invoking the metaphor of epidemic creates its own logic, which in turn has political and policy repercussions. Since an epidemic is something that must be controlled and contained, the pervasiveness of the metaphor functions as "political logic . . . [and] social rationality" (27).[3] Singer explores this epidemic logic, seeing it in, for example, the calls for quarantining and testing of people "at risk" for HIV. This logic functions as tool, according to Singer, for the conservation of certain forms of hegemonic authority as well as the propagation of an ideology marked by buzzwords such as "family values." The rhetoric surrounding Kimberly Bergalis offers a telling case study of the functioning of epidemic logic.

Kimberly Bergalis made news headlines instantly in 1990 when it was announced that she had AIDS. While the precise mode of her infection has never been ascertained, her case and four others were linked to her dentist, Dr. David Acer. When he treated Bergalis, Acer was working within Centers for Disease Control (CDC) guidelines for disease control; these cases of infection have thus remained a mystery to epidemiologists, who have never been able to pinpoint how HIV was transmitted during a routine dental procedure. This unusual case received great media attention. Bergalis was consistently represented as the consummate victim: a young, beautiful student, a loving and loved daughter, who never had sex, hardly ever dated, and studied hard. Initial coverage depicted her as the last person anyone would ever have expected to contract HIV. Her parents were devastated and resigned, although according to her father, "Her sickness would have been easier to accept if she'd been a slut or a drug user. But she had everything right" (Johnson 77). Coverage in *People* showed Bergalis at home with her family, thoughtful but not especially angry or bitter. "I don't think he ever meant for this to happen," she said of Dr. David Acer (Johnson 78). She further noted her wish to have a positive impact on society as a result of her illness, foreshadowing her later work to promote legislation requiring HIV testing for health care workers.

The progression of Bergalis's illness was widely documented in videotaped and still pictures that showed her markedly thinner, laying listlessly on her parents' couch. By April 1991, Bergalis was obviously physically weakened, and wrote a letter to Florida health authorities which her family released for publication in late June. This letter, obviously a highly personal response to her own illness, illustrates and enacts many of the rhetorical strategies and cultural beliefs discussed above. Bergalis's discourse crystallizes many of the issues in AIDS debates. Her letter opens with a description of symptoms:

> I have lived to see my hair fall out, my body lose over 40 pounds, blisters on my sides. I've lived to go through nausea and vomiting, continual night sweats, chronic fevers of 103–104 that don't go away anymore. . . . I lived through the fear of whether or not my liver has been completely destroyed by DDI and other drugs . . . I lived to see white fungus grow all over the inside of my mouth, the back of my throat, my gums and now my lips. It looks like white fur and it gives you atrocious breath. Isn't that nice? (in Helms S9477)

Especially in combination with the photographic representations of her illness, Bergalis's description offers a moving commentary on the physical devastation AIDS can cause. The list of symptoms effectively documents the multitude of ways HIV can affect the body, each symptom adding to the rhetorical impact. Towards the end of the description her shift to direct address ("it gives you atrocious breath") invites the reader into her illness, conflating Bergalis and the unknown reader, inviting us to speculate on how thrush, the "white fungus" Bergalis describes, would feel on our lips. The sarcastic rhetorical question at the end of the paragraph ("isn't that nice?") draws us in even more.

The final portion of Bergalis's letter reflects the tendency to respond to AIDS by finding someone to blame for infection. While the first step in response to any pandemic should be to identify the cause of the illness and the mode of transmission, responses to AIDS have tended to focus more on identifying moral causes for illness rather than viral ones. When Bergalis asks, "Who do I blame? Do I blame myself?" she opens the issue of moral culpability for her illness, constructing the reader as someone who assumes that the establishment of blame is the first step in analyzing the epidemic, as though we have asked her, "who is to blame here?" In answer to the question, Bergalis replies:

I sure don't [blame myself]. I never used IV drugs, never slept with anyone and never had a blood transfusion. I blame Dr. Acer and every single one of you bastards. Anyone that *knew* Dr. Acer was infected and had full-blown AIDS and stood by not doing a damn thing about it. You are all just as guilty as he was. You've ruined my life and my family's. I forgive Dr. Acer because I believe the disease affected his mind. He wasn't able to think properly and he continued to practice. (in Helms S9477)

The release of this letter galvanized efforts to enact legislation that would restrict the practices of HIV-infected health care workers and institute mandatory HIV-testing programs for them. Bergalis's indictment of Acer and the "bastards" who ignored this situation is a clear statement of the position that personal immorality is a fundamental part of the etiology of AIDS (see Wall, 229–30; 235– 37, for a more complete presentation of this point). One of the interesting aspects of this portion of her letter is the way in which, in the public view, the moral responsibility for Bergalis' infection is shared by not only Acer and Florida health officials who oversee and license medical professionals, but by the generalized "you" of the letter's audience. The previous paragraph had seemed to draw the reader into an identification with Bergalis, but in this paragraph, the you shifts: suddenly it refers to "bastards" who are complicit with authorities who simply stood by allowing a tragedy to unfold.

Perhaps the most striking element of Bergalis's letter, and indeed of her family's response to her illness, is the desire to find someone to blame for it. This response is a normal, human response: in the face of any tragedy, we seek to find a cause or even a scapegoat. This response has colored many responses to AIDS. Watney sees the rhetoric of AIDS going beyond this need to find a scapegoat: the compelling and persistent nature of this discourse appeals to "deep psychic anxieties that run far beneath the tangible divisions of the social formation" (74). AIDS, as it forces us to confront cultural attitudes about sex, sexuality, public health, and privacy, among other things, appears to threaten the structures labeled as "family," or "nation." One cultural response to this perceived threat is to defend against it by regulating morality. In the service of that end, epidemic logic requires powerful symbols of the threat. Kimberly Bergalis functions as one such symbol, and her remarks thus became a powerfully effective focus for conservative forces leading the fight to contain HIV by containing what they perceive to be immoral behavior.

The most obvious way in which Bergalis's remarks feed into epidemic logic is in the way her case was a catalyst for the movement to contain the epidemic, at least in part, through mandatory testing of health care workers. A desire to manage and suppress the epidemic is clear in Bergalis's position that Florida health authorities ought to have done something to prevent this from happening. The raw emotional appeal of Bergalis's letter is undeniable. Yet a more rational logic comes to a different conclusion. While responding compassionately to the individuals involved, it is still possible to view Bergalis against the larger picture of the epidemic, in which one anomalous infection out of more than one million infections in the United States alone is not the case on which public policy should be based. Statistically, Bergalis's case is an outlier, a case of interest for the epidemiological challenge it poses, but not a case suitable for the basis of national policy. As C. Everett Koop, then surgeon general, asserted in his Congressional testimony, the "Florida case is too bizarre to be helpful in determining policy" (Hearings 56). Educational materials and prevention policies that address greater numbers of people will have the greatest long-term public health benefits, as Angela Wall argues elsewhere in this volume.

The rhetoric of blame became even more pronounced in Bergalis's 1991 testimony before the House Subcommittee on Health and the Environment at hearings about the Kimberly Bergalis Patient and Health Provider Protection Act, which would have mandated HIV testing for all health care workers. Bergalis was quite ill at the time of the hearing and could speak only briefly:

> I would like to say that AIDS is a terrible disease that we must take seriously. I did nothing wrong, yet I am being made to suffer like this. My life has been taken away. Please enact legislation so that no other patient or health care provider will have to go through the hell that I have. Thank you. (Hearings 131)

The rhetorical structure of these remarks differs in some significant ways from her letter; in this more formal setting, she is less angry, but her claim that she "did nothing wrong" outraged many AIDS activists. Implicit in her disavowal of wrong-doing is acceptance of the notion that AIDS is punishment for sin. Just below the surface hovers the notion that ethics explains the etiology of AIDS. However, the passive construction ("my life has been taken away") elides the agent responsible for her death. Blame is diffused, although after months of media coverage there could be little doubt whom she considered to be at fault.

George Bergalis, Kimberly's father, testified after his daughter, calling her "God's messenger on Earth." In his remarks he almost disclaimed any authority to speak, noting, "I am not a medical professional. I am not a scientist. I am not a politician, a civil libertarian or a homosexual. But I am a father who is profoundly enraged by the impending loss of his daughter, a loss that was preventable" (Hearings 131). This list serves to supply the elision in Kimberly Bergalis's passive construction, naming those responsible for her illness. As he told the House committee, Kimberly is "all of Congress' shame because of the fact that she is the result of your unwillingness or inability to deal with this monster that you created: the HIV virus and AIDS disease which is the result of it" (Hearings 131).

Parts of such rhetoric are certainly appealing: conservatives and liberals alike can agree with Kimberly Bergalis's claim that the government should take AIDS seriously, and the raw emotion in their remarks cannot be denied. Their remarks are even in some senses reminiscent of other attacks on the federal government's lack of response to AIDS (a criticism frequently leveled by ACT-UP, for instance). Despite the effectiveness of the personalization of her illness, the construction of the audience, and the call for action, however, the Bergalises' rhetoric encourages the idea AIDS activists work to counter: that some people with AIDS are innocent victims whose lives are worth more than others who deserve to be sick. It is not surprising that Bergalis's testimony was received warmly by conservative politicians like Jesse Helms who have been working for years to prevent federal funding for AIDS education, as Angela Wall points out in her essay.

Many people testified before the House subcommittee: people living with AIDS, representatives of AIDS service organizations and medical associations, and family members of people living with AIDS. Kimberly and George Bergalis received by far the greatest amount of national media attention. Why should they alone, of all those who testified, figure so prominently in this debate? Even the testimony of Barbara Webb, another of Acer's patients who supported the Bergalis Act, made little impact on the headlines. But Webb's remarks differed from Bergalis in one significant way. Webb pleaded for mandatory HIV testing for health care workers, arguing that not all humans act rationally and responsibly all of the time, but she also told the subcommittee: "There are no guilty victims of this disease. There are people who have gotten it in different ways, but none of us, of them—and there really is no 'us' or 'them' in this. No one is guilty" (Hearings 131). This statement does not support epidemic logic as clearly as Bergalis's, despite Webb's support for the mandatory testing legislation. Her rhetoric explicitly rejects the dualistic separation of people living with AIDS into two camps, whether those camps are labeled us and them, gay and straight, or guilty and innocent. Webb's support of the Bergalis Act is rooted in compassionate concern for others, but her unwillingness to engage in the rhetoric of blame apparently made her less newsworthy.

Arguments that attempt to separate the moral analyses of AIDS from epidemiological analyses are not dramatic enough to capture widespread attention. When Belinda Mason, an Eastern Kentucky journalist with AIDS and a member of the National

Commission on AIDS, wrote a letter to President Bush taking a position contrary to that of Kimberly Bergalis on testing of health care workers, the story received front page coverage in the *New York Times* for one day and then faded from view. Mason, self-conscious of her atypical position in the epidemic, told the President that "[i]f I was a young woman of color in the Bronx, I wouldn't be standing up and talking AIDS. I'd be home worrying about how to pay the rent" (Hilts A1). In sharp contrast to Bergalis, Mason asserted that "doctors don't give people AIDS—they care for people with it. The blanket screening of health care workers will create the false illusion that people with AIDS are a threat to others." In a telephone interview Mason questioned the bitterness evident in Bergalis's—and others'—accounts of the epidemic:

> It seems to me that [the bitterness] is based on an assumption that things are supposed to be easy in life, that what happened is not fair and shouldn't have happened to me. This occurs to people, particularly people like me who got AIDS from a blood transfusion and Kimberly Bergalis who got it from an unfortunate contact with her dentist. But the question is, why should it happen to anybody? I never felt I was a member of an exclusive club that should go through life unscathed. (Hilts A14)

The same day that Kimberly Bergalis testified in Washington, Iowa nurse Barbara Fassbinder testified as well. Fassbinder, who was infected in 1986 during an emergency room procedure while treating a patient who probably did not know that he was HIV-positive, testified that "since there is no cure for the disease of AIDS caused by HIV, our best and only weapons are education and prevention of the transmission of that virus. We have further protection through the diligent and consistent use of the universal precautions as outlined by the CDC, regardless of a health care workers' knowledge of a blood borne infection in themselves or their patients" (Hearings 144–45). Fassbinder called the proposed mandatory testing legislation "simply cruel," asserting that it would "not prevent one single infection in the health care setting. It will only serve to perpetuate fear and misunderstanding regarding HIV" (Hearings 145). Like Webb, Fassbinder made no attempt to dichotomize people affected by HIV.

The Congressional responses to Bergalis's letter and testimony reveal further dimensions of the workings of epidemic logic.

Two themes emerged in Congressional responses to Bergalis's letter: the loss of her beauty, and her saintliness. Bergalis's perceived innocence enabled her to become a persuasive symbol for conservative legislators. The Bergalis family's willingness to publicly articulate the view that there are guilty and innocent victims made Kimberly Bergalis the perfect spokeswoman for this point of view. In order to confer greater authority on her speaking position, representatives stressed her purity, her beauty, her simplicity, her innocence. Jacob Weisberg's analysis of the Congressional hearings notes that while Bergalis's anger is understandable,

> no member of Congress says that furious gay activists have a unique qualification to speak about the public policy aspects of their disease. To the contrary, homosexuals who claim that those who did not prevent their infection are murderers are kept far from the hearing room. In Bergalis' case, however, the victim's irrational blasts of rage are taken as sober policy recommendations by legislators who want to make the most of her anomalous tragedy. (13)

Yet Bergalis, precisely because of her pristine appearance, was viewed as an authority. References to her "innocence" abound. She was described by Representative Burton of Indiana, for instance, as "the young lady who is a beautiful, vibrant young American, very pretty. I have seen pictures of her in her earlier days" (H 5203). Senator Jesse Helms called her "once-beautiful" (S9778). Bergalis' beauty sheds no light on the issue in front of Congress, preventing HIV transmission, but it does illuminate the ways in which Bergalis functioned as a political and ideological symbol.

Perhaps the most interesting aspect of the Congressional responses to Bergalis' testimony, however, is the characterization of her as a saint. Representative Dornan, following Danton, characterized Bergalis as "very religious . . . you could tell that in the talk shows." He speaks of her almost as a prophet, noting that

> In this jaded, sexually obsessed society, when she said, "I am a virgin, I was saving myself for my husband, I wanted to have a good marriage and children," in this cynical, sleaze-ball world of popular culture, people scoffed and jeered at her and said, "Check her out. She is probably promiscuous." But when [other patients were found to be infected] the world had to say, "Maybe this beautiful young woman is telling the truth." (H 5205)

Senator Jesse Helms, too, quotes Florida governor Lawton Chiles saying that visiting Bergalis is "a lot like being in the presence of a saint" (S7799), a comment echoed by Representative Dornan as he described his meeting with her in Senator Dannemyer's office:

> tears came to my eyes. My throat closed because I was in the presence of a saint. This young lady from Florida who is close to death from AIDS, is a young saint. I felt like I was in the presence of Mother Teresa, and anybody who has met that lady knows they are in the presence of somebody very spiritual, or a word we do not use too much these days, very holy. She is a very holy person. (H 6921-22)

What is it about Bergalis' situation that evoked these responses? Terminal illness in any young person evokes a strong emotional reaction. And living through AIDS no doubt affected Bergalis's view of the world and may well have given her insights some of her peers lacked. In light of the moral dimensions of AIDS discourse, though, the image of Bergalis as saint creates spiritual authority for the conservative side of the debate, making containment strategies the correct response to AIDS from a social, political, and spiritual perspective. The discussion of blame already identifies innocent and guilty parties, but the canonization of Bergalis increases the distance between those two groups.

The rhetorical position from which this view is articulated is one which easily enables the speaker to engage in broader criticism of those identified as guilty. Representative Dornan, for instance, having begun by describing Bergalis's beauty, quickly moves into rambling, sharp attacks on homosexuality. Dornan's speech is itself rhetorically fascinating. His lack of focus reveals how easy it is to associate homosexual men with the "threat" of HIV, even in a discussion of a woman with AIDS. Towards the end of his remarks, Dornan complains that in the past few decades, the word *gay* has lost its meaning. He notes parenthetically that *homophobia* is not in the House dictionary: "folks, a made-up word" (H6924), and thus erases the real experiences of many gay people, rendering them invisible. Yet, as he continues, he shifts pronouns and directly addresses gays, almost as though all the representatives before him were gay. Dornan's main point is that the changing meaning of *gay* is a public relations move designed to convince people that you are more cheerful, more mirthful, more happy than everybody else. So we are supposed to stop having gala balls, stop singing at Christmas time "Now we don our gay apparel". . . . . What person can claim that they are a healthy person, mentally and physically, if they get their kicks going to men's johns, like at the Washington Monument, or I stumbled on a scene across from the beautiful Willard Hotel in a little park dedicated to my father and other veterans of World War I. . . . I remember one time up here at a Greenbelt park one of the policemen told me, "They are scaring the horses, they are scaring the children, rustling in the bushes, and not even using the bushes sometimes."

From a discussion of a particular woman with AIDS comes scathing criticism of gay people—or criticism of what gays are presumed to be like, as Dornan here claims that all gays are unhealthy men who have sex in public places.[4] In this process, the female body is constructed as that of a saint, or a chaste martyr. The contrasts between AIDS and beauty, and between innocent female victims and unhealthy gay men scaring children and horses in the park create a compelling view of the AIDS epidemic as a moral phenomenon. It will take concerted political and social action and analysis to shift the emphasis to the epidemiological issues which know no gender or sexual orientation.

We can see, then, that the figure of Kimberly Bergalis became a powerful symbol in an increasingly polarized and moralized debate about how to respond to HIV and AIDS; elements of her own rhetoric and rhetoric of others speaking about her reinforced each other, ultimately representing her as a fragile innocent sacrificed as a result of moral laxity. This emphasis on moral issues takes a slightly different form in material written for women in the popular press. Publications directed at middle-class, largely white, women frequently stress that meaningful, intimate sex will enable them to avoid infection; this vague discussion encourages women to examine the nature of the relationship in which sexual encounters may happen and gives them no information about what actually causes HIV infection (or any other sexually transmitted disease). In short, the epidemiological aspects of AIDS involving women have been given little attention. While reporting about AIDS in women's magazines has improved somewhat since *Cosmopolitan* magazine's now-infamous article by Robert Gould (which suggested that only African women can get HIV because

African men treat women roughly during sex and have gay sex more often than North American men do, and because Africans have more anal sex than do North Americans), a complete view of the epidemic remains lacking. Gould's view of the epidemic was roundly criticized by medical professionals and AIDS activists who pointed out that his assertions about sexual practices in both Africa and North America were based on no confirmed data or responsible studies, yet the magazine never printed a correction or retraction. Instead, features in *Cosmopolitan* and other women's magazines have continued to stress that rationality and self-help approaches will eradicate AIDS; the implication is that being white, middle-class, and in a stable relationship will protect readers from AIDS. Coverage in *Cosmopolitan* or *Vogue* never details specific modes of transmission or discusses frankly the ways women can be sexually active more safely. Women are never told that unprotected, monogamous sex with an infected partner is far more dangerous than protected sex with multiple partners. Instead, the ideal of monogamy is held up as prophylactic against HIV and other sexually transmitted diseases, as though one's philosophy about sexuality or one's moral fiber can protect against a virus.

While neither *Cosmopolitan* nor *Vogue* should be viewed as reflecting the beliefs of most American women, these magazines do reflect ways in which the moralizing beliefs about AIDS we see played out in political debates seep into more personal discussions of sexuality and health. A good example of this influence is found in perhaps the most bizarre of all the women's magazine articles, the 1990 *Cosmopolitan* article, "The Risky Business of Bisexual Love," in which Susan Gerrard and James Halpern offered women advice about ways to tell if their husbands are bisexual. Relatively few women diagnosed with AIDS have contracted HIV as a result of sexual contact with bisexual men, something the authors overlook (as of June 1994, only .08 of all women infected through heterosexual contacts were partners of bisexual men [Centers for Disease Control 10]).[5] Gerrard and Halpern's advice to women relies on stereotypes: "If he looks into another man's eyes for even a microsecond longer than it takes to make socially acceptable eye contact, beware. Heterosexual men do not do it" (Gerrard and Halpern 204). And lest readers of *Cosmopolitan* missed this fine advice, in November 1994 the magazine ran another article, "When Straight Women Marry Gay Men," in which more advice on how to identify gay men is proffered. The consistent emphasis is on the risk from without; as in Bergalis's rhetoric, the suggestion is that women are at risk only if they are victimized by others, and the solution is to control others' behavior, not to learn to protect oneself. Thus women must know how to identify bisexual or gay men, rather than learn how to take more active roles in sexual relationships.

From a disease-control perspective, Gerrard and Halpern and other *Cosmopolitan* authors have missed several crucial facts. One is, simply, that to be a bisexual male is not necessarily to be a HIV-infected male. And how a man or woman identifies him or herself—as gay, bisexual, or straight—tells spouses or partners little about potential risk factors for HIV. Simply being bisexual or gay is not a risk factor for HIV; having had unprotected sex with any partner is. A heterosexual man who has used intravenous drugs and shared needles may well be at risk for HIV infection. To judge their own risks, women need information about how HIV is transmitted, between men, between women, between men and women; women need information about how to broach this sensitive topic with potential sexual partners. And yet in late 1994 a *Vogue* article on stamping out sexually transmitted diseases neglected any mention of HIV (Pike), and a *Cosmopolitan* article opened with the telling title and blurb: "What should you tell him about your sexual history? The answer to this hoary question resides in 'six little words': Ab-so-lute-ly no-thing!" (Heyn 154–55). Telling women that they should suspect their husbands are bisexual if they work in the travel or hotel industry, as Gerrard and Halpern suggest, plays into stereotypes about gay and bisexual men; Heyn's advice to stay away from discussions of sexual history makes it impossible to discuss the possibility of AIDS. This response to AIDS relies on the view that morality is a better defense against infection than information. And even as the epidemic progresses, as "facts" about AIDS become better known, as education programs (however precarious their federal funding) are in place for longer periods of time, this moral view of AIDS does not fade.

If morality is really the answer to HIV and AIDS, then it would logically follow that most people in the "general public," who are, after all, assumed to share the most conservative social moral standards, would have little to be concerned about. Even as the figure of Kimberly Bergalis became a symbol representing the need to control HIV, she also represented the notion that the "general public" did not need to be concerned about HIV: their risk factors would be unusual, external, unpredictable factors (like those encountered during a visit to the dentist), and these unusual factors could be controlled by legislation. To support this notion, the popular press provides "scientific" information designed to allay any fears. After Magic Johnson revealed his sero-status, *Cosmopolitan* published yet another article telling women they did not have anything to worry about. The table of contents for the March 1992 issue noted that Daniel Lynch's "AIDS: The Real Story About Risk" told "reassuring, rarely reported facts." Lynch argued that since cancer and heart disease kill more Americans than AIDS, AIDS has been misrepresented as a serious problem (a view also articulated by, among others, Senator Carl Levin of Michigan). This argument ignores several factors about the HIV pandemic. While it is true that chronic diseases like cancer and heart disease kill more Americans each year than AIDS does, AIDS affects younger people, people in their childbearing years and people in the prime of their careers. From a solely economic standpoint, AIDS creates further burdens for a society in that it decreases productivity and collective income, and in that it creates a situation in which many children whose parents are ill or have died require financial and emotional support. The effects of any disease are not limited to those who suffer from it, and from a demographic perspective, the age range most affected by AIDS dictates that the rest of the culture cannot avoid being affected in the long-term. Furthermore, by comparing AIDS to heart disease and even cancer Lynch maintains that providing information and education about HIV/AIDS is worthwhile, for efforts to lower heart disease and cancer rates have demonstrated the success of national educational campaigns. Changes in diet and stress levels, for instance, have been effective in lowering the rate of heart disease, and this experience should teach us that providing information about the causes of disease will help the population respond to it effectively.

Lynch does not provide such information, however. Instead he insists that a "large segment of the public believes homosexuals are degenerates . . . and that intravenous-drug users are even worse" (197). He suggests that AIDS advertisements showing women at risk are designed "to scare the hell out of everybody" (197). If anyone is inciting fear, it is Lynch, with his impassioned and self-righteous remarks about gay people and drug users. *Even if* it were somehow shown to be true that certain groups of Americans are degenerate, we would know nothing about HIV transmission. Responding to AIDS with personal attacks does not enable Americans to take the steps necessary to protect their health. Counseling drug users into treatment centers (and ensuring the funds for wider availability of treatment centers, including centers for women with children and women who are pregnant), advising women how to ask their partners to use dental dams or condoms, telling women and men how to evaluate and eliminate health risks by cleaning needles and modifying sexual practices would all be calm, useful, and compassionate responses to AIDS. The indictment and dismissal of medical knowledge about HIV is not.

Since I have been studying these issues, more and more women's bodies have figured in the public debate. Elizabeth Glaser told the Democrats that her experiences with AIDS taught her how unfair America can be, and challenged the nation to do something about the "crisis of caring" afflicting the nation (Trafford 6). Mary Fisher told the Republicans that AIDS "is winning" despite previous government attempts to prevent it, and she went on to say baldly that "we have killed each other—with our ignorance, our prejudice, and our silence" (Trafford 7). Glaser and Fisher stood before the conventions, as did Clinton's aide Bob Hattoy, white, apparently healthy, speaking of challenge, compassion, and bridge-building. And while all three speeches moved delegates to tears, none of the three penetrated public consciousness with the force of Kimberly Bergalis. Their bodies were not decaying (and when Glaser was dying, in 1994, her physical deterioration was not an issue), and their messages were not divisive.

The ever-widening spread of HIV is a great tragedy for all those infected (not to mention their families and friends). The story of Kimberly Bergalis should have heightened awareness of the prevalence of HIV. When Ryan White, another "innocent young victim" of AIDS, went public with his experiences, he helped all Americans, especially children, understand more about HIV and AIDS, understand more about how HIV is spread and, just as importantly, how it is not, and understand more about what it is like to live with HIV in a society that stigmatizes AIDS. Bergalis had the same opportunity to educate people about HIV transmission, but chose not to ally herself with other people with AIDS and instead her anger became a force for increased regulation of the HIV infected and thus a force encouraging, albeit unwittingly, greater misunderstandings about AIDS. The Bergalis case added momentum to fears and attitudes about AIDS that predated Bergalis's infection, and these same fears and attitudes continue to inform discourse about women and HIV. The constant suggestion that women need not fear HIV if they are in meaningful relationships, accompanied by misleading "scientific" data, can have only a deleterious affect on women's and men's ability to make informed judgments about sexual activity and other types of behavior. This discourse serves only to reinforce arbitrary social barriers set up to keep out unacceptable social elements. Gayle Rubin's analysis of sexual hierarchy is familiar to feminist theorists; she posits that rhetoric about sex maintains a hierarchy of sexual practice, built on what she calls "a domino theory of sexual peril. The line appears to stand between sexual order and chaos. It expresses the fear that if anything is permitted to cross this erotic DMZ [demilitarized zone], the barrier against scary sex will crumble and something unspeakable will skitter across" (282). Representations of women in AIDS discourse are becoming another barrier against unspeakable perils. That the holy, virginal, saintly body of a Kimberly Bergalis could be so desecrated by opportunistic infections causes such fear and panic that major steps must be taken to prevent further desecrations, no matter how high the cost. Such images and such rhetoric must be subjected to more careful scrutiny to foster more understanding of what we must do in order to prevent the spread of HIV. We must understand the ways in which women's bodies function as symbols in debates about AIDS to resist the pull of epidemic logic, and we must resist inscriptions of the body that signify only saint or sinner. Left unexamined, the discourse about women with AIDS will foster a continuing lack of compassion for people with AIDS, and result in public policies that will continue to withhold the information people need to make choices that could save their lives.

Notes

1. Many thanks are due to Ellen Armstrong, Helen Fox, Phyllis Lassner, and Becky Reed for their role in the formulation of the arguments presented here.

2. Since Angela Wall's essay examines educational materials in great detail, I have omitted such analysis from my work.

3. Similar logic was used by Newt Gingrich in his discussion of why legislation protecting the civil rights of gay and lesbian people is unnecessary. He observed that employers needed the right to fire a man who came to work in a dress, thereby narrowing the meaning of "gay" to include only men who wish to cross-dress at work. His remarks played on negative stereotypes of gay people, ignored the diverse realities of gay

and lesbian life, and further obscured the fact that civil rights legislation is not an absolute ban on the firing of members of protected groups; such legislation would simply prevent the firing of gay employees *because* they are gay.

4. When George Bergalis testified before a House of Representatives subcommittee, he said that AIDS is a "political issue. It is not a disease, it is a political disease " (Hearings 136). The notion of a "political disease" could only emerge in such a climate.

5. By the time this essay appears in print, the statistics quoted here will be outdated. Although the raw numbers of women with AIDS have been steadily increasing, the proportion of women infected through sex with a bisexual man have not changed in the six years I have been studying this issue.

Nearly half (45 percent) of the people in the United States diagnosed with AIDS are between 30 and 39 years old; 24 percent are between 40 and 49; and 18 percent are between 20 and 29 (Centers for Disease Control 13). These proportions have not significantly changed in the past years. See Treichler, *passim*, for a more extended discussion of the ways in which scientific "data" function in public understanding of HIV and AIDS.

11

CONFLICTS IN AIDS DISCOURSE: FOUCAULT, SURGEON GENERALS, AND THE [GAY MEN'S] HEALTHCARE CRISIS[1]

Angela Wall

The media and congressional coverage of the dismissal of former Surgeon General Joycelyn Elders has raised for me many of the concerns regarding trends in public health that have become particular to the AIDS healthcare crisis of the eighties and the Clinton administration's attempts to formulate (with minimum success) a national system of healthcare provision. The concerns to which I refer deal particularly with the insistence of many healthcare legislators that morality and family values come before education and lived sexual practices.

Predominantly expressed in the discursive accounts of Joycelyn Elders's dismissal are concerns about her lack of social etiquette and her ability to be "too outspoken" and to "go too far" in her comments and policies regarding sex education and health care. Elders has stated with regard to anti-abortionists that they "love little babies as long as they're in someone else's uterus rather than caring about children after they're born" (*Ebony* 154); in regard to how sex education is taught, she has suggested that "we teach teenagers what to do in the front seat of the car, and now we should teach them what to do in the backseats," and she believes that condom distribution in high schools could help curb the spread of AIDS among teenagers, stating that "I support abstinence as much as anyone, but if I know from the facts that young people are not being abstinent, I can't bury my head in the sand and pretend we don't have a problem" (160); in response to the current drug and crime crisis facing many Americans she proposed that "we'd markedly reduce our crime rate if drugs were legalized. I don't know all the ramifications, but I do feel we need to do some studies" (156). The culmination of her indiscretion was a comment made in December 1994 at a United Nations-sponsored conference in New York commemorating World AIDS Day. Responding to a question inquiring after a more explicit discussion of her reference to masturbation as a means of curbing the spread of AIDS, Elders replied that she supported "comprehensive" sex education for children, and said of masturbation, "I think that it is something that is part of human sexuality and it's part of something that perhaps should be taught" (*Facts on File*, 937). The contrast between her indiscreet thoughts regarding what should be done to combat the healthcare problems of America versus the discrete, indirect approach recognizable in the response of the Reagan government of the 1980s suggests a radical difference in how healthcare problems are perceived. Throughout her controversially labeled performance as surgeon general, Joycelyn Elders was cited consistently in and by the press for being outspoken and did little to moderate her views once she was confirmed. Elders's comments on masturbation are commonly reported as the cause for her dismissal, yet a clear shift in Clinton's perception of how her policies were contributing to the democratic image contributed to the decision to dismiss rather than support her as Clinton had done previously when Elders had seemingly made more controversial statements. What seems evident here is a serious shift in how the healthcare needs of the U.S. are being constructed.

For many, Joycelyn Elders spoke to the needs of communities where the failure of adequate education and information concerning, for example, sexual practices clearly contributed to severe healthcare problems within such environments. She spoke of healthcare policies that sought to address healthcare problems that are not typically perceived as being universally experienced: AIDS, drug addiction, crime, masturbation—practices that supposedly only take place in certain "unhealthy" moral environments. This popular misconception seems particularly unfeasible given that Elders's own son was convicted on cocaine charges. Of the many characteristics associated with Elders is her remarkably disciplined and orthodox upbringing: interviews with her that discuss her childhood pay particular attention to the fact that she graduated as her high school valedictorian at age 15, and that considerable sacrifices were made by her family so that she could become a doctor. Equally emphasized is her determination that "every single one [of her siblings] who wanted to go to college was going to go" (*Ebony*, 158): Elders helped put five of her seven siblings through college. Thus, a somewhat contradictory image of Elders is constructed for public consumption: praised as having a healthy moral outlook and work ethic, she is at the same time chastised for continuing to remind people of the obligation and responsibility of government legislators to raise the level of education among those who remain in need, particularly those at risk of healthcare problems.

Elders's dismissal, the response to her recognition of the radical differences between the educational needs of diverse communities, indicates a problematic failure or unwillingness by the Clinton administration among other policymakers to acknowledge the complex make-up and needs of groups requiring changes in healthcare policy. However, the implications for a healthcare policy that would recognize such a diversity of sexual practices and lifestyles is not unique to the Clinton administration, rather this issue seems to have been the root of problems in the healthcare system for over a decade now. Historically, this point has been best demonstrated by the initial responses by government healthcare workers and community health activists to the AIDS crisis.

In the midst of the AIDS pandemic of the eighties, we were offered a wide variety of texts that participated in the identity construction of those diagnosed with AIDS or as HIV positive. We were offered differing definitions of what it was to be an AIDS "victim" by, for instance, the Centers for Disease Control and by the surgeon general; of what it was to live with AIDS by AIDS artists and by people living with AIDS. In the various texts of popular culture, the identity of the body with AIDS was based on the possibilities for codification offered by the disease the body had become. Or to put it in the words of cultural critic Paula Treichler, "Whatever else it may be, AIDS is a story, or multiple stories, read to a surprising extent from a text that does not exist: the body of the male homosexual."[2]

As a cultural, social, and political moment as well as a disease, AIDS is a site for the ideological reproduction of dominant beliefs about racial, national, class, ethnic and sexual identity. Within this context, challenging the marginalization of "other" interests (feminist, gay, lesbian, bisexual, Latino/a, and African American, for example) and examining the implications of the systematic reproduction of this process of othering enables a close look at how institutions, meanings, and values are discursively produced, legitimated, and maintained in the hegemonic system of discipline and compliance. The emergence of the "AIDS body" alongside an increasing array of challenges to and criticism of what constitutes and contributes the composition of an "HIV+ body" has caused a crisis in the construction of more traditional others.

In his article "The Spectacle of AIDS," Simon Watney uses psychoanalytic understandings of identification to explain how "the homosexual body" is publicly consumed at a specific cultural moment and how "the gay personality" is constituted and specified by a series of identifications. Drawing from the argument made by Laplanche and Pontalis that the subject "assimilates an aspect, property, or attribute of the other and is transformed, wholly or partially, after the model the other provides," Watney claims that the substantive process of identifying operates in two modes: "the transitive one of identifying the self in relation to the *difference* of the other, and the reflexive one of identifying the self in a relation of *resemblance* to the other."[3] An application of the transitive mode of identification would explain how the homosexual body is an object that can only enter "public" visibility as different from the public— in the "transitive mode," the representation of difference is contingent upon the scrupulous refusal of any possibility of identification.

More recently, many critics have argued that the threat to heterosexual stability posed by homosexuality is based not on its difference from heterosexuality but on its resemblance to it. Judith Butler provides a highly articulate and intricate argument to this end in her essay, "Imitation and Gender Subordination."[4] Writing prior to the publication of this piece and the subsequent move toward theorizing the process of identification between heterosexuality and homosexuality in terms of resemblance, Watney relies on a model of difference. To this end, Watney demonstrates how the homosexual body is given various identifiable marks that typically serve to identify sexual and ideological differences. However, these differences serve only to restrict the ideological perpetuation of homosexuality. The homosexual body is positioned as other in relation to the general public as both a spectacle of difference and as a reminder of public contempt for such difference. At the center of many public representations of the homosexual body is then the construction of a homosexual "them" whose identifying traits need publicly to be specified in order to confirm what the general public "we" are not. When AIDS is introduced as a contributor to the identificatory specifics of homosexuality, the construction of ideological boundaries based on sexuality and lifestyle is shown to be not only false, but dangerously fictitious.

Using the coverage of homosexuality in several British tabloids as examples, Watney demonstrates how these fictions are produced and reproduced for public consumption. The popular daily newspaper *The Sun* sells homosexuality as an "exclusive" in its coverage: "Exclusive: Ryan's kinky secret revealed—Maniac Rambo was my gay lover," and inside; "Exclusive! Liberace and Pal who Died of AIDS." Another tabloid, *The People*, offers "Secrets of the Gay Vicars." These stories map out the psychological and physiological construction of the homosexual male as different. Yet the impossibility of immediately being able to recognize this difference is evident in the surprise expressed at the discovery that someone who was thought to be heterosexual—indeed as manly as the hetero-icon Rambo—is in fact homosexual. Being gay is sold for consumption under a warranteed bill of difference: kinky, secretive, maniacal. The homosexual body, a promiscuous, duplicitous, self-satisfying, pleasure-seeking saboteur of morality and family values, "becomes an impossible object, a monster that can only be engendered by a process of corruption through seduction."[5] When this image is made synonymous with AIDS, the gay male identity is "reduced to a topology of signs that promises to identify the dreaded object of desire in the final moments of its own apparent self-destruction" (Watney 79). We are shown "'death-as-the-deserts-of-depravity'. . . the 'homosexual body' is 'disposed of,' like so much rubbish, like the trash it was in life" (80). The "comfort" of this image to the "general population" may be because it finally does mark the homosexual body as verifiably different. As a result, AIDS is thus made to rationalize the impossibility of the "homosexual body," an impossibility based not only on societal precautions and policies to keep homosexuality invisible but also one that confuses the visual categories of identity: it is not just different but is both different and alike. In refusing the possibility and viability of the homosexual body, the traditional family is further inscribed as a one source of protection against an increasingly destabilized and destablizing social world. Indeed, at the cultural moment of AIDS, "the family" becomes a keyword through which the world and the self are to be understood.

Yet, as a nondiscriminatory virus which holds no race, class, or sexual prejudice, AIDS has successfully disrupted such traditional understandings and processes of moral value and belief legitimation: strong Christian values and high moral standards offer little protection against the HIV virus. A contradiction arises between the illicit, "immoral" gay lifestyle lived out in excess by those supposedly responsible for the disease, and the spread of the disease into the "decent" heterosexual community. The "promiscuous" spread of the virus leads us to question what constitutes "normal" sexual practices. AIDS has served to expose overt discrimination against any kind of cultural diversity, revealing the limitations of a collapsed cultural condition that attempts to avoid addressing this crisis by variously describing it as "a curse from God against homosexuality," "a gay man's disease," and as "begun in Africa by natives having sex with monkeys." AIDS has exposed the existence of a set of hegemonic appropriations that can no longer be regarded legitimately as innocent, natural, unavoidable, or just a part of everyday life.

Michel Foucault's work on a disciplinary society (and the disciplined self) provides a useful theoretical framework for understanding how it is that a universalized "we" is created and then divided into an "us" that does the monitoring and a "them" who are monitored. Although Foucault has been criticized for his failure to directly address the oppression of marginalized groups, particularly women, his discussion of technologies of power helps us to understand how it is "that dominated groups participate in their own domination."[6] For example, Foucault's model becomes a useful way to read current healthcare/civil rights crises in relation to both the current AIDS pandemic and the struggle for control over women's bodies. In white, westernized American culture today, power is not so centrally located nor is it governed only by the principle of visibility. As a result, traditional systems of beliefs about how women should behave and look are readily available for consumption. Women learn to monitor and police themselves and in so doing, they learn to take on the responsibility of their own discipline. Calorie counting, exercise routines, body-fat analysis, diet fads, are all technologies of surveillance, methods of monitoring discursively produced identities that are internalized and imposed upon the self. A checklist of western, late capitalist identities is offered under the guise of either consumer advertising or "what women want." Here the agents of oppressive power are less a faceless "them" and more a self-disciplined body.

If we follow along with Foucault, one of the ways in which this power is disseminated is through the interiorization of what he terms "the gaze": a standard, normal, and universalized way of looking at the world. However, this process is itself complicated by the reality that instead of one central overseer performing the surveillance from a visible panopticon, we each learn how to internalize the gaze and police ourselves. Thus those interested in exercising power are no longer, nor arguably have they ever been, an identifiable they, but are rather an all-encompassing, all-projected virtual "we." Or a bunch of we's with no they.

At the cultural moment of AIDS, the "systemized network of power" articulated in Foucault's theory can be identified at the various intersections between the U.S. and British governments' responses to the AIDS crisis, the emphasis on testing, the monitoring and surveillance of those diagnosed as HIV antibody positive on the one hand, and the actions and demands of AIDS activist groups for improved healthcare for people with AIDS and for better funding of AIDS research on the other. If we are to effectively intervene in these systemized networks of power so as to open them up for change, then we must examine how we come to engage in such effective strategies of self-surveillance. Recognizing the process by which we police our own behavior is a crucial and valuable site of inquiry if we are to effect momentary, yet crucially significant, acts of intervention.

The strategies of surveillance and the subtle methods of managing control discussed by Foucault are particularly relevant in an examination of how public responses to the AIDS pandemic have been guided. In 1988 a brochure, entitled *Understanding AIDS* was put together by Ronald Reagan's surgeon general, C. Everett Koop. At the time of its publication, this document was considered a radical move for an administration that had up until that time failed to publicly recognize the devastation being wreaked on Americans by the AIDS epidemic. This "do-it-yourself" health pamphlet, mailed to all United States Americans by the United States Government— mailed, that is, to all U.S. citizens except the homeless and those residing in State Correctional Institutions—was considered by many Americans to be a major step forward in the government's response to a health crisis. The brochure aimed at educating the American family—itself an interesting mode of address—about AIDS by addressing the issues of "How You Get AIDS," "What Behavior Puts You at Risk," "What Does Someone with AIDS Look Like?" and "Should You Get an AIDS Test?"

A close reading of the first page tightly focuses the brochure's agenda: a photograph of the then surgeon general, C. Everett Koop; a list of his credentials including the title "doctor of medicine"; and further validation of his expertise through his consultation with "top health experts" in preparing the brochure. These all establish him as someone who "really" knows what he's talking about. What we read then in this brochure is the construction of a hierarchy of knowledges, with the knowledge of the surgeon general at the top, supported by lower positioned government health "experts," who in turn are positioned just slightly above the next rung of health education organizations found in "schools, churches, synagogues and community groups" (in order of ideologically approved merit), all of which are positioned higher than the person living with AIDS, who is firmly at the bottom.

The effort to get us to internalize the brochure's agenda begins as we are told on the first page of the brochure that "Stopping AIDS is up to you, your family and your loved ones." If we can only take control of our own lives, take control of our own behavior patterns, then we can prevent the spread of this "Public Enemy Number One." While this may seem like good, sound advice, the subtext dictates to the reader a very particular code of conduct. In telling us what we can do to prevent contracting the disease, we are told also what those who have contracted the disease did not do. The surgeon general offers us a "personal greeting as a postal customer" in a separate section of the brochure titled "A Message from the Surgeon General" and signed. Heading the pamphlet, it encourages us to practice responsible behavior based on understanding and strong moral values. What comes across clearly is that, in this brochure, the discursive identity of the AIDS body is subtly constructed as the social and cultural "Other." "We"—the postal customers who receive the brochure—are assumed not to have AIDS; clearly we are warned about how to avoid it. Our responsible behavior and strong moral agenda will protect us from the disease. Those already afflicted are the unnamed others in this mass mailing. It is as if the very pronoun "we" will magically protect us from the dread infection.

Reagan's domestic policy discretely avoided addressing the healthcare crisis as it directly and drastically affected the lifestyle of the gay population of the U.S. His AIDS policy agenda was firmly grounded in promoting a very specific family structure. In an attempt to track developments in AIDS education, PBS produced "AIDS Quarterly," a television news–style show, hosted by Peter Jennings, that aired four times a year during the late eighties and early nineties.[7] The show aimed to analyze the steps being taken by the government. These were discussed by Gary Bauer, Reagan's Domestic Policy Advisor, who stated in an interview that "We felt on this particular controversy that public health advice seemed to correspond with good moral advice. And the best public

health advice was to refrain from having numerous sexual partners, monogamy [sic], etc." Here, the emphasis on a moral agenda
is given priority over AIDS healthcare. AIDS is being written as a
disease that will not affect those who take "good moral advice." The
"public" is seen as those not diagnosed as HIV antibody positive,
and as those not involved with numerous sexual partners.
Members of the public are assumed to be monogamous,
heterosexual, and engaging in "normal" reproduction-oriented
sexual practices.

In a letter he later sent to the secretary of Health and Human
Services, Bauer spelled out the Reagan Administration's moral
agenda: "The resources we have to fight AIDS must not be used to
promote homosexual activity which most Americans find deeply
offensive." This specific moral agenda and the notions of normalcy it
seeks to reify serve not only to dangerously misinform the "public"
about the way AIDS is spread, but also to promote a "natural"
lifestyle which this nondiscriminatory "epidemic" has already shown
to be an elaborate cultural fiction.

The Understanding AIDS brochure repeatedly stresses a specific moral agenda, and emphasizes the individual's behavior and
responsibility. The brochure states that "some [people] should be
worried [about contracting AIDS] and need to take some serious
precautions. But many are not in danger of contracting AIDS."
This discursive distinction between those who are and those who
are not in danger relies confidently on the self-policing, self-
moralizing standards of "most Americans" who confidently take
refuge in the illusion of an inviolate heterosexuality. It is not
difficult to determine, then, who those discursive "Others" might
be: they are those who engage in sharing needles and syringes;
those who practice anal sex, "with or without a condom"; and
those who have sex with a "pickup or prostitute or with someone
you don't know well." Since few patriotic, heterosexual Americans
would openly confess to such practices, "we" can assume it is
"them"—the drug addicts, homosexuals and sodomites—who are
the only ones at risk.

If we can identify those who do not have AIDS as those who
have strong personal values and who practice responsible behavior,
we can identify those who are HIV positive by their lack of values
and irresponsible behavior. An antithetical picture of who has HIV
offered by the brochure is then used to describe how to avoid HIV.
To be safe from the disease, the brochure recommends the following short and unimaginative behaviors:

Not having sex.

Sex with one mutually faithful, uninfected partner.

Not shooting drugs.

In contrast to pamphlets from gay organizations and other groups involved in AIDS education that aim at informing about actual safe-sex practices rather than preaching moral behavior under the guise of safe-sex guidelines, the government agenda behind understanding AIDS becomes one that denies difference and advocates sexual prudery rather than education as the means of avoiding contact with HIV.

In 1987, the Gay Men's Health Crisis published a pamphlet aimed at educating a sexually diverse public about the spread of the HIV antibody. *The Safer Sex Condom Guide For Men And Women* is a color pamphlet of air-brushed graphics. The front page offers no message from the president or organization chair. It offers no quotation from a patron, and certainly it offers no signed message of endorsement from the surgeon general and by extension the president. The authority of the GMHC to speak on these issues is thus grounded in an entirely different frame of reference and one that is entirely "unofficial" in comparison to the *Understanding AIDS* brochure. The GMHC pamphlet explicitly and graphically shows an at-risk public how to use condoms. Authorship is openly registered with the Gay Men's Health Crisis, alongside a slogan "First in the Fight Against Aids." Sensational though this slogan may sound, the date of publication puts the GMHC a whole year ahead of the U.S. Public Health Service in addressing the public on how the HIV virus is spread, and several years ahead of the government in addressing AIDS as a sexually transmitted disease amongst all sexually active persons rather than one isolated to the sexual practices of the gay community. The GMHC establishes a set of credentials based on its volunteer status. The group does not boast ownership of a medical and scientific authority that gives it permission to speak on the crisis of AIDS. This contrasts with the hierarchy of credibility offered by the government brochure, and reveals the polemical approaches to the AIDS crisis taken by the government and AIDS Service Organizations.

Instead, we are shown the curvaceous, stretching mid-torso of a clothed, rather muscular man posing with his legs slightly apart. Clearly visible in the back pocket of his tightly worn jeans is the circular indent of a condom. The effect of the air-brush combines with the curves and poise of this body to subtly eroticize the image. The torso is a contained snapshot in a square frame, and this type of seductive graphic is used throughout to visually contextualize the written text. Here, the "them" that the *Understanding Aids* brochure seeks to protect "us" from is clearly controlling the gaze.

The *Safer Sex Condom Guide* pamphlet opens out to show us the top half of a tanned, naked man holding a condom close to his mouth. He is staring, lips pouting, directly at "us." A hand is entering the illustration, with fingers (possibly male) poised to take hold of the condom. The air-brushed graphics turn into several color photographs showing us how to put condoms onto an erect penis, showing us where to put lubricants, showing men how to put condoms on themselves. While the men are shown in various stages of undress, their clothes indicate their diverse lifestyles: clothing ranges from business shirts and "city" ties, to unzipped jeans and black vests implying occupations or fetishized roles that range from city executive to construction worker. Concurrent with these graphics, under the heading "What's in a Name?" are the various names given to condoms, the types of condoms available, and the connection between rubbers and safer sex. Clearly, we are being made to understand the connection between safe sex and AIDS:

> Rubbers, condoms, prophylactics, bags, skins, raincoats, sheaths, hats, letters; they're all the same thing.
>
> They can be lubricated or non-lubricated, have reservoir tips or plain end.
>
> Some are colored, some have ribs or bumps.
>
> The choice is yours.
>
> The virus that causes AIDS will not go through a latex rubber. If it does not leak, break or fall off, a latex rubber will block the AIDS virus.

Here the person who might get AIDS is arguably identified as anyone, regardless of social class, formal education, or ethnic background, who is engaging in any kind of sexual intercourse. While this universal/global approach is not necessarily always useful—it avoids recognizing and subsequently framing specific safer sex practices to the particular needs of certain communities—such an approach at least moves toward a more explicit application of safer sex methods. Nevertheless, this pamphlet is clearly produced by the GMHC, and deals with condoms, not dental dams or condams—consequently, lesbians remain unquestionably unrecognized and excluded as an at-risk group.

Understanding AIDS is here at least directed towards comprehending how the virus is transmitted. And implicit in understanding AIDS is at least an acknowledgment that sexual pleasure, in all its variations and multiplicity, is not the cause of the spread of HIV. Sexual lifestyle is not addressed as a "high-risk behavior." Instead, the GMHC pamphlet focuses on practicing safer sex and using a condom—"colored, flavored, or ribbed."

The Safer Sex Condom Guide does not offer ways to identify "us" and "them" in terms of gay and straight. Instead all who are sexually active, at least with penile penetration, are recognized to be at risk. The distinction between those at risk and those less at risk becomes one based not on one's sexual preference, lifestyle, or the number of sex partners encountered in one night, but on one's sexual practices—unsafe sexual practices. "We," the readers, are shown the available preventative materials and told "the choice is yours." But the subtext of this choice clearly places the responsibility to practice safe sex on "us," the "at-risk" reader. Here, the separation between "us," the sexually diverse readers, and "them," the volunteers of the Gay Men's Health Crisis, is one defined by an agenda of practical experiences in dealing with AIDS in the gay male community. Contrast this with the moral agenda of the Reagan (and then the Bush) administration and the Centers for Disease Control: their objectives have been to prevent the spread of AIDS—but not if it means promoting a lifestyle that it has decided is unacceptable to "most Americans." In the short time scheme of HIV antibody transmittance, "we" become those who remain at risk, and ultimately "we" will become those responsible for spreading HIV. For the GMHC, understanding AIDS means understanding how to live with AIDS in a system where the stigmas of association serve to prevent a person with AIDS from receiving health insurance, housing, healthcare, and employment. For the government, on the other hand, it involves understanding what types of sexual behavior to warn against: sexual behavior that directly challenges the traditional value systems of a Western, late-capitalist heterosexual system of government.

In her analysis of AIDS service industries, Cindy Patton discusses the way in which the media uses the ideology of altruism to strip service industry volunteers of political exigency. The term *altruistic* serves to undermine the ability of those not coded as healthcare experts to intervene effectively and change the course of the epidemic. In a survey study of New York Gay Men's Health Crisis volunteers carried out by Philip Kayal, volunteers were asked whether their motives were political or altruistic. Respondents said "altruistic." However, Kayal points out that further questions revealed that they volunteered not for some "abstract greater good, but because they saw a direct relationship between their volunteer work and community-building work toward political goals of the gay movement, and because they felt less hopeless and more personally engaged through their work." Of particular interest is the manner also in which the terms "altruistic" and "political" are positioned in opposition to one another. Patton argues that the fact that many volunteers do have political and self-interested reasons for their involvement in AIDS service organizations "would suggest that there is at least a latent 'political consciousness' or 'minority identification' among AIDS service volunteers which may be at odds with the media representations of AIDS volunteers."[8] Self-interest is here defined in an expanded way, aligned more with community than with the individual. The politically motivated involvement of volunteer workers, as well as the absolute necessity of their involvement (due to the government's refusal to provide adequate health caretaking facilities), serves to challenge not only the implied power of government in attempts to ignore and deny its responsibility for the loss of human lives; it also challenges hegemonic practices and ideologies. As part of their "credentials," the GMHC lists the following services: "[The GMHC] develops and distributes materials that address the various aspects of AIDS (general information, risk reduction, medical and psychological issues, testing, health insurance and legal concerns) to meet the needs of different audiences." The recognition of "different audiences," of differently positioned subjects, is a crucial distinction between the government response and the response of the GMHC. In its role as an AIDS service organization, the GMHC makes available legal advice for people with AIDS who face discrimination based on their HIV-positive status. In so doing, they redefine understanding the AIDS crisis. Rather than defining AIDS as "just" a healthcare crisis, the Gay Men's Health Crisis includes in its agenda of dealing with AIDS an understanding of the politics of being HIV positive. In this way then, we read their explicit graphics on safe-sex procedures as not merely demonstrating how and when to use a condom, but as actually challenging a hegemonic system of values which seeks to make taboos out of sexual practices that challenge the family, the patriarchal system, and "traditional American values."[9]

This shift in concern toward a "how-to"-style safer-sex education for the recognized "different audiences" is discussed by Cindy Patton and a number of gay, safer-sex video makers, in her essay "Safer Sex and the Pornographic Vernacular." In an effort to make safer sex practices "the norm" in sex acts, Patton and her coworkers considered the important connection between safer sex, responsible sexual fantasy, and diverse sexual cultures. Inevitably, in this framework, fantasy has a broad landscape and the question of what constituted the representation of safe sex became an impossible one to answer.[10] As their work progressed, the group raised a series of questions problematizing the use of "native tongue" phrasing to convey safer sex practices to certain "at-risk" communities. The terms consistently used in descriptions of these "alternative" perspectives on safer sex typically project a style that is attempting to be "culturally sensitive" and "sexually explicit." Observing how safer-sex education evolved through the eighties, Patton suggests that these phrases have been "bandied about as if the former were a category of narrative preference and the latter a marker of realistic representation" (39). Patton argues that these terms suggest that sexuality is a "culture in itself," rather than, she argues, an "artefact of cultures." Outside of the gay community's grappling with its own diversity, she writes, "cultural sensitivity became a new form of voyeurism for public health officials and clinicians." She continues that those in "need" of cultural diversity are measured against a middle-class, white norm, and are therefore found lacking in both the decoding skills and the behavioral and social values of the mainstream society (40). Indeed, those deemed in "need" of a safer-sex language that they are sure to comprehend are also considered those who are "truly at risk." They need to be reached no matter how bawdy the language, no matter how explicit the material.

Patton's project then becomes one of exploring how to discursively address sex practices in ways that celebrate safer sex as the "norm not the problem" (32) as well as to successfully speak in ways that recognize diverse sexual cultures without othering them as representing sexual lifestyles more at-risk than white, middle-class heterosexual cultures. Patton argues for reeducating people about sex in such a way that broadens what constitutes sexual activities for all people. She proposes that the term "sexually explicit" defines the spectrum of sexuality in extremes—with discreet euphemism acting as the repressed extreme of explicit. Instead, she suggests that a better term might be "sexually consistent material, that is, material consistent in form—oral, written, pictorial, gestural—in style, and in mode of the cultural circulation" (46).

The arguments made by Patton et al. carefully work through many of the problems that arose in early attempts to educate a diverse array of cultural practices about safer sex. One of the common misconceptions about "gay-oriented" or "explicit" literature was the equation that visual representations of sexual gratification leads to moral bankruptcy and social disorder. This is addressed by Watney in a chapter of *Policing Desire*. He quotes T. R. Witomski's discussion of pornography and AIDS:

> The opponents of pornography, from fundamentalists to radical feminists, are in agreement: pornography is "sick." Not bad, boring, silly, useless . . . Porn is described as an epidemic in the same way that AIDS has [sic]. The pornographer is seen as a vampire: he wishes to 'infect' society and must be wiped out . . . Jerry Falwell inveighs against smut as if it's a sub-genre of sick homosexuality; for Robin Morgan, 'pornography' is the theory, and rape is the practice . . . Pornography can't be 'sick' because sexuality isn't 'sick.' The pornographic 'sickness' doesn't reside in the works of pornography, but in the minds of erotophobes . . . Attacking porn for contributing to the number of AIDS cases betrays a fundamental misunderstanding of both porn and disease. A disease has no conscience. Being 'good'—for example—will not prevent you from getting sick. [11]

In the case of AIDS education, a "sick mindset" is often associated with the safe sex practices of a particular culture. In the 1989 issue of the *AIDS Quarterly*, the GMHC is shown to be one of many gay-oriented AIDS education projects severely criticized (primarily by Senator Jesse Helms of North Carolina) and financially dismissed on such "sick" mindset allegations. The hidden agenda in such rulings is based on cultural fictions of what is "natural," "good," and "normal."

The female body is similarly a site of inscription to promote a moral agenda and lifestyle that organizes women's lives completely around the family unit.[12] Here, an identity concurrently constructed for women serves to establish and maintain a patriarchal system of values; women are placed in roles to which they are "naturally" suited, roles which usually involve upkeeping and maintaining a hegemonic system of patriarchy. To ensure that such value systems can be continually maintained, women who fall outside of such roles are variously defined as resisting their natural inclination to motherhood, loose and selfish, or psychologically imbalanced. In terms of AIDS information material, gay organizations that approach safer sex education through graphic representations or named sex acts in an attempt to prevent the spread of HIV are seen as trying to pervert others; they are suspected of using AIDS education as an excuse to show "gay pornography," and promote homosexuality in the name of AIDS education.

In the government brochure *Understanding AIDS*, the identity of the person with AIDS becomes equated with lifestyles that are considered immoral: homosexuality, non-monogamy, using drugs, premarital sex, bisexuality. This desire to make visible, to identify a person with AIDS as different, is crucial if the traditional moral codes of "right" and "wrong" behavior are to be confirmed and legitimized. In short, these "others" have to be identified and maintained in the eyes of power for current standards and values to survive. But the dangers of continuing to believe in a "we" versus "them," in which the "we" are those upstanding Americans who are presumed not to have to practice safe sex and who don't require "explicit" sex education—and the "them" are those self-identified as gays, bisexuals, or drug users, will be increasingly risky. In the AIDS crisis, the boundaries between "us"—heterosexuals, non-IV drug users, and "them"—homosexuals, IV drug users, sex workers, are shown to be cultural fictions aimed at keeping safe the values of those identifying themselves as "not at risk" and eliminating the lifestyles of those who directly challenge such values. Paradoxically, at the cultural moment of AIDS, the map of self-policing traditionally encoded onto the female body now figures into the regime for how men are to discipline and police themselves.

The hysteria of racism, sexism, and homophobia that AIDS and AIDS activism unearth suggests that the standards and values of this ubiquitous identity named "most Americans" are unable to stand up to close scrutiny. In terms of body politics this reveals, and contests, a paradoxical moment in the construction of two typically hysterical bodies. The historically written pathological and diseased female body is, at the cultural moment of AIDS, mapped onto the homosexual body. The identification of AIDS with homosexuality encourages our culture's distaste for, and anxiety about, homosexuality. Yet the recognizable transfer of this anxiety and hysteria from the female body to the homosexual body raises a variety of questions concerning the current state of Western, late capitalist culture and society. The question most constantly arising in my own critical inquiry asks what crisis of legitimation is occurring within the bounds of Western, late-capitalist culture that has conveniently permitted AIDS to serve as an excuse for a late-twentieth-century witch hunt? The subsequent manifestations of male panic/anxiety/hysteria that AIDS has revealed goes some way toward suggesting the complexity of this crisis. The largest indication of just how serious a crisis of legitimation AIDS, and the subsequent activism and intervention, has posed inheres in the moral panic that has erupted and now consistently informs government domestic policy.

Returning to more recent history, the controversy inspired by former surgeon general Joycelyn Elders's dismissal has been consistently attributed to her use of bawdy terms and taboo language. *New York Times* journalist Frank Rich reported that her reference to masturbation was not in vain and "actually achieved its intended effect, which was to yank a ludicrously taboo subject completely out of the closet."[13] Rich contends that "Mr. Clinton deliberately misconstrued [Elders's] meaning; she called for including masturbation information, not instruction, in sex education." The continued reluctance of successive governments to heed the work being done by a broad spectrum of healthcare activists severely impairs the implementation of a number of educational programs that could successfully speak to the diverse cultural practices of various groups and perhaps reduce the numbers of unwanted pregnancies and the spread of sexually transmitted diseases.

Notes

1. I would like to thank Sherrin Fitzer for her collaboration on an earlier version of this paper. I would also like to thank Anne Balsamo and particularly Lynne Joyrich for their encouragement and constructive comments on the various recent drafts of this paper.

2. Paula Treichler, "AIDS, Homophobia, and Biomedical Discourse: An Epidemic of Signification" (42).

3. Simon Watney, "The Spectacle of AIDS" (78).

4. Butler, among others, has done much to elaborate the mimetic relationship between homosexuality and heterosexuality focusing on "likeness" instead of "otherness." This line of thinking has proved powerful at a time of increasing political shrewdness amongst homophobic conservatives. Butler questions, through a complex series of gestures, the notion of an original and proper (hetero)sexual identity and its "derivative," "secondary," "imitation," or "copy," homosexual identity. She argues that if it were not for the notion "of the homosexual as copy, there would be no construct of heterosexuality as origin. Heterosexuality here presupposes homosexuality. And if the homosexual as copy precedes the heterosexual as origin, then it seems only fair to concede that the copy comes before the origin, and that homosexuality is thus the origin." But, she continues, "the inversions are not really possible. For it is only as a copy that homosexuality can be argued to precede heterosexuality as the origin." She suggests that the instability of this framework "confounds the possibility of any stable way to locate the temporal or logical priority of either term." Hence she moves toward a rendering of gay and lesbian sexuality in relation to heterosexuality not in terms of derivatives but "imitation" which she argues "does not copy that which is prior, but produces and inverts the very terms of priority and derivativeness" suggesting that gay identities are implicated in heterosexuality (22).

5. Watney, 77.

6. Nancy Harstock, "Foucault on Power: A Theory for Women?" (169).

7. As a result of much criticism for its failure to connect AIDS to broader social and legislative issues, "AIDS Quarterly" was taken off the air. It returned in 1993 as *"Medicine at the Crossroads."* The program now addresses AIDS as a global healthcare crisis rather than one peculiar to U.S. domestic policy.

8. Cindy Patton, *Inventing AIDS* (137).

9. In regard to the Gay Men's Health Crisis "Safer Sex Shorts" film released in 1989, coproducer Gregg Bordowitz comments that in the conceptualization process of the tapes "there was a black men's task group, a Latino group, a women's group, and people interested in making an s&m tape." Bordowitz continues, "that's what's unique about our project: it's trying to be very focused in its address and its distribution" (*How Do I Look*, 52). This focus on distribution as well as address marks an important shift in safer sex education and is a point often forgotten as different groups react to varying responses to safer-sex education. Bordowitz and his coproducer, Jean Carlomusto, work to create "vernacular safe-sex representations."

10. Patton addresses this issue in detail in her essay, posing questions and disputing the "relation (or distinction) between fantasy sex and 'actual sex'"; here she explores the nature of porn watching: is porn watching a sexual activity? Or do porn videos serve as an aid to imagination, which produces the fantasy for the viewer? Do viewers practice what they see? Does watching unsafe sex provide a viable substitute for practices now out of bounds? Do unsafe videos image and stabilize activities that ought to be erased from any moment of desire? (36) As Patton states, "the arguments outlined . . . represent the heart of a struggle for group self-determination." While I think in the context of her essay she is referring to her working group of critics, activists, and video makers, this struggle is evident in many of the concerns she raises within the safer-sex guides produced by and examined between groups practicing sex in culturally diverse ways.

11. Watney, *Policing Desire: Pornography, AIDS and the Media* (63).

12. See feminist critiques of feminist responses to anti-pornography campaigns in works like *Caught Looking: Feminism, Pornography and Censorship* by Kate Ellis et al.; and Donna Turley, "The Feminist Debate on Pornography" in *Socialist Review* 87–88: May–Aug, 1986; Andrew Ross's "The Popularity of Pornography" in *No Respect: Intellectuals and Popular Culture* and in the films of Annie Sprinkle, Suzie Sex Bright, and the work of Candida Royalle's Femme Productions, to name but a few.

13. Frank Rich, "The Last Taboo."

CONTRIBUTORS

Alice E. Adams is Assistant Professor of English and Women's Studies at Miami University in Oxford, Ohio. She is the author of *Reproducing The Womb: Images of Childbirth in Science, Feminist Theory, and Literature* (Ithaca: Cornell University Press, 1994). She is currently working on a book about the social and cultural impact of interracial reproduction.

Susanmarie Harrington is Assistant Professor of English and coordinator of placement testing at Indiana University–Purdue University, Indianapolis.

Catherine Hobbs, Associate Professor of Rhetoric and Cultural Studies at the University of Oklahoma, Norman, completed her doctoral work in rhetoric and composition at Purdue University. She currently researches and publishes on the history of literacy, especially as it concerns women, and on nonfiction prose in the eighteenth and nineteenth centuries. Recent projects include feminist perspectives on Locke in *Rhetoric Society Quarterly*, an article on Condillac for *Rhetorica*, a book chapter on the social rhetoric of Jane Addams of Hull House, and a collection of essays entitled *Nineteenth Century Women Learn To Write: Past Cultures and Practices of Writing* (Charlottesville: University of Virginia Press, 1995).

Cynthia Huff was Director of Women's Studies at Illinois State University for six years, and is now an Associate Professor of English. The recipient of a Fulbright Research Grant, her publications include *British Women's Diaries* and articles on women's diaries and autobiographies, feminist theory, and the cultural ramifications of childbirth. She is currently working on women's childbirth accounts and the Carlyles's letters, and has co-edited *Inscribing the Daily: Critical Essays on Women's Diaries.* (Amherst: University of Massachusetts Press, 1996).

Christine Moneera Laennec holds a Ph.D. in French from Yale University, where she studied art history as a secondary subject. Most of her publications to date have been on the medieval writer

Christine de Pizan, but her teaching and academic areas of specialization also include feminist theory and women in all periods of history. She currently teaches French and Women's Studies at the University of Aberdeen, Scotland, where she has also been studying Gaelic. Her work appears in *Tulsa Studies in Women and Literature* and in the collections *Anxious Power* and *Une Femme de lettres au Moyen Age*.

Cathy Peppers is writing her dissertation on the uses of scientific origin stories in contemporary feminist theories and women's novels. She has also published articles on works by Octavia Butler, Toni Morrison, and William Faulkner.

Roberta Schreyer received her Ph.D. in English from the State University of New York at Buffalo. She teaches courses in psycho-analysis, women and literature, fantasy, folklore, and mythology at Potsdam State College in Potsdam, New York. She has written critical articles in these areas, some of which have appeared in the journals *Literature and Psychology*, *American Imago*, and *The Melanie Klein and Object Relations Journal*. The DePalma piece included here is her first foray into film criticism.

Julie Shaffer's work focuses on British novels of the late eighteenth and early nineteenth centuries. She has published on women writers' use of the marriage plot to challenge and subvert ideologies repressive for women in such texts. Her most current work focuses on incest, extramarital sexuality, and illegitimacy in novels by women in the decade following the French Revolution. Her work appears in *Criticism: Studies in The Novel*; *Misogyny in Literature*, edited by Katherine Ackley; *Dialogue of Voices: Feminist Theory and Bakhtin*, edited by Karen Hohne and Helen Wussow; and elsewhere. Shaffer is currently an assistant professor of English at the University of Wisconsin, Oshkosh.

Torri L. Thompson teaches Shakespeare and Renaissance literature at Illinois State University. Her current research focuses on feminist analyses of the connections between traditional literature and early modern English domestic texts. Recently, she published on feminist pedagogy in the Renaissance literature classroom for *Feminist Teacher* and gender ideology in seventeenth century surgical texts for "Social and Cultural Aspects of Visual Communication," a special issue of IEEE's *Transactions on Professional Communication*, December 1995.

Angela Wall is working on a dissertation that uses feminist cultural theories of science and technology to analyze various cultural formations of gender as they are presented in medical journals, social policy statements, news magazines, science fictions, and popular films. She is currently a Brittain Fellow at Georgia Institute of Technology.

Deborah S. Wilson took her Ph.D. in English from the University of California, Irvine. Her other areas of expertise include feminist pedagogy and women's literature. She is currently at work on a study of feminist incursions into American popular culture, especially computer games and science-fiction/adventure films, tentatively entitled *Feminism for The Colonially Challenged.* Since 1989, she has been a writer and editor for the *Post Amerikan,* Bloomington-Normal's alternative community newspaper, the oldest, continually published newspaper of its kind. She teaches English at Illinois Central College, and is also a trained massage therapist.

BIBLIOGRAPHY

ACT-UP Women and AIDS Group. *Women, AIDS, and Activism.* Boston: South End P, 1990.

Adam, Annmarie. "Architecture in the Family Way: Lying-in and the Design of Middle-Class Motherhood." Paper presented at the Interdisciplinary Nineteenth-Century Society Meeting, Yale Center for British Art, New Haven, Conn., 1991.

Adams, Alice E. *Reproducing the Womb: Images of Childbirth in Science, Feminist Theory, and Literature.* Ithaca: Cornell U P, 1994.

Adams, Henry. *The Education of Henry Adams.* New York: Modern Library, 1931.

The AIDS Quarterly. "Money and Morals." PBS (Station WILL, Champaign,Ill.); Winter 1990.

Alleman, Richard. "Waist Not." *Vogue* June 1993, 126–27.

Amitt, Lucie. *Where No Man Has Gone Before: Women and Science Fiction.* New York: Routledge, 1991.

Amussen, Susan Dwyer. *An Ordered Society: Gender and Class in Early Modern England.* New York: Basil Blackwell, 1988.

Armstrong, Nancy. *Desire and Domestic Fiction.* New York: Oxford U P, 1986.

Armstrong, Nancy and Leonard Tennenhouse. "The Literature of Conduct, Conduct of Literature, and the Politics of Desire." *The Ideology of Conduct.* Eds. Nancy Armstrong and Leonard Tennenhouse. New York: Methuen, (1987): 1–24.

Ash, Juliet and Elizabeth Wilson, eds. *Chic Thrills: A Fashion Reader.* London: Pandora P, 1992.

Auerbach, Nina. "Magi and Maidens: The Romance of the Victorian Freud." *Writing and Sexual Difference.* Ed. Elizabeth Abel. Chicago: U of Chicago P, (1981): 281–300.

Austen, Jane. *Mansfield Park.* 1814. New York: Oxford U P, 1990.

————. *Pride and Prejudice*. 1813. New York: Oxford U P, 1990.

Bakhtin, M. M. *The Dialogic Imagination: Four Essays*. Ed. Michael Holquist. Trans. Caryl Emerson and Michael Holquist. Austin: U of Texas P, 1981.

Balsamo, Anne. "Assembly-Line Gender and the Postmodern Body." Paper presented at the Midwest/Modern Language Association Conference, November 1991, Chicago, Ill.

————. *Technologies of the Gendered Body: Reading Cyborg Women*. Durham, N.C.: Duke U P, 1995.

Barr, Marlene S. *Lost in Space: Pro Feminist Science Fiction*. Chapel Hill: U of North Carolina P, 1993.

Bassuk, Ellen L. "The Rest Cure: Repetition or Resolution of Victorian Women's Conflicts?" *The Female Body in Western Culture: Contemporary Perspectives*. Ed. Susan Rubin Suleiman. Cambridge: Harvard U P, (1986): 139–51.

Bauer, Dale M. "Twilight Sleep: Edith Wharton's Brave New Politics. *Arizona Quarterly* 45 (1989): 49–71.

de Beauvoir, Simone. *The Second Sex*. 1952. Trans. H. M. Parshley. New York: Vintage Books, 1974.

Belenky, Mary Field, *et al. Women's Ways of Knowing: The Development of Self, Voice, and Mind*. New York: Basic Books, 1986.

Benjamin, Jessica. "A Desire of One's Own: Psychoanalytic Feminism and Intersubjective Space." *Feminist Studies/Critical Studies*. Ed. Teresa de Lauretis. Bloomington: Indiana U P, 1986: 78–101.

Benjamin, Walter. "The Work of Art in the Age of Mechanical Reproduction." *Illuminations*. Trans. Harry Zohn. New York: Schocken Books, 1969: 217–52.

Bennington, Geoff. "The Perfect Cheat: Locke and Empiricism's Rhetoric." *The Figural and the Literal: Problems of Language and the History of Science and Philosophy, 1630–1800*. Eds. Andrew E. Benjamin, Geoffrey N. Cantor, and John R. R. Christie. Manchester: Manchester U P, 1987: 103–23.

Benstock, Shari. *Textualizing the Feminine: On the Limits of Genre*. Norman: U of Oklahoma P, 1991.

Bentley, Thomas. *The Monument of Matrones: Conteining Seven Severall Lamps of Virginity*. STC #1892, reel #174. (5th, 6th, and 7th lamps are on reel #377.)

Berger, John. *Ways of Seeing.* New York: Penguin, 1977.

Boffin, Tessa and Sunil Gupta. *Ecstatic Antibodies: Resisting the AIDS Mythology.* London: Rivers Oram, 1990.

Boose, Lynda E. "Scolding Brides and Bridling Scolds: Taming the Woman's Unruly Member." *Shakespeare Quarterly,* 42 (Summer 1991): 179–213.

Bordo, Susan. "Feminism, Postmodernism, and Gender-Scepticism." *Feminism/Postmodernism.* Ed. Linda Nicholson. New York: Routledge, 1990: 133–56.

———. *The Flight to Objectivity: Essays on Cartesianism and Culture.* Albany: State University of New York P, 1987.

Browne, Dallas L. "Christian Missionaries, Western Feminists, and the Kikuyu Clitoridectomy Controversy." *The Politics of Culture.* Ed. Brett Williams. Washington D. C.: The Smithsonian Institution P, 1991: 243–72.

Burford, W. J. and Sarah Shulman. *Of Bridles and Burnings: The Punishment of Women.* New York: St. Martin's, 1992.

Burney, Frances. *Camilla.* 1796. London: Oxford U P, 1972.

———. *Cecilia.* 1782. London: Virago , 1986.

Butler, Judith. *Bodies that Matter: On the Discursive Limits of "Sex."* New York: Routledge, 1993.

———. "Imitation and Gender Insubordination." *inside/out: Lesbian Theories, Gay Theories.* Ed. Diana Fuss. London: Routledge, 1991: 13–31.

Byers, Thomas B. "Good Men and Monsters: The Defenses of *Dracula.*" *Literature and Psychology,* xxxi (1981): 24–31.

Cadigan, Pat. "Rock On." *Mirrorshades: The Cyberpunk Anthology.* Ed. Bruce Sterling. New York: Arbor House, 1986: 34–52.

———. *Synners.* New York: Bantam, 1991.

Carpenter, Carole H. "Tales Women Tell: The Function of Birth Experience Narratives." *Canadian Folklore Canadien* 7 (1985): 21–34.

Centers for Disease Control. *HIV/AIDS Surveillance Report.* June 1994.

Certaine Questions by Way of Conference Betwixt a Chauncelor and a Kinswoman of His Concerning Churching of Women. 1601. STC #20557, reel #1639.

Certaine Sermons or Homilies Appointed to be Read in Churches in the Time of Queen Elizabeth; and Reprinted by Authority From King James I., A.D. 1623. To Which Are Added, The Constitutions and Canons of the Church of England. Philadelphia: George and Wayne, 1844.

Chapkis, Wendy. *Beauty Secrets: Women and the Politics of Appearance.* Boston: South End Press, 1986.

Charlton, Mary. *The Wife and the Mistress.* London: Lane, 1803.

Chopin, Kate. *The Awakening and Selected Stories.* Ed. Sandra M. Gilbert. Hammondsworth: Penguin, 1984.

Clover, Carol. "Her Body, Himself: Gender in the Slasher Film." *Representations* 20 (Fall 1987): 87–228.

Collected Letters of the International Correspondence Society of Obstetrics and Gynecology. 23 (January 1982).

Congressional Record. House. Burton. June 26, 1991. H 5203–5205.

Congressional Record. House. Dornan. September 26, 1991. H 5205-5208.

Congressional Record. Senate. Helms. July 10, 1991 S 9476-9796.

Corea, G., *et al*, eds. *Man-Made Woman: How Reproductive Technologies Affect Women,* Bloomington: Indiana U P, 1987.

Cosslett, Tess. "Childbirth from the Woman's Point of View in British Women's Fiction: Enid Bagnold's The Squire and A. S. Byatt's *Still Life.*" *Tulsa Studies in Women's Literature* 8 (1989): 263–86

———. "Childbirth on the National Health: Issues of Class, Race, and Gender Identity in Two Post-War British Novels. *Women's Studies* 19 (1991): 99–119.

———. *Women Writing Childbirth: Modern Discourses of Motherhood.* New York: St. Martin's P, 1994.

Couless, Inge and Mary Pittman-Lindeman, eds. *AIDS: Principles, Practices, and Politics.* Cambridge, N.Y.: Hemisphere Books, 1988.

Craik, Jennifer. *The Face of Fashion: Cultural Studies in Fashion.* London and New York: Routledge, 1994.

Cressy, David. "Purification, Thanksgiving, and the Churching of Women in Post-Reformation England." *Past and Present* 141 (November 1993): 106–46.

Csiscery-Ronay, Istvan. "Cyberpunk and Neuromanticism." *Storming the Reality Studio: A Casebook of Cyberpunk and Postmodern Fiction.* Ed. Larry McCaffery. Durham: Duke U P, 1991: 182–93.

———. "Futuristic Flu, or, the Revenge of the Future." *Fiction 2000.* Eds. George Slusser and Tom Shippey. Athens: U of Georgia P, 1992: 26–45.

Dally, Ann. *Women Under The Knife: A History of Surgery.* New York: Routledge, 1991.

Daly, Mary. *Gyn-Ecology.* Boston: Beacon, 1978.

Darnton, Nina. "Is Brian De Palma Crossing the Line between Art and Pornography?" *New York Times* 134, November 18, 1984, section 2, 1–7.

de Laurentis, Teresa. *Alice Doesn't: Feminism, Semiotics, Cinema.* Bloomington: Indiana U P, 1984.

———. "Feminist Studies/Critical Studies: Issues, Terms, and Contexts." *Feminist Studies/Critical Studies.* Ed. Teresa de Lauretis. Bloomington: Indiana U P, 1986: 1-19.

———. *Technologies of Gender: Essays on Theory, Film, and Fiction.* Bloomington: Indiana U P, 1987.

Devlin, Polly, ed. *The Vogue Book of Fashion Photography.* New York: Conde Nast, 1979.

De Zayas, Marius and Agnes Meyer. "Mental Reactions." *291* 2 (1915) Beinecke Library, New Haven, Conn.: Yale University.

Doane, Janice and Devon Hodges. *Nostalgia and Sexual Difference: The Resistance to Contemporary Feminism.* New York: Methuen, 1987.

Doane, Mary Ann. "Technophilia, Technology, Representation and the Feminine." *Body/Politics.* Eds. Mary Jacobus *et al.* 163–76.

Donawerth, Jane L. and Carol A. Kolmerten, eds. *Utopian and Science Fiction By Women: Worlds of Difference.* Syracuse: Syracuse U P, 1994.

Dorkenoo, Efua. *Female Genital Mutilation: Proposals for Change.* London: Minority Rights Group, 1992.

Dull, Diana and Candace West. "Accounting for Cosmetic Surgery: The Accomplishment of Gender." *Social Problems* 38 (February 1991): 54–70.

Dworkin, Susan. *Double De Palma: A Film Study with Brian De Palma.* New York: Newmarket P, 1984.

Edgeworth, Maria. *The Absentee.* Vols. 5 and 6 of *Tales of Fashionable Life.* 1809, 1812. 6 vols. London: Lane, 1812.

——. *Vivian.* London: Lane. Vol. 4 of Tales of Fashionable Life.

Eisenberg, Carola, M.D. "Medicine Is No Longer a Man's Profession." *The New England Journal of Medicine.* 321 no. 22 (November 30, 1989): 1542–1644.

Facts on File 54 no. 2820 December 15, 1994: 937.

Farson, Daniel. *The Man Who Wrote Dracula: A Biography of Bram Stoker.* London: Michael Joseph, 1975.

Ferrier, Susan. *Marriage.* 1818. 3 vols. London: Oxford U P, 1971.

Fillin-Yeh, Susan. *The Technological Muse.* Katonah, N.Y.: Katonah Museum of Art, 1990.

Fitz, Linda T. " 'What says the Married Woman'?: Marriage, Theory, and Feminism in the English Renaissance." *Mosaic* 13 (1980): 1–22.

Foucault, Michel. *Discipline and Punish: The Birth of the Prison.* Trans. Alan Sheridan. New York: Pantheon Books, 1977.

——. "The Eye of Power." *Power/Knowledge: Selected Interviews and Other Writings 1972–1977.* Ed. Colin Gordon. New York: Harvester, 1980: 146–65.

——. *The History of Sexuality: An Introduction.* Vol I. Trans. Robert Hurley. New York: Random House, 1980.

——. *The Use of Pleasure, The History of Sexuality.* Vol. II. Trans. Robert Hurley. New York, Pantheon Books, 1985.

Frantz, Andrea B. *Redemption and Madness: Three Nineteenth-Century Feminist Views on Motherhood and Childbearing.* Las Colinas, Tex.: Ide House, 1993.

Freud, Sigmund. "Instincts and Their Vicissitudes." *Standard Edition of The Complete Psychological Works.* Vol. 14. Trans. James Strachey. London: Hogarth, 1966: 111–40.

Fumaroli, Mark. "Rhetoric, Politics, and Society: From Italian Ciceronianism to French Classicism." *Renaissance Eloquence.* Ed. James J. Murphy. Berkeley: U of California P, 1983: 253–73.

Fuss, Diana. "Fashion and the Homospectatorial Look." *Critical Inquiry* 4 (1992): 713–37.

Gaines, Jane and Charlotte Herzog, eds. *Fabrications: Costume and the Female Body.* New York and London: Routledge, 1990.

Gallagher, Catherine. *Nobody's Story: The Vanishing Acts of Women Writers in the Marketplace.* Berkeley: U of California P, 1994.

Gardner, Richard. *Sex Abuse Hysteria: Salem Witch Trials Revisited.* Cresskill, N.J.: Creative Therapeutics, 1986.

Gay Men's Health Crisis. *The Safer Sex Condom Guide for Men and Women.* New York: Gay Men's Health Crisis, Inc., 1987.

Gentile, Kathy. "Monstrous Absence: The Maternal Body and *Frankenstein.*" Paper presented at the Midwest/Modern Language Association Conference, November 1989, Minneapolis, MN.

Georgiade, Nicholas, M.D., Gregory Georgiade, M.D., and Ronald Riefkohl, M.D., eds. *Aesthetic Surgery of The Breast.* Philadelphia: W. B. Saunders, 1990.

Gerassi, John. *The Boys of Boise: Furor, Vice, and Folly in An American City.* New York: Collier Books, 1968.

Gerrard, Susan and James Halpern. "The Risky Business of Bisexual Love." *Cosmopolitan,* October 1990, 203, 205.

Gibson, William. "Burning Chrome." *Burning Chrome.* New York: Ace, 1987.

———. "The Gernsback Continuum." *Burning Chrome.* New York, Ace, 1987.

———. *Count Zero.* New York: Ace, 1986.

———. *Mona Lisa Overdrive.* New York: Bantam, 1988.

Gilmore, Leigh. *Autobiographies: A Feminist Theory of Women's Self-Representation.* Ithaca: Cornell U P, 1991.

Glut, Donald. *The Frankenstein Legend.* Methuen, N.J.: The Scarecrow P, 1973.

The Golden Boke of Christian Matrimonye. 1542. STC #1723, reel #25.

Gouge, William. *Of Domesticall Duties.* London, 1622. #803, The English Experience. Norwood, N. J.: Walter J. Johnson, 1976.

Gould, Robert. "A Doctor Tells Why Most Women are Safe from AIDS." *Cosmopolitan.* January 1988: 146-148, 204.

Grant, Meg. "An Anguished Voice Falls Silent." *People,* December 23, 1991, 114+

Haraway, Donna. "The Biopolitics of Postmodern Bodies: Determinations of Self in Immune System Discourse." *Difference* 1 (Winter 1989): 3–43.

———. "A Cyborg Manifesto: Science, Technology, and Socialist Feminism in the Late Twentieth Century." *Simians, Cyborgs, and Women.* New York: Routledge, 1994: 149–81.

Harstock, Nancy. "Foucault on Power: A Theory for Women?" *Feminism/ Postmodernism.* Ed. Linda J. Nicholson. New York: Routledge, 1990: 157–75.

Heale, William. *An Apologie for Women. or an Opposition to Mr. Dr. G. his assertion. Who held in the Act at Oxforde.* Anno 1608. *That it was lawfull for husbands to beate their wives.* 1609. #665, The English Experience. Norwood, N.J.: Walter J. Johnson, 1974.

Henderson, Katherine Usher and Barbara F. McManus. *Half Humankind: Contexts and Texts of the Controversy about Women in England, 1540–1640.* Urbana: U of Illinois P, 1985.

Heyn, Dalma. "What Should You Tell Him About Your Sexual History?" *Cosmopolitan.* December 1994, 154–57.

Hilts, Philip. "Mason Writes President." *New York Times*, August 4, 1991: A1, A14.

Hirsch, E. D. *Cultural Literacy: What Literate Americans Know.* Boston: Houghton Mifflin Company, 1987.

Hodgkinson, Darrill, M.D. and Glen Hait, M.D. "Plastic Vaginal Labioplasty." *Plastic and Reconstructive Surgery* (September 1984): 414–16.

Hoffmann, E. T. A. "The Sand Man." *Best Tales of Hoffmann.* Ed. E. F. Bleiler. New York: Dover Publications, 1967: 183–214.

von Hoffman, Nicholas. *Citizen Cohn.* New York: Doubleday, 1988.

Hollenberg, Donna K. *H. D.: The Poetics of Childbirth.* Boston: Northeastern U P, 1991.

Hollinger, Veronica. "Cybernetic Deconstruction: Cyberpunk and Postmodernism." *Mosaic: A Journal for the Interdisciplinary Study of Literature* 23 (Spring 1990): 29–44.

Horney, Karen. "The Distrust Between The Sexes." *Feminine Psychology.* New York: W.W. Norton Company, 1967: 107–18.

———. "The Dread of Woman." *Feminine Psychology.* New York: W.W. Norton Company, 1967: 133–46.

Hosken, Fran. *The Hosken Report: Genital and Sexual Mutilation of Females.* Lexington, Mass.: Women International Network News, 1982.

Howell, Ann. *Georgina, or the Advantages of Grand Connexions.* London: Lane, 1796.

Huff, Cynthia. "Delivery: The Cultural Re-presentation of Childbirth. *Prose Studies* 14 (1991): 108–21.

Hull, Suzanne W. *Chaste, Silent, and Obedient: English Books for Women, 1475–1640.* San Marino: Huntington Library, 1982.

Hunt, Lynn. "Foucault's Subject in *The History of Sexuality.*" *Discourses of Sexuality: From Aristotle to AIDS.* Ed. Domna C. Stanton. Ann Arbor: The U of Michigan P, 1992: 79–93.

Huyssen, Andreas. "Mass Culture as Woman: Modernism's Other." *Studies in Entertainment: Critical Approaches to Mass Culture.* Ed. Tania Modleski. Bloomington: Indiana U P, 1986: 188–207.

Irigaray, Luce. "On The Maternal Order." *je, tu, nous: Toward a Culture of Difference.* New York: Routledge, 1993: 3–44.

Jacobus, Mary, Evelyn Fox Keller, and Sally Shuttleworth, eds. *Body/Politics: Women and the Discourses of Science.* New York: Routledge, 1990.

Jehl, Douglas. "Surgeon General Forced to Resign." *New York Times,* December 10, 1994: A1.

Johnson, Bonnie, Meg Grant, and Don Sider. "Kimberly Bergalis." *People,* October 22, 1990, 72+.

Jordan, Constance. *Renaissance Feminism: Literary Texts and Political Models.* Ithaca, N.Y.: Corneli U P, 1990.

Kaminer, Wendy. *I'm Dysfunctional, You're Dysfunctional: The Recovery Movement and Other Self-Help Fashions.* Reading, Mass.: Addison-Wesley Publishing Company Inc., 1992.

Keller, Evelyn Fox. *Reflections on Gender and Science.* New Haven: Yale U P, 1985.

———. *Secrets of Life, Secrets of Death: Essays on Language, Gender, and Science.* New York: Routledge, 1992.

Kelley, Edith Summers. *Weeds.* Afterword by Matthew J. Bruccoli. Carbondale: Southern Illinois U P, 1972.

Kelly, Joan. *Women, History, and Theory: The Essays of Joan Kelly.* Chicago: U of Chicago P, 1984.

Kelso, Ruth. *Doctrine for the Lady of the Renaissance*. Urbana: U of Illinois P, 1956.

King, Margaret L. *Women of the Renaissance*. Chicago: U of Chicago P, 1991.

Kipnis, Laura. "(Male) Desire and (Female) Disgust: Reading *Hustler*." *Cultural Studies*. Eds. Lawrence Grossberg, Cary Nelson, and Paula Treichler. New York: Routledge, 1992: 373–91.

Klein, Joan Larsen, ed. *Daughters, Wives, and Widows: Writings by Men about Women and Marriage in England, 1500–1640*. Urbana: U of Illinois P, 1992.

Kristeva, Julia. *Desire in Language*. Trans. Leon S. Roudiez *et al*. New York: Columbia U P, 1980.

————. "Woman Can Never Be Defined." Trans. Marilyn A. August. *New French Feminisms: An Anthology*. Eds. Elaine Marks and Elizabeth de Courtivron. New York: Shocken Books, 1980: 137–41.

Kroker, Arthur. "Body Digest: Theses on the Disappearing Body in the Hypermodern Condition." *Canadian Journal of Political and Social Theory*. 11 (1987): 1–2.

Kroker, Arthur and Marilouise Kroker. *Body Invaders: Panic Sex in America*. New York: St. Martin's, 1987.

————, eds. *The Last Sex: Feminism and Outlaw Bodies*. New York: St. Martin's P, 1993.

Lakoff, Robin, and Raquel L. Scherr. *Face Value: The Politics of Beauty*. Boston: Routledge, Kegan, & Paul, 1984.

Leavitt, Judith. "Birthing and Anesthesia: The Debate over Twilight Sleep." *Journal of Women in Culture and Society* 6 (1980): 147–64.

————. *Brought To Bed: Childbearing in America, 1750–1950*. New York: Oxford U P, 1986.

LeFanu, Sarah. *Feminism and Science Fiction*. Bloomington: Indiana U P, 1989.

Le Guin, Ursula K. "The World of Science Fiction." *Ms.*, November/December 1990, 52–54.

————. *Prisoners of Ritual: An Odyssey into Female Genital Circumcision in Africa*. New York: Haworth P, 1989.

Lightfoot-Klein, Hanny. *The Left Hand of Darkness*. New York: Ace, 1969.

Locke, John. *An Essay Concerning Human Understanding*. Ed. Peter H. Nidditch. Oxford: Clarendon P, 1975.

Lynch, Daniel. "AIDS: The Real Story About Risk." *Cosmopolitan*, March 1992, 196–98.

Lyon, Elizabeth. "The Unspeakable." *Camera Obscura* 24 (1990): 5–6.

MacCannell, Dean and Juliet Flower MacCannell. "The Beauty System." *The Ideology of Conduct*. Eds. Nancy Armstrong and Leonard Tennenhouse. New York: Methuen, 1987: 206–38.

Macfarlane, Alan. *Marriage and Love in England, 1300–1840*. New York: Basil Blackwell, 1985.

"Machine Age Exposition," exhibit catalogue printed in *The Little Review* 11 (1927).

Maclean, Ian. *The Renaissance Notion of Woman: A Study in the Fortunes of Scholasticism and Medical Science in European Intellectual Life*. Cambridge: Cambridge U P, 1980.

de Man, Paul. "The Epistemology of Metaphor." *Critical Inquiry* 5 (1978): 13–30.

Marcus, Steven. *The Other Victorians: A Study of Sexuality and Pornography in Mid-Nineteenth Century England*. New York: Basic Books, 1966.

Marter, Joan. "Review of Susan Fillin-Yeh's *The Technological Muse*." *Art Journal* 50 (Summer 1991): 75–77.

Martianus, Capella. *Martianus Capella and the Seven Liberal Arts. Vol II: The Marriage of Philology and Mercury*. Trans. William Harris Stahl and Richard Johnson with E. L. Burge. New York: Columbia U P, 1977.

Martin, Emily. "Body Narratives, Body Boundaries." *Cultural Studies*. Eds. Lawrence Grossberg, Cary Nelson and Paula Treichler. New York: Routledge, 1992: 409–23.

———. *The Woman in The Body: A Cultural Analysis of Reproduction*. Boston: Beacon P, 1987.

McCaffery, Larry, ed. *Storming the Reality Studio: A Casebook of Cyberpunk and Postmodern Fiction*. Durham: Duke U P, 1991.

McCaffrey, Anne. *The Ship Who Sang*. New York: Ballantine, 1969.

McGregor, Deborah Kuhn. *Sexual Surgery and the Origins of Gynecology: J. Marion Simms, His Hospital and His Patients*. New York: Garland Publishing, 1989.

McHale, Brian. "Elements of a Poetics of Cyberpunk." *Critique* 33 (Spring 1992): 149–75.

McKendrick, Neil, John Brewer, and J. H. Plumb. *The Birth of a Consumer Society: The Commercialization of Eighteenth-Century England.* Bloomington: Indiana U P, 1982.

McLuhan, Marshall. *The Mechanical Bride: Folklore of Industrial Man.* New York: Vanguard P, 1951.

McRobbie, Angela, ed. *Zoot Suits and Second-Hand Dresses: An Anthology of Fashion and Music.* Basingstoke and London: Macmillan, 1989.

Meade, W. W. "When Straight Women Marry Gay Men." *Cosmopolitan,* November 1994, 218–21.

Mellor, Anne K. *Mary Shelley: Her Life, Her Fiction, Her Monsters.* New York: Methuen, 1988.

———. "Possessing Nature: The Female in *Frankenstein.*" *Romanticism and Feminism.* Ed. Anne K. Mellor. Bloomington: Indiana U P, 1988: 220–32.

Modleski, Tania. *Feminism Without Women: Culture and Criticism in a "Postfeminist" Age.* New York: Routledge, Kegan, Paul, 1991.

Moers, Ellen. *Literary Women.* Garden City: Doubleday & Company, Inc., 1976.

Monette, Paul. *Borrowed Time: An AIDS Memoir.* New York: Avon Books, 1990.

———. *Last Watch of the Night: Essays Too Personal and Otherwise.* New York: Harcourt Brace & Co., 1994.

Montagu, Ashley. *Coming into Being among the Australian Aborigines: A Study of Procreative Beliefs.* Boston: Routledge and Kegan Paul, 1974.

Morano, Elizabeth. *Sonia Delaunay: Art into Fashion.* New York: George Braziller, 1986.

Morgan, Kathryn Pauly. "Women and the Knife: Cosmetic Surgery and the Colonization of Women's Bodies." *Hypatia* 6 (Fall 1991): 25–53.

Morrison, Toni. *The Bluest Eye.* New York: Washington Square, 1970.

Mulvey, Laura. "Visual Pleasure and Narrative Cinema." *Visual and Other Pleasures.* Bloomington: Indiana U P, 1989: 14–26.

Myers, Mitzi. "Reform or Ruin: 'Revolution in Female Manners.'" *Studies in Eighteenth-Century Culture* 11 (1982): 199–216.

Navasky, Victor. *Naming Names*. New York: The Viking P, 1980.

Newton, Judith Lowder. *Women, Power, and Subversion: Social Strategies in British Fiction, 1778–1860*. New York: Methuen: 1981.

Nietzsche, Friedrich. *Friedrich Nietzsche on Rhetoric and Language*. Eds. and Trans. Sander L. Gilman, Carole Blair, and David J. Parent. New York: Oxford U P, 1989.

Nixon, Nicola. "Cyberpunk: Preparing the Ground for Revolution or Keeping the Boys Satisfied?" *Science Fiction Studies* 19 (July 1992): 219–35.

Patton, Cindy. "Safe Sex and the Pornographic Vernacular." *How Do I Look? Queer Film and Video*. Seattle: Bay P, 1991: 31–63.

Pearsall, Roland. *The Worm in The Bud: The World of Victorian Sexuality*. New York: Macmillan, 1969.

Penley, Constance and Andrew Ross. "Cyborgs at Large: Interview with Donna Haraway." *Technoculture*. Eds. Constance Penley and Andrew Ross. Minneapolis: U of Minnesota P, 1991: 1–20.

Pike, Deborah. "Health and Fitness: Stamping Out STDs." *Vogue*, September 1994, 384–86, 388.

Plath, Sylvia. *The Bell Jar*. New York: Bantam, 1971.

Poe, Edgar Allan. "The Philosophy of Composition." *Great Short Works of Edgar Allan Poe*. Ed. G. R. Thompson. New York: Harper Collins, 1970: 528–42.

Pollard, A. W. and G. R. Redgrave. *A Short Title Catalogue of Books Printed in England, Scotland, and Ireland, and of the English Books Printed Abroad, 1475–1640*. London: Bibliographical Society, 1926. Revised edition, ed. W. A. Jackson *et al*. London: Bibliographical Society, 1976.

Poovey, Mary. *The Proper Lady and the Woman Writer*. Chicago: U of Chicago P, 1984.

———. *Uneven Developments: The Ideological Work of Gender in Mid-Victorian England*. Chicago: U of Chicago P, 1988.

Randolph, Laura B. "In The Eye of the Storm: Surgeon General Jocelyn Elders Challenges the Status Quo." *Ebony*, February 1993, 154–60.

Reiss, Timothy J. *The Discourse of Modernism*. Ithaca: Cornell U P, 1982.

Ricci, James. *One Hundred Years of Gynecology, 1800–1900*. Philadelphia: Williams and Wilkins, 1945.

Rich, Adrienne. *Of Woman Born: Motherhood as Experience and Institution.* New York: Norton, 1976.

Rich, Frank. "The Last Taboo." *New York Times.* December 18, 1994, E15

Roberts, Robin. *A New Species: Gender and Science in Science Fiction.* Urbana: U of Illinois P, 1993.

Rollins, Roger B. "Triple X: Erotic Movies and Their Audiences." *The Journal of Popular Film and Television* 10 (Spring 1982): 2–21.

Ross, Andrew. *No Respect: Intellectuals and Popular Culture.* New York: Routledge, 1989.

Rubin, Gail. "The Traffic in Women: Notes on the Political Economy of Sex." *Towards and Anthropology of Women.* Ed. Rayna Reiter. New York: Monthly Review, 1975: 157–210.

Rubin, Gayle. "Thinking Sex: Notes for a Radical Theory of the Politics of Sexuality." *Pleasure and Danger: Exploring Female Sexuality.* Ed. Carole S. Vance. Boston: Routledge Kegan and Paul, 1984: 267–319.

Rudd, Andrea and Darien Taylor, eds. *Positive Women: Voices of Women Living with AIDS.* Toronto: Second Story P, 1992.

Rule, John. *Albion's People: English Society, 1714–1815.* London: Longman, 1992.

Russ, Joanna. *The Female Man.* Boston: Beacon, 1975.

Ryan, Michael, and Avery Gordon, eds. *Body Politics: Disease, Desire, and the Family.* Boulder: Westview P, 1995.

Sandelowski, Margarete. *Pain, Pleasure, and American Childbirth: From the Twilight Sleep to the Read Method, 1914–1960.* Westport, Conn.: Greenwood, 1984.

Schultz, Gladys Denny, ed. "Journal Mothers Report on Cruelty on Maternity Wards." *Ladies Home Journal,* May 1958, 44–45, 152+.

Scully, Diana. *Men Who Control Women's Health: The Miseducation of Obstetricians and Gynecologists.* Boston: Houghton Mifflin, 1980.

Seebohm, Caroline. *Conde Nast.* New York: Conde Nast, 1983.

Shaffer, Julie. "The High Cost of Female Virtue: The Sexualization of Female Agency in Late Eighteenth– and Early Nineteenth–Century Texts." *Misogyny in Literature: An Essay Collection.* Ed. Kathy Ackley. New York: Garland, 1992: 105–42.

Shelley, Mary. *Frankenstein; or, the Modern Prometheus.* 1818. Ed. Johanna M. Smith. Boston: Bedford Books of St. Martin's P, 1992.

Shilts, Randy. *And The Band Played On: People, Politics, and the AIDS Epidemic.* New York: St. Martin's P, 1987.

——. *Conduct Unbecoming: Gays and Lesbians in The U. S. Military—Vietnam to the Persian Gulf.* New York: St. Martin's P, 1993.

Siebert, Bessie. Manuscript Autobiography, in possession of Cynthia Huff.

Silverman, Kaja. "Fragments of a Fashionable Discourse." *Studies in Entertainment: Critical Approaches to Mass Culture.* Ed. Tania Modleski. Bloomington: Indiana U P, 1986: 139–52.

Simpson, D. "Examining the Episiotomy Argument." *Midwife, Health Visitor, and Community Nurse* 24 (January/February 1988): 6–14.

Singer, Linda. *Erotic Warfare: Sexual Theory and Politics in the Age of Epidemic.* New York: Routledge, 1993.

Smith, Henry. *A Preparative to Marriage.* London: 1591. STC #22685, reel #1395.

Smith, Sidonie and Julia Watson, eds. *De/Colonizing the Subject: The Politics of Gender in Women's Autobiography.* Minneapolis: U of Minnesota P, 1992.

Sowerman, Ester. "*Ester hath hanged Haman*; or An Answer to a lewd Pamphlet entitled *The Arraignment of Women*." Eds. Katherine Esher Henderson and Barbara F. McManus. *Half Humankind: Contexts and Texts of the Controversy over Women in England, 1540–1640.* Urbana: U of Illinois P, 1985: 217–43.

Spark, Muriel. *Mary Shelley.* New York: E. P. Dutton, 1987.

Spoto, Donald. *Dark Side of Genius: The Life of Alfred Hitchcock.* New York: Little, 1983.

Stafford, Barbara. *Body Criticism: Imaging the Unseen in Enlightenment Art and Medicine.* Cambridge: MIT P, 1993.

Stanton, Domna C. *Discourses of Sexuality: From Aristotle to AIDS.* Ann Arbor: U of Michigan P, 1992.

Starkey, Marion Lena. *The Devil in Massachusetts: A Modern Inquiry into the Salem Witch Trials.* Magnolia, Mass.: Peter Smith Publishers, Inc., 1969.

Steichen, Edward. *Steichen: A Life in Photography.* New York: Doubleday, 1963.

Sterling, Bruce. "Preface." *Burning Chrome.* New York: Ace, 1986: ix–xl1.

————. "Preface." *Mirrorshades: The Cyberpunk Anthology.* New York: Ace, 1986: vii–xiv.

Stevenson, John. "The Vampire in the Mirror: The Sexuality of *Dracula.*" *PMLA* 103 (1988): 139–49.

Stoker, Bram. *Dracula.* 1897. New York: Oxford U P, 1989.

Stone, Lawrence. *Family, Sex, and Marriage in England, 1500–1800.* New York: Harper, 1977.

Suleiman, Susan Rubin, ed. *The Female Body in Western Culture: Contemporary Perspectives.* Cambridge: Harvard U P, 1986.

Sunstein, Emily W. *Mary Shelley: Romance and Reality.* Boston: Little, Brown and Company, 1989.

Tatsumi, Takayuki. "Some Real Mothers: An Interview with Samuel R. Delany." *Science Fiction Eye* 1 (March 1988): 5–11.

Thacker, Stephen B. and H. David Banta. "Benefits and Risks of Episiotomy: An Interpretive Review of the English Language Literature, 1860–1980." *Obstetrical and Gynecological Survey* 38 (1983): 322–38.

Thewelweit, Klaus. *Male Fantasies, Vols. 1 and II.* Minneapolis: U of Minnesota P, 1987, 1989.

Thomas, Keith. "The Double Standard." *Journal of The History of Ideas* 20 (1959): 195–216.

Thompson, James. *Between Self and World: The Novels of Jane Austen.* University Park: Pennsylvania State U P, 1988.

————. *Models of Virtue: Eighteenth-Century Political Economy and the Novel.* Durham, N.C.: Duke U P, 1996.

Tiptree, James (Alice Sheldon). "The Girl Who Was Plugged In." *The Other Woman: Stories of Two Women and a Man.* Ed. Susan Koppelman. Old Westbury, Conn.: Feminist P, 1984: 283–321.

Trafford, Abigail. "Messengers on AIDS." *Washington Post Health,* August 25, 1992, 6+.

Treichler, Paula J. "AIDS, Homophobia, and Biomedical Discourse: An Epidemic of Signification." *AIDS: Cultural Analysis, Cultural Activism.* Ed. Douglas Crimp. Cambridge: MIT P, 1988: 31–70.

Tuana, Nancy. *The Less Noble Sex: Scientific, Religious, and Philosophical Conceptions of Woman's Nature.* Bloomington: Indiana U P, 1993.

Underdown, David. *Revel, Riot, and Rebellion: Popular Politics and Culture in England, 1603–1660.* Oxford: Oxford U P, 1987.

Upton, Lee. "Women's Creation Stories." *Denver Quarterly* 23 (1988): 119–24.

U.S. Congress. House. *Hearings Before the Subcommittee on Health and the Environment of the Committee on Energy and Commerce.* September 19 and 26, 1991.

U. S. Department of Health and Human Services. *HIV/AIDS Surveillance Report.* U.S. GPO: December 1990.

———. *Understanding AIDS.* U.S. GPO: 1988.

Wajcman, Judy. *Feminism Confronts Technology.* University Park: The Pennsylvania State U P, 1991.

Walker, William. "Locke Minding Women: Literary History, Gender, and the Essay. *Eighteenth Century Studies* 23 (990): 245–68.

Watney, Simon. "The Spectacle of AIDS." *AIDS: Cultural Analysis, Cultural Activism.* Ed. Douglas Crimp. Cambridge: MIT P, 1988: 71–86.

———. *Policing Desire: Pornography, AIDS, and the Media.* Minneapolis: U of Minnesota P, 1989.

Wayne, Valerie. "Historical Differences: Misogyny and Othello." Ed. Valerie Wayne, *The Matter of Difference: Materialist Feminist Criticism of Shakespeare.* Ithaca, N.Y.: Cornell U P, 1991: 152–77.

Weisberg, Jacob. "The Accuser." *The New Republic,* October 21, 1991, 12–14.

Weldon, Fay. *Life and Loves of a She-Devil.* New York: Pantheon, 1983.

Wertz, Richard W. and Dorothy C. Wertz. *Lying-In: A History of Childbirth in America.* Expanded Ed. New Haven: Yale U P, 1989.

West, Jane. *Letters to a Young Lady.* 1806. 3 vols. New York: Garland, 1974.

Whately, William. *A Bride-Bush, or a Wedding Sermon.* London, 1623. In the Folger Shaespeare Library Collections, Washington, D.C.

Wicke, Jennifer. "Vampiric Typewriting: *Dracula* and Its Media." *ELH* 59 (1992): 409–23.

Williams, Linda. *Hard Core: Power, Pleasure, and the "Frenzy of The Visible."* Los Angeles: U of California P, 1989.

Wilson, Elizabeth. *Adorned in Dreams: Fashion and Modernity.* Berkeley: U of California P, 1985.

Winship, Janice. *Inside Women's Magazines.* London and New York: Pandora Press, 1987.

Witomski, T. R. "The 'Sickness' of Pornography." *New York Native.* July 29–August 11, 1985, 121.

Wolf, Naomi. *The Beauty Myth: How Images of Beauty Are Used Against Women.* New York: William Morrow, 1991.

Wolmark, Jenny. *Aliens and Others: Science Fiction, Feminism, and Postmodernism.* Iowa City: U of Iowa P, 1994.

Wood, Anthony. *Athene Oxonienses.* London, 1691.

Woodbridge, Linda. *Women in the Renaissance: Literature and The Nature of Womankind, 1540–1620.* Urbana: U of Illinois P, 1986.

Woolf, Virginia. *A Room of One's Own.* 1928. New York: Harcourt Brace Javonovich, 1957.

Yeager, Patricia. "The Poetics of Birth." *Discourses of Sexuality: From Aristotle to AIDS.* Ed. Domna C. Stanton. Ann Arbor: U of Michigan P, 1992: 262–96.

Yeazell, Ruth Bernard. *Fictions of Modesty: Women and Courtship in the English Novel.* Chicago: U of Chicago P, 1991.

Yolton, John W. *Thinking Matter: Materialism in Eighteenth Century Britain.* Minneapolis: U of Minnesota P, 1983.

Zimmerman, Bonnie. "Feminist Fiction and the Postmodern Challenge." *Postmodern Fiction: A Bio-Biographical Guide.* Ed. Larry McCaffery. Westport, Conn.: Greenwood, 1986. 175–88.

NAME INDEX

SUBJECT INDEX